What people are saying about

Beyond Sex and Soup

Anna Parkinson's book, *Beyond Sex and Soup*, is a guidebook, a handbook and a book of wisdom. Rooted in personal experience and true stories, this book elucidates the ways of self-fulfilment and self-realisation. Readers will discover the place of beauty, integrity, mutuality and spirituality in everyday life in this outstanding and inspiring book. I thoroughly recommend it to all who are seeking healing and wholeness in their lives.
Satish Kumar, Editor Emeritus, *Resurgence & Ecologist* magazine, founder Schumacher College

I have two passions: one is to demystify healing, making it available to everybody, and the other is to bring together spirituality and science.

That is what Anna delivers in her book, a practical approach to healing based on practical experiences. She provides tools for reaching this deep inner reconciliation that so many are seeking. An inner journey to the source with simplicity and love – the two major ingredients of spirituality to me.
Annick Brofman, author and healer

Beyond Sex and Soup

Living a Spiritual Adventure

Beyond Sex and Soup

Living a Spiritual Adventure

Anna Parkinson

BOOKS

Winchester, UK
Washington, USA

JOHN HUNT PUBLISHING

First published by O-Books, 2021
O-Books is an imprint of John Hunt Publishing Ltd., 3 East St., Alresford,
Hampshire SO24 9EE, UK
office@jhpbooks.com
www.johnhuntpublishing.com
www.o-books.com

For distributor details and how to order please visit the 'Ordering' section on our website.

ISBN: 978 1 78904 846 9
978 1 78904 847 6 (ebook)
Library of Congress Control Number: 2021932064

A CIP catalogue record for this book is available from the British Library.

Design: Stuart Davies

UK: Printed and bound by CPI Group (UK) Ltd, Croydon, CR0 4YY
Printed in North America by CPI GPS partners

We operate a distinctive and ethical publishing philosophy in all areas of our business, from our global network of authors to production and worldwide distribution.

Contents

Previous books by Anna Parkinson

Nature's Alchemist: John Parkinson, Herbalist to Charles I
London: Frances Lincoln Ltd., 2007
ISBN 978-0-7112-2767-5

*Change Your Mind, Heal Your Body: when modern medicine has no
cure, the answer lies within*
London: Watkins Publishing, 2014
ISBN 978-1-78028-683-9

I dedicate this book to the beauty in you who reads this.

"Why can't I read the alethiometer[1] any more? Why can't I even do that? That was the one thing I could do really well, and it's just not there any more – it just vanished as if it had never come."

"You read it by grace," said Xaphania, looking at her, "and you can regain it by work."

"How long will that take?"

"A lifetime."

"That long...?"

"But your reading will be even better then, after a lifetime of thought and effort, because it will come from conscious understanding. Grace attained like that is deeper and fuller than grace that comes freely, and furthermore, once you've gained it, it will never leave you."

Philip Pullman, *The Amber Spyglass*

---

1. The 'alethiometer' is a fictional instrument that enables the user to read events past, present, and future by means of interpreting signs.

Preface

This book is written to help you uncover the beauty in you, in your life and your purpose.

The beauty is always there but sometimes it is shrouded for all of us by fear, anger, anxiety or pain. We can learn to understand these reactions in ourselves and, in so doing, we can be free of them, liberating our essential energy to engender more creativity, more love, and more joy. I have brought together tools to help you uncover the beauty from the everyday drama of your life, tools that I have found to be powerful for my own healing and my practice of healing others over the past fifteen years.

This is also a story about death, the knowledge of which makes us so much more joyful about living. Along the way, you'll encounter some of the everyday drama of my life and the characters it's been my privilege to share the adventure with. I have to thank those people for all they have given me and I offer them my profound love and respect as I offer you this story they have generated.

Chapter 1

Introduction – *'Increasingly Transparent'*

Sometime after her 90th birthday, my mother and I went to stay with friends for a night so she could attend a family party. It had been a long while since we had lived together. I had my own home and family, and she, now widowed, maintained her independence fiercely. We had grown apart in many ways, but our familiarity as mother and daughter was still strong and we were happy to share the bathroom in the morning, washing to get ready for the day. Suddenly my mother said,

"There's a question I've been meaning to ask you, but it's probably a complicated answer so I'd better not ask you now." Curiosity would not let me wait.

"No please, ask me now," I said as I started to brush my teeth.

"What's it like to be you?" she asked.

When I heard the question I thought, *Oh god! I'll never answer that!*, but at the same time words came out of my mouth that I felt summed it up.

"Increasingly transparent," I said.

I understood why she had asked the question. About ten years before this I had become a healer, for reasons that will become clear in this book. Exploring the world of healing is like a journey into the invisible which nevertheless changes all the tangible world around you. This was a mystery to my mother who did not let herself understand what I did or why I was doing it, but this 'mystery' had become a vital part of my reality. It was a dimension to my life that I would no more do without than I would choose to see the world in black and white instead of colour. To me it is an adventure that has brightened my life immeasurably and helped me to brighten others. The

3

'transparency' is simply a matter of allowing myself to get out of my own way and continue the journey with open eyes, learning as I go along. This book is an account of some things I have learned, offered to you with methods that will allow you to explore and apply them in your own life. These methods, 'invisible tools' as I call them, do, I believe, change your life and your environment for the better.

Chapter 2

Different Realities

Everyone thinks of changing the world, but no one thinks of changing himself.
Leo Tolstoy

August, 2018. Kent, England
I am driving along the M23 about to join the M25 travelling toward Dartford. The traffic is crawling steadily like a millipede intent on its destination. I have collected my brother from the airport where the crowds of arriving travellers were so thick it was hard to make out who was waiting and who was arriving. The airport is designed so that the only information board is a long way from where the travellers arrive. Worry too much about what should be happening and you're likely not to see what is happening. Engrossed in the various greeting rituals of the crowd around me, I nearly miss the tall, pale figure of my brother who suddenly appears. I go to greet him, and we move on.

Now I am steering the car into available spaces in the collective millipede on the motorway, listening to my brother talk.

My brother is talking about his present reality. He has plenty to say. For about forty years he has been a devoted follower of a Tibetan Buddhist teacher. He knows all the texts, and the teachings and the history, and I am struggling to keep up. He talks about Guru Rinpoche. I know that means 'most revered teacher'. He talks about how Guru Rinpoche travelled from India into Tibet and changed a lot of things in Tibet.

"He changed the geography," says my brother. "He moved the earth to show them his power." Suddenly I understand he is talking about something this Guru Rinpoche did 800 years ago, and I wonder how my brother can be so sure that he did anything at all. Stories of human beings making a profound alteration to apparently fixed material abound. They have always caused wonder and admiration and are passed down through generations of teaching: the Vedas, the bible, all the great myths and stories from Bhagavad Gita to the 12th century Welsh tales of the Mabinogion. I have no reason to doubt these stories. I've experienced this unexpected change myself, but in spite of my own experience of apparently magical events, the sceptical part of my mind is still alive. And kicking!

"The more people believe in something the more power it has," my brother is saying. "So he needed to dismantle the devotion to the demon, Dorje Shugden, by overturning that. And then there was another teacher from the Gelugpa sect who reversed this and decided to bring the demon back. So the demon agreed to serve him, but you can never leave the demon once you have devoted yourself to him."

We have jumped forward another 600 years, but we are still a couple of centuries away from today. Even so, all this is explaining a very present and painful reality for my brother. It is not empty theory. This battle with the demon is something he devotes his life to. My brother's reality was the murder, four years ago in China, of the teacher he loved. His bond with this teacher is deeper than any family ties, overarching the whole purpose of his being, and though the man is dead, my brother still believes that he is in contact with him and that the feelings in his heart echo what the man himself would say.

Hence his foray into the dangerous world of Tibetan religious politics, where demons wield power that rivals the power of love and compassion, where hungry ghosts that can drag your soul to eternal depths roam around, where supernatural signs are very real heralds of devastating events, and where, for my brother at least, all of this wild wonder is governed by the inexorable eternal influence of the planets and stars.

I have looked upon this world with trepidation since my early twenties. I rejected then the fierce and bloody images of the demon gods that the Tibetan teachers brought with them to the West. And yet gradually and nervously I have learned the value of embracing the darkness. It makes the light shine brighter. The more I have come to understand the nature of love, the more I begin to understand evil too.

My brother rattles on with tales of mystical skulduggery that have very real effects in the present. I know several Tibetan Buddhist teachers who keep a low profile or hide their whereabouts, whether in Britain, Spain or India, for fear of the power of the followers of the dark side of this long history. The most respected of all Tibetan teachers, the Dalai Lama, feels he is fighting a lone battle for the purity of the Buddhist teachings, according to them.

I lose track of where we are as we trickle along the lanes of traffic. The names on the signposts are familiar but I cannot quite place them. I glance to my right as we join another motorway crossing the flyover. "Shit!" I can see the traffic stretching endlessly into the distance. But it makes no difference. We have no way of being where we need to get to any faster. We are stuck in the present. Suddenly it seems as though the frozen traffic itself is the whole human race. We are striving in our vehicle, our car, our body, to get somewhere, to do something, borne on the wings of desire to be in a better place than this present moment.

In our present, without the dressing of ambitions, desires, fears, relationships and reputation, we feel lost. We want to climb out of the traffic, express our strength, walk on the shoulders of others who block us, and yet they are us. The confluence of our desires and fears has created the reality we experience. Our thoughts and feelings can be contagious and have a decisive impact on our world. We are ourselves and at the same time the collective whole. Currently stuck and going nowhere.

My brother continues to talk, oblivious to any reality other than the one that occupies his imagination. This, I think, is the paradox we all have to negotiate. Each individual has a unique view of the present, governed by so many influences that are invisible to others: memories, feelings, desire and imagination. To some extent the world we experience as reality is the sum of these collective invisible influences: machines that fly; voices that carry ten thousand miles; new hearts to replace the old one. We live in a very magical world! Whether we experience this reality as pleasant or unpleasant, we are all affected by it. Yet we know, deep in ourselves, that we have a unique power. We have a mission and a destiny that no one else shares. As a tiny cell in this vast moving millipede of living beings, our thoughts and feelings matter and are the instrument of change for the whole being.

Sometimes we need to see the limitations of the thoughts and feelings that create our world so we can let them go. Sometimes we need to perceive the magnitude of them, so we can build a better reality for ourselves and those we love. It can be a confusing journey which I have been helping people to navigate since breaking through a major barrier of my own a couple of decades ago.

The flow of the work I love to do has been interrupted by a very different reality that has overtaken me in the past month or so. The reason my brother has left his life of semi retreat in Spain and come to join me, is that our mother has been in hospital. In the course of six weeks, she has changed from a feisty 94-year-old, fiercely maintaining her independence and managing to live on her own, to a weak and dependent old woman preoccupied by the gradual understanding that her reality bears no relation to anyone else's. She is dying, but neither she, nor I or my brothers, are yet quite sure what that looks like.

She has brain damage. Two weeks before she had been taken back into hospital because the carers who had come to get her up in the morning had found her "difficult to rouse." Difficult enough that they had called the paramedics and by the time I tracked down the hospital the ambulance had taken her to and got there, she was lying on a trolley in the accident and emergency department muttering crossly about being "on a train."

For four or five hours she lay on this trolley, complaining of being hungry and demanding something to eat. The only physical aspect of her behaviour that seemed alarming was that every now and then she would sit up and angrily demand food, or to see the doctor, or the nurse, and every time she did so, her blood pressure readings would lurch into the red and the machine she was hooked up to would bleep. She knew who we were and she knew where she was. She kept on repeating her name, loudly and firmly, over and over again to no one in particular, just in case. She could say the Queen's name but not the year the Second World War ended. She knew with crystal clarity that she wanted to go home, and she knew she was hungry. My daughter tried to calm her down. "Think of Tara."

"Tara, who's Tara?" said my mother.

"You know, white Tara, green Tara, the goddess of love and compassion."

My mother has told my daughter about Tara since she was a little girl.

"Oh yes, yes," said my mother impatiently. "Get me something to eat!"

Waiting to see a doctor with her, we wiled away the time listening to my mother discussing the other people in the bays in a loud voice. It was amazing that she could hear really. But perhaps her senses were heightened.

"That man over there would rather spend £14 twice than £28 once."

But we could not reach her. Great spaces seemed to have opened up in the engine that drove her. I did not know where the train was. She did not know who Tara, the Buddhist goddess of compassion was, even though she had been a practising Buddhist for over 45 years. She scratched incessantly and hung her head, the blood pressure raising weals and blotches on her face. She was itching so much she was even scratching me as I sat by the bed and held her hand.

She weed pee the colour of brick dust into a cardboard container and they told her she had a urine infection. The nurse refused to give her food because they wanted to wait and see what the doctors wanted to do. She demanded food all the same.

We tried to calm her with sips of water until eventually a doctor came in and asked her to raise her arms and legs in succession. She did this with little problem, her chin jutting forward and her toothless mouth pursed in an expression of angry determination.

"When can I go home? You can't keep people here against their will in the 21st century you know!"

She snatched the mild-mannered doctor's papers from him and appeared to study them intently. I didn't think she was reading them as her glasses had been left behind in the rush to get her to hospital, along with her teeth.

"Illegal drugs!" she snorted. "I haven't had any illegal drugs!"

The doctor gently took his papers back. He asked her to count backwards from 20 to 1, demonstrating the first few numbers. "20, 19, 18..."

"20, 19..." she repeated slowly and deliberately. "19..." she faltered. Her head sunk to her chest again and she was lost in this meaningless maze.

"It doesn't matter," said the doctor lightly, but my mother was fixed on proving she was up to the task. My daughter sat beside her quietly encouraging her by getting her back on the launchpad. "20, 19..."

Meanwhile the doctor disappeared and came back through the blue curtain a few minutes later looking puzzled.

"Your mother has had a stroke."

I was astonished. From every sign that I could see it was the morphine again: the itching, the dazed confusion, the complicated burbling about intellectual abstractions. She was stoned, as far as I could tell. But it turned out that there was some method in her madness. She had been in a scanner that morning before I arrived. *Ah, the train.* I thought.

The scan had revealed an infarct on the right side, the doctor showed me. Of course, I didn't know what that was, but he assumed it to be a stroke. Despite this she showed no physical signs and was ready to go home right after she'd had a good meal. She wolfed down a hospital puree and a yogurt that I fed her from a spoon. But they kept her in for the night.

Hospitals brought out a deeply rebellious hostility in my mother. When I first found her there, she was terrified of losing her identity and never being herself again. She was under the illusion that the hospital staff were part of a conspiracy to do this to her, so she decided to resist all treatment. Overnight she twice ripped out the drip that they had put in her arm to rehydrate her, saying the next day that you never knew what kind of food they put in these things. By the time I arrived in the morning with her teeth, glasses, clothes and other trappings of normal life for her, the nursing staff were showing signs of having had a difficult night. She sat in an armchair gazing doggedly at a patch of grass through an open door that represented the outside world, the real world that she could relate to, where grass grew and butterflies flew. But she was not calm.

She greeted me like her prodigal child returned from outer space, while the nurses told me she was refusing to take the antibiotics they had given her for the infection. "Will you take them, Mum?" I asked. "You have an infection and they want to treat it."

"I'll take them if you're here. I trust you," she said, gripping my arm with a vice-like bony grip. And while I stood by, she shakily tipped a mysterious liquid from a paper cup down her throat, spilling half of it on to her hospital gown, already heavily bloodstained from where she had scratched herself raw.

Enough, I thought. *I have let you look after yourself as you wanted, but it's like leaving a two-year-old alone in a chemist's shop.* I walked with my mother back to the room where she had been put for closer observation by the night nurses.

"This stuff you have been taking has got to go," I said. My mum unsuspectingly became a drug addict in her nineties with the full authorisation of her doctors.

"You've been taking zopiclone to make you sleep. It doesn't make you sleep. You just forget you've taken it in the night and go round angrily looking for more. And still it doesn't make you sleep. The morphine is even worse. It's the reason you're back in hospital. You don't take it for pain. You take it to make you sleep and although it does that, it makes you shaky, weak, and scratch furiously all the time. These drugs are making you ill."

She listened patiently, already beginning to come back to earth, although she gave some friends who visited a long account of the Machiavellian schemes of the "bossy nursing staff" who would have fed her poison through the drip in her arm if she hadn't ripped it out. In the afternoon the consultant came.

"You haven't had a stroke, recently at least. There is damage to the brain."

"Why? How did this happen?" she asked, a little disappointed, I thought, that this dramatic explanation for her change of circumstances had been taken away from her.

"A combination of old age and overuse of sleeping pills and strong painkillers," he answered firmly. "Don't take them. You don't need to sleep at night. You don't have to get up and go to work in the morning. You can sleep during the day if you like, and you'll get as much sleep as you need."

With her permission he showed me the scan of her head. I could see the large dark patch in the right-hand lobe. I accepted and was grateful for his explanation of her deterioration.

"Could it be an effect of the anaesthetic also?"

"Anaesthetic?" He looked surprised. "Has she had an anaesthetic?"

"Yes. A few weeks ago she had an operation for a femoral hernia. It was a successful operation, but I wonder whether it could have affected her brain." It had been in a different hospital and I forgave him for not having had time to call up all her notes.

"It could, yes. With the other factors."

So there we were. It felt like the care of my mother's brain was now in my hands. If the anaesthetic had contributed to this altered reality she was experiencing then there was a chance that it would get better. I had felt the aftereffects of anaesthetic myself, as a heavy depression that lifted after eight weeks or so. It wasn't clear whether that would happen in such an old brain as hers, but I was pretty sure that throwing away all the painkilling, reputedly sleep-inducing and hypnotic medicine she had been taking would help.

She could no longer take her own medicines, however, which meant that she could no longer be left to live on her own. For a while, at least, I would need to stay with her or she would never be able to leave hospital. The next day she was still muttering her sympathy for prison inmates loudly to anyone who would listen and announcing her intention to join Amnesty International. The nurses were called on to dial my mobile number at least a dozen times, although unfortunately my mother was not able to speak into the phone once I was reached. But the message was clear. I had to do anything I could to get her out of hospital. And that meant, for me, staying close by her side.

For a while my reality changed. I was taken up with the business of being nurse and carer during the day, cleaning, washing, getting food and supplies, straightening out the chaos of the night so that my mother, who could barely stagger to the bathroom, could lie back on clean sheets and tell everyone who asked how she looked after herself independently at home, fetched her own meals and was able to drive to the doctor. She was aware, however, that something was not right. There was an unreachable chasm that had opened up inside her.

At night she plunged into the depths of darkness and despair. Still restless, I would be woken up by the sound of her running all the taps in the kitchen. Wearily I would tear myself out of bed because I knew that meant she would be trying to make herself a hot water bottle, despite temperatures in the high twenties, which she hadn't the strength to do. These night-time conversations in the kitchen were dark.

"I wish I could go to the cliffs," she'd say. "I've always wanted to throw myself off. That's why I've never been able to go near the edge. Take me to Dover Cliffs."

"We'd never get there," I say brightly. "Long traffic jam just now. Everyone's been held up and it's taking six or seven hours to get to Dover."

She'd look at me, astonished, and I would take her back to her room with her hot water bottle, pick up the lamp from the floor, collect her teeth, remake the bed, turn down the electric blanket and pray that we'd both get some sleep.

In the morning she would have forgotten the night. Brooding, she lay and listened to the whirring thoughts that rambled in her head.

An assessor came from the neuro rehab unit and asked her a lot of questions. Impatiently, my mother explained in a high, haughty voice how she read, did her own cooking, and even cooked for herself.

"What sort of thing do you cook?" asked the doubtful assessor.

"Oh vegetables, mostly," my mother answered hopefully. "I like vegetables."

I explained that this picture of independent living didn't correspond with my reality. My mother began to get angry.

"In families you know, it's very difficult, because people have their own agenda."

A steely edge had crept into her voice. The assessor moved on and asked to see how my mother walked. With a great effort she grasped her stick and levered herself off the bed, grabbing the furniture for support. She tapped, limped and staggered to the bathroom. The assessor watched. On the way back to her bed, my mother leaned on the wall and studied the floor tiles. The assessor asked her why she was looking at the floor.

My mother snapped.

"Why shouldn't I look at the floor? Don't people ever look at the floor? I've a right to look at the floor in my own house!"

Furiously, she limped back to her bed and brooded on the insult. The assessor left, confused. Friends visited, and my mother seemed to become aware that there were more people who shared my reality than hers. When they left, I found her lying prone, considering this problem.

She could not understand why everyone else seemed to have a different reality. It was as though she had gone to sleep on the same train as her fellow passengers and woken up to find they were all on a different platform. The anger had gone, to leave only the fear. The fear that, alone in her separate reality, she had, as she put it, gone mad.

"Of course, we do all have different realities, don't we?" she asked me.

"Yes," I agreed. "We all see the world in our own way. We see it through our feelings, our memories, our desires, and those are different, for each of us."

15

She nodded.

"What we call 'reality' is just a way of keeping safe, I suppose."

"Yes, we need to keep ourselves safe, otherwise we can't be here to experience our lives. And we have agreed realities that do this for us. If you see the motorway as yellow, and I see it as purple, you have a perfect right to do that. But if I am going to drive on the motorway, I want to do it with other people who see the road as purple. Having someone there who sees the road as yellow would be dangerous for all of us."

This explanation seemed to satisfy her and she relapsed for a while into patiently allowing herself to be looked after. Meanwhile I set about getting reinforcements to help me do this job.

I have plunged you into an everyday domestic tale. How can this glimpse of a family saga matter to you in your life?

My mother has found herself in the hands of medical professionals who overwhelm her independence. She is frustrated that she can no longer make her own choices as this system tries to 'save her life', which it is bound to do. But this life they are trying to save is not the one that has meaning for her. The one that has meaning is the one she lived when she still had energy and vigour to choose how to act and react. The one I live and the one, I trust, you do too.

As I watch her face her fear of death, and to the best of my ability, help her with this, it seems to me that the choices we make about how to live when we can still make those choices independently are even more critical. Life is too precious to waste time with fear, regret, anger, jealousy or disappointment. There are ways to overcome these feelings we all experience, and to use them to help us explore a different reality, rather than keep us stuck as they tend to do. The more I watch my mother go through her rite of passage, the more vital I feel these tools of living are. Our mother's perspective on life is critical to how we first perceive 'reality' so that it can be hard to see that we do not have to have the same approach to life. We are all partly our mothers and partly our fathers, but not many of us want to be them. Our soul is embarked on an adventure, from the moment we are born. The journey is unique to us even though all souls may meet in the same place at the end of it. Our journey is to make different choices and achieve different results in our lives than the ones our parents or siblings make, to find our own ways to be happy.

The starting point is to understand our relationship with mother, which tells us so much about how we began this life. Then, like a tulip bulb, we can split off from the mother bulb, put down our roots and flourish independently. A tulip, for the non-horticulturally minded, never grows true from seed. It reproduces by creating little bulbils which split off from the mother bulb when they grow big enough and find their own soil. Separating from the mother bulb and putting down our own roots is something that must be done to develop our individual strength, and it can be done painlessly, using the tool of your mind, as you'll see. This doesn't mean not having a relationship with your mother. On the contrary, it makes it easier to appreciate what she has been able to teach.

There was, as Shakespeare has Polonius say of Hamlet, 'method' in my mother's madness. Even within the narrow confines of practical daily life and the bounds of families that are born of the same parents and brought up in the same way, we all have different realities. Each of us is unique and our reality is generally invisible to others. Understanding the uniqueness of your reality, what is shared and what is different, can free you to live your life to the fullest, in a way that is fruitful, healthy and happy.

Helping people to do that has become a daily reality for me. I describe what I do as healing, and it has been largely concerned with the way people's bodies express deep and sometimes forgotten feelings as illness or disease. But whether or not those bodies have disease, they always have feeling. And healing is about accessing and releasing feeling. So I have developed some methods to give you the tools to do this job for yourself. Once you begin to use these 'tools of the invisible', you will find yourself on a fascinating journey into the fullness of your life. In the process you will discover paradox. You will find strength in accepting your weakness, meaning in your fragility, purpose in your being with no purpose. I trust, as you read the stories in this book, and practise some of the tools, you will fall in love with your life, and if you can do that, you will have done me and everyone one else who knows you, an immeasurable favour.

I became a healer, which meant exploring my life and energy in an unfamiliar way, because I had to.

In 2002 I was diagnosed with a brain tumour. I had piercing headaches and double vision, which made me sick and dizzy all the time. This tumour proved to be inoperable, deeply buried as it was, and since the medical profession could not help me, eventually I began to turn to other ways to free myself of it that I knew very little about. I explored the effects of different diets, of herbal treatments and acupuncture with little perceptible results. Looking for anything that could help me, I also explored healing, and gradually realised that although I didn't understand what was happening, I could feel that another person's energy had a physical effect on my body. Still exploring blindly, eventually I met a healer whose work turned the lights on for me. Like Alice, in Lewis Carroll's story, I stepped through the Looking Glass and experienced the same world in a completely different way.

I have already told this story in another book, *Change Your Mind, Heal Your Body*, which I wrote because I wanted people to understand that, for me at least, healing was not an instant miracle, but a process, which the book explains. That process is logical but also mystical. In the course of uncovering healing, you discover the link between the measurable practicality of your life and unmeasurable invisible. The more you are aware of the relationship between those two forces, the better you can navigate all the challenges, pains, and problems you encounter. Because you will have pains, challenges and problems. Without them you wouldn't be living, in the fullest human sense. Understanding the impact of the forces that surround you will help you navigate your journey in peace.

Ironically, for me at least, seeing both the tangible and intangible world at once is a kind of double vision. Ironic, because the nature of the physical problem that forced me to stop and view my life in a different way manifested initially as double vision. That physical problem has been corrected now, but it launched me on the path of a different kind of double vision that I do not want to let go of, where logic and mystery are intertwined.

We see that things are as they are in our shared reality, so as to be able to negotiate them, but we see also that they are more than that for us personally. The events and even the physical circumstances that surround you are an energetic resonance with your deepest self, and the more you recognise that, the greater your power to change them and use your energy to create something you like better.

Chapter 3

Gulls – *Hunting For Survival*

On that particular evening, peculiarly warm and clear, I looked up at the pink sky of the closing day and saw, spread across the wide expanse of my vision, an arrow of seagulls emerge from the north, heading directly in perfect formation towards the south. I watched them as they spread out far above my head, their wings beating out the message of their powerful intent to fly in the slipstream of the bird just ahead, a message of harmony and consciousness, yet focused on the practical task of travelling so many miles, taking the path of least resistance through the air. As they disappeared towards the south, another wave came, and then another, shooting like a quiver of arrows across the pink tinged sky. High above them, puffs of cloud bubbled, catching the light of the sinking sun. These clouds gather at 18,000 feet in a formation called cirrocumulus that is commonly known as a 'mackerel' sky. Never before had I seen sharp billed noisy seagulls show their strength and beauty with such grace, and never before had I seen these hungry keen-eyed fishing birds fly unconsciously under their fish! The 'mackerel' clouds looked down peaceably on the passing arrows of gulls without fear of disturbance.

The unusual beauty of the gulls this evening told me a story. Like the gulls we are fully focused on pursuing our goals, aware of our relationship to each other and the distance we are travelling. We try to keep up with the group, not to get isolated, where the going would be harder and we can feel so alone in the wide-open space around us. Like the gulls, we strive to be in harmony with our race, and everything works better when we are. However, like the gulls, we may be blind to the 'food' we need to keep going, innocently flying under the 'mackerel' that sustain us, leaving us hungry for something we cannot see.

Chapter 4

The Quest – *To Find Your Self*

Unless and until the human body, from the foot to the head, right to left, is known very well, the unknown cannot be approached.
BKS Iyengar

When my mother was recovering in hospital from surgery to her bowel, her mind was wandering restlessly trying to grasp a secure reality that she could recognise. I was that reality in a physical form. She would look at me, dazed and grateful, and utter her astonishment at the fact that I had emerged from her body.

"I have the feeling that you came out of my head!" she cried to all who would listen, raising her thin arms in a dramatic arc from the crown of her head and sweeping them outward. "And then, as soon as you came out, you stood up and shouted!"

In other moments it was the difficulty and fear that had haunted her at the time of my birth that she recalled.

"I was all alone in that room," she told me darkly, "and I was in so much pain I thought I would die. You were so big!"

She didn't die. It was a long labour, but not an especially difficult birth. Nor was I, at 9 lbs, a particularly big baby. To hear her, you would think that no woman had ever had a baby before, let alone two previous babies as she had. Yet I think I understand what she is talking about. She has come close to the other great journey of her life. She is looking down the tunnel of leaving life, gripped with fear. In her current state of mind, the distinction between her own physical body and mine has disappeared. I tell her this and she agrees enthusiastically, unreproached.

"Yes! Isn't that strange? I used to be me and now I'm you!"

Facing death, she is constantly recalling the first journey of her life, something in her pre-conscious memory, when she herself came into the world in July 1923.

My mother's state of mind could well be called madness or dementia. It doesn't bear much resemblance to measurable facts. But there is a deep truth in it that I have seen again and again in my work as a healer: that the body records and retains the memory of every emotional reaction you have ever experienced in your life and will offer this up as information when you face a similar situation.

You live in a truly remarkable instrument whose genius we have scarcely begun to understand. Your body itself is a source of wisdom and guidance in your life. It does not make a neat distinction between physical and non-physical reality but swiftly transmutes one into another. When you begin to understand this exchange, you can live in your body much more comfortably. Neither does your body make a distinction between one part of you and another. Each organ and muscle functions individually but also in relationship to other parts, communicating problems, referring pain and lending support where it is needed. We have a lot to learn from the way our bodies function, even when those bodies show signs of wearing out and getting ready to die.

My mother was in hospital because she had had a femoral hernia. This is when the bowel pokes through the wall of muscle deep in the groin and gets trapped. The muscles close against the bowel and shut off its blood supply. The bowel quickly begins to die and so nothing can be eliminated from the body this way. In these circumstances, the bowel sends a message to stop the traffic entering the system. Autonomic reflexes further up the line shut down. My mother found herself unable to swallow. She vomited anything that she was able to swallow. It was because of this that the doctors recognised a femoral hernia and returned her bowel to working order by cutting out the dead piece and re-stitching the cut ends together. Two days later the patient was eating and drinking normally and her bowel was working perfectly.

There is a great deal that medicine is still discovering about the intelligence of our body tissues themselves, and their ability to repair and regrow. Much of what is known functions so perfectly naturally that science can only admire the process, without yet having found a way to copy or change it. My mother is frightened as she lies in her hospital bed. She has come close to death and she knows it. Accustomed to driving herself forward by sheer effort of will, she is confronted with an overwhelming power in which her will has no place. For a while, all her reactions seem like those of a small child. She wants to understand what is happening. She wants to understand her body.

Her brain is not retaining information. The internal computer is not making the connections that it did. But as she lies in her bed I talk to her about the process that is going on inside all of us from the moment of our conception to the moment of death, a tiny powerful process that sums up so perfectly the paradox of existence that I think of it often. It is the process called apoptosis – selective cell death.

"The cells in our bodies are constantly being created and constantly dying. This begins to happen when you form in the womb. The organs and the limbs somehow know what shape they should be, what they can discard, and what they need to function. It's because of apoptosis that you have spaces between your fingers and toes, nostrils in your nose and so on. Places where the tissue cells are not. So this process gives you shape and form, as it does the leaves, the trees, the cats, the elephants."

She looks delighted and smiles.

"But this process goes on through your whole life. Your skin is being remade. Your bowel is being remade while some cells die and are flushed away. So you are always living and dying at the same time. At some point, and no one knows when or why, the speed of cell death is faster than the speed of creation and growth. You begin to weaken and shrink, just as the leaves turn brown in the autumn."

My mother's attention has wandered. She is tired. But she looks peaceful as she closes her eyes.

Before a leaf falls off its tree, the cells at the top of its stem gradually form a seal and close the stem off from the branch. The leaf no longer feeds light and energy into the tree. The tree which has grown the leaf to capture the light has absorbed the energy it has sent back and stored it. So the leaf is discarded and falls to the ground where it feeds the bacteria and moulds that in turn feed the tree. We can only admire this perfect pattern. We would not want it any other way. But when we consider the process in our own bodies, it is not so easy to contemplate, not so perfect or harmonious, or peaceful. We have consciousness that perhaps the leaf does not possess. And our consciousness perplexes us.

This book will offer you ways you can change the complicated effects of your active mind on your living being that I have found to be useful. We can work better with our consciousness if we learn to understand it and, in that way, to master it to some extent. Very few of us can see it clearly, but nearly all of us can see it better than we do and use it to help us rather than hinder us. Our physical bodies are a powerful ally in this journey of understanding.

One reason that the intelligence of our body's tissues is so hard for medical science to uncover is that much of it cannot be measured. The engine of the body's functioning is deep within our invisible selves. We know this to be true instinctively. When you are in love you have the energy and optimism to climb mountains and make magic. When you are lonely, your body aches and disease flourishes. When you fear what faces you, you tell yourself you will fail, and you do. When you trust that you will 'try 'til you die', you achieve more than you thought possible. All these aspects of your being: love, fear, memory, will, are what make the life of a human being. We all know that. Yet none of them can be measured, copied, exchanged or given away to another. You are uniquely in charge of these invisible aspects of your self. They are energy. They are life. They are the parts of your consciousness that you are free to master.

Strangely, given that we all understand what a powerful part they play in our lives, none of them is considered important in medical science. This is because they are inherently unscientific, since they are unmeasurable. But if you want to improve your health, to make the most of the life you have, you can start by exploring those feelings in yourself.

It can be hard to see ourselves. Think of what you notice when you go into a stranger's house: the carpet, the colours and style of the furniture, the pictures on the wall. Compare that to what you actually see of your own home. It has grown so familiar that you see only glimpses of what you like or don't like. It's hard to view it with the root and branch clarity with which you react to somewhere unfamiliar. Yet, in fact, the information we need to see ourselves is coming back to us all the time. It is in our bodies, in the events in our lives, in our interactions with family, friends, work colleagues and strangers. As we learn to relate to all these things as information, they become as helpful as the mirror we use to judge the clothes we are wearing or the shape of our hair. We can look on them gratefully, even when we don't like what we see, and, strangely, this humility gives us power.

This process, of learning humility and acceptance in the face of an apparently immoveable physical object, in my case: a brain tumour, is one I was forced to learn for my own healing. It is natural to carry on enjoying our bodies and our lives until we encounter a block that seems to arrest our progress. Some event, or some physical symptom that causes us pain stops us in our tracks. It really doesn't make much difference whether the pain we encounter is emotional or physical. We actually need to experience pain in order to learn and develop as human beings, although we spend much of our energy trying to protect ourselves and our loved ones from it. Pain is a signpost that leads us forward on our soul's journey.

I have learned through this healing process that the physical form of pain is just an expression of the non-physical form: emotional pain which has perhaps become so habitual and so ingrained that it has altered the smooth harmony of your body's natural processes. This may seem like a far-fetched claim to you. It is not medical science, although, as I will show you, there are developments in medical science that are beginning to support it. It is *beyond* medical science, as we ourselves are organisms that medical science cannot comprehend. I have no way of proving it, other than anecdotally through the stories and experiences of the people I have worked with as a healer. If you entertain the ideas and use the methods I describe in this book to explore your inner world, however, you'll be surprised by how powerful an effect this has on your outer, physical world.

I am not advocating that you uncover the ancient history of your emotional reactions and treasure them like artefacts in a museum. You need to let go of the old stuff. Once old emotions are revealed to your current conscious mind, you will find yourself making swift decisions to resolve the situation, and you will feel better.

I am often asked how you can access and release old feelings. This is, in fact, remarkably simple to do, although, like many simple and powerful processes, it can take time, and can be complicated by other feelings such as fear, pride and shame. Still, it's not rocket science. The methods and means of growing towards what makes you happy are accessible and available to every human being. I have been teaching them for years in workshops that I designed to focus on particular practical problems: the ones we are all familiar with in our lives: fear, insecurity, anxiety, addictions, anger, lack of confidence, jealousy, frustration and so on. Most of us have felt these at some time in our lives, and even if they are not a current reality, the memory of them can define our experience of the present. If you feel any of these things on a regular basis, in yourself or your loved ones, wouldn't it be nice to live without them?

To free yourself you may need to rely on some of your natural faculties more powerfully than you have been accustomed to. Most of us who read this book in English have been schooled into understanding that 'reality' consists of measurable physical facts, regardless of knowing that immeasurable love, joy, pain or grief is very real indeed. This wouldn't have been true if we had been born in England 400 years ago, or if we had been born into a culture without a Western education. Our ancestors were accustomed to treating the invisible as a real power in their lives, and often spoke about feeling the power of God, or being possessed by the devil. Country tales in England treated fairies and spirits as regular inhabitants of certain places alongside their human residents.

The English diarist, John Aubrey, writing in 1687, lamented the fact that his contemporaries no longer talked about spirits – non-physical entities that they perceived as part of their physical reality with senses other than sight and touch, and he attributed this to the ready availability of books.[1] New methods were being developed to master the natural environment, but Aubrey clearly felt the 'old information' was a valid counterpart to the way the nature of the world was being measured by new generations of educated men. The Renaissance method of measuring experience 'rationally' through observation and repeated experiment had spread into every branch of life. It's a form of enquiry that has built our modern world and we are grateful for it, but it is not the only reality. It is not even the reality we live as human beings. Humans are possibly the least rational of all mammals.

Since the days of Albert Einstein the frontiers of physics have measured reality in terms which are almost incomprehensible to the 'rational' mind, since they embrace two contradictory truths at once. On 28th November 1919, the *London Times* published a telling commentary on an article in the paper by Albert Einstein.

Einstein had written an enthusiastic tribute to the impartiality of English scientists whose experiments during the solar eclipse in May of that year had decisively confirmed his Theory of Relativity, regardless of the fact he could be regarded as from the opposite side in the war that had so recently devastated Europe. *The Times* leader writer attempts to sum up Einstein's theory:

> *Gravitation, hitherto regarded as an absolute proposition, becomes relative. The simple majesty of the square of the distance has lost its isolated splendour as an expression of the conformity between abstract thought and observation of the fabric of the universe.*[2]

In other words, the fabric of our universe had been shown to be different from the reality we observe with our eyes. Space can no longer be described by straight lines, as it curves and moves. Even so, the leader writer assures his readers, they needn't worry. The theory would make "little difference to the practical world... We may measure our land and believe in our clocks as we did before Einstein."

And so we do. Generally, we treat our space, our home, our bodies as though they were composed of fixed matter that can be defined and calculated by straight lines. It is a way for us to cope with the limitations of our physical senses. But it is not all we are, and we know it. Just as a physicist's knowledge of the difference between the appearance and substance of matter have in fact made a profound practical difference to our lives, through invisible applications of waves of energy that were not dreamed of by a London journalist in 1919, so our knowledge of our inner energy makes a powerful practical difference to our world. Grasping, as journalists do, at unseen possibilities to balance his remarks, the leader writer concedes that while this theory and its proof does not change anything practically, knowledge of it does, in some way, change everything.

"On the other hand, the change in philosophy and metaphysics is fundamental."

Undoubtedly, the physical world we inhabit would have been unrecognisable to my grandfather who probably read that article in 1919. This theory of Einstein's, which opened the door to our understanding that apparently contradictory realities coexist, was the start of it.

Even so, as individuals, each one of us would have been immediately recognisable to my grandfather. Human nature doesn't change much, and he was ready to recognise the human spirit in people of all backgrounds and cultures. While the way we can live our lives has altered almost beyond recognition in the last century, many of us know little about the one constant in a fast-changing world: how to manage our own emotions through the challenges of the inevitable stages of life. Childhood, adolescence, romance, employment, maturity, old age and death are characterised by our relationships with each other, often by storms, anger and a legacy of hurt or bitterness. We have not yet learned to manage our lives with joy. The biggest contradictory reality we face is that, while we are all the same, we all see the world differently.

We find it hard to accept that our world view is only 'our reality', a bunch of facts that we have created to suit our emotional experience. Sometimes this works and we are in universal agreement: we agree that a block of ice is solid and can be picked up and transferred, even though a physicist would see it as a bunch of moving molecules with space in between them. But we don't agree on the invisible: whether one person treats another in a way that is reasonable, or fair, or kind and so on. We are all invisible, essentially, and we inhabit different real worlds.

Around the world, many cultures respect our human capacity to perceive information beyond the physical, and in the decades since Einstein's theory, more and more of those educated in Western rationalism have sought knowledge of these 'irrational' skills.

Throughout history, human societies have relied on the faculty of intuition, spoken through the language of imagination, as the powerful, creative aspect of our intelligence that it is. Of course, this element of our intelligent energy is alive and well in developed commercial nations just as it has been in more primitive societies. We use it as individuals and society gets great joy from it when it delivers wonderful stories, powerful art, beautiful films. But somehow Western society fails to give it the respect it deserves. We learn early on to dismiss its power in ourselves. We don't give it time to express itself. We don't listen to it when it does. And we don't value it enough in ourselves because we have come to regard ourselves as purely physical beings, while behaving in a very different way. The process of healing is about acknowledging, understanding and liberating your emotional self so that you can clear your way forward. Until you can do this, no amount of instruction, medication or counselling can change things for you. To do it you need to learn to trust your own perceptive faculties and act on them.

We've all had the experience of the way our intuition and imagination can take us forward in a split second, while our rational faculty is struggling to keep up. *Thinking, Fast and Slow* is the title of a best-selling book by psychologist Daniel Kahneman who won a Nobel prize for his work showing that humans are a lot less rational than we think we are. We feel safest with rapid decisions based on emotion and memory of the past, and we have a tendency to use this to narrow our vision of what is 'real' or 'possible' to something already familiar that we know how to cope with.

Understanding our bodies and how they function is an example of this. While every human body functions like any other, different cultures have various ways of describing how they do it. If you have studied or received acupuncture you will know that it follows an extraordinarily detailed map of connections in the body along so-called meridians. These invisible pathways intersect at important junctions known as acupuncture points. For decades after acupuncture came to the West it was regarded with deep scepticism by the medical profession because none of these pathways could be seen and therefore they were considered not to exist. Even though that is still the case, the practice has been widely accepted now because Western medical science knows no other way to overcome pain than to deaden the nerves that feel, and of course that has other undesirable effects. Acupuncture often acts like pain relieving medication without the side effects.

Acupuncture and its meridian map is thousands of years old, we know. In the 1960s, a North Korean scientist named Bong Han Kim made it his life's work to use the most modern microscope technology he could obtain to prove that acupuncture meridians were a physical reality. Before his research centre was summarily and mysteriously closed by the North Korean government in 1965, Bong Han published five papers, some in English, detailing his physical examination of a system of almost invisible ducts carrying liquid that spread from the surface of all internal organs of the mammalian body to the skin. These pathways, which correspond to the meridians, and particularly to the important junctions between them, carry DNA, stem cells, that have the ability to repair wounds and damage in the body, and immune cells whose function is to destroy toxins.

North Korean medical research was not highly rated by international scientists in the 1960s, so Bong Han's discoveries remained on ice, until the late 1990s when Professor Fujiwara of Osaka claimed to have reproduced his results, and working with researchers from Seoul and Hong Kong, made such definitive discoveries that these points have acquired a new name. Known until that time as Bong Han ducts, that are now known as the Primo Vascular System and further research into their possibilities is under way, principally in China, the USA and South Korea.[3]

You don't need to wait for scientific approval before you can find and use methods that make a powerful positive difference to your life. In the West we need to get over our cultivated distrust of intuition. Our mistrust is there for a very good reason. It is there to keep us safe. But our mistrust also keeps us confined. We need to have the courage to go beyond our safe boundaries and start a new adventure. We find this courage in particular circumstances: extreme fear and extreme pain.

I've said that my own breakaway from confinement to rational thinking came from having an inoperable brain tumour and discovering that through uncovering old feelings and changing my thinking, I was able to make the journey from tumour to no tumour. I've told this story in my book *Change Your Mind, Heal Your Body*,[4] but all I need to say here is that if, at the beginning of this journey, I'd been able to make an appointment with a surgeon who could cut the tumour out for me so that I could go back to the life I had before, with no mental effort on my part, I would simply have marked the date in my diary and made the necessary arrangements. That is what we expect our doctors to do for us and I was no exception. We treat ourselves like machines with occasional faults that our medical system can correct for us, so we can drive the car away from the garage and resume functioning. It was only because I could not do that, because the tumour stayed with me with all its imposing effects and the doctors, in the nicest possible way, shrugged and said there was nothing they could do, that I was forced to take responsibility for this new reality in my life. It was *my* head that was affected and, I finally found myself saying, it was *me* that had to do something about it.

In the course of finding my way to a solution I was introduced to a map. This map is as ancient as the map of acupuncture meridians but it concentrates on the core of the nervous system that runs along your spine. It is the map of *chakras*, wheels of energy along your spine that connect to different activities and experiences that you go through in your life. To some extent this map is entirely logical. If you look at even a nineteenth century map of the body's nervous system, such as in *Gray's Anatomy*, you will see that the nerves branch out from the spinal cord at certain points and reach deep into the organs that make your body function. The places where these vital nerves intersect with the spinal cord are called ganglia, and it is these intersections that are known as *chakras* in the old Sanskrit map of the human body. *Chakra* means wheel, and like wheels, these energetic nervous bunches send and receive messages to the surrounding areas and their connected organs, relating all essential parts of the body to all other parts via the coherent coordinating organ which is your brain.

This map departs from logic, however, in that it was arrived at by intuition rather than visual observation. The chakra 'map' also confounds logic by being conceived of as spherical as well as linear. What appears to be at the top of the linear map, the crown chakra, is known to be at the centre of your energy field, the piece in the middle, with all the other chakras radiating out from it in sequence, like layers of a multicoloured ball.

Just as with the acupuncture map of the body, if you dissected a human body, you would find the ganglia of tiny nerves along the spinal cord, but not the energy that passes along them – obviously! The more we learn about how the brain works, the more we discover that what we thought was fixed is in fact mutable, that what we thought was distinct, one organ from another, for example, or parts like your little toe, a long way from the physical brain, is in fact part of a communicating system that affects and changes the whole.

Until recently we were unable to discover much about how the brain and the nervous system work because once it was possible to examine either one or the other, it was no longer working. But magnetic resonance imaging and EEGs, that show activity taking place in a living organism, have changed that and gradually science is charting the powerful physical effect of non-physical perceptions on our bodies. Understanding of how the living human body works in practice relies partly on anatomical logic, and partly on other forms of perception, which have been largely unmeasurable and so essentially 'unscientific'. The latter are all the more powerful for the fact that they take us into the world we actually experience: emotion, pain, memory, imagination.

Some time ago I worked in the professional world as a news and current affairs journalist for the BBC with a strong preference for measurable and 'provable' facts. My illness changed all that, and afterwards I began to work directly with individuals to help them bridge difficulties in their lives, whether pain or illness. For those who need it I use healing. Others have come to me for massage – a Hawaiian form of massage known as 'lomilomi'. When I massage someone's body it 'speaks' to me. I touch a part of the body and it feels 'full' or 'empty'. Or it squeals with pain and tells me where else in the body the pain is felt and what the connection is between these two points. Someone asked me recently how I knew she felt pain where she did.

"*I* know," she said. "I can feel it. But how do *you* know?"

I struggled to put an answer into words.

"It's as though I can feel it in my own body. It doesn't hurt me, but my body knows you feel it in the parts where it hurts you."

The ability to do this is not peculiar to me. It is a human

faculty of perception that comes to most massage therapists with experience. It plays a vital role in healing one person by another and it is entirely instinctive.

When I work with people to give them healing, it is my instinctive, intuitive perceptions that are working. Just as the power of massage works not through physical touch alone but through the exchange of energy between one human being and another, so in healing it is the internal energy of the person I am healing that I see.

Inside each one of us there is a technicolour picture created by our invisible selves. It is a rainbow of the energy generated by our emotional reactions, our desires, our expectations, our memories and our unique path of discovery in this life. This energy has physical effects, but it is not immediately physical. It can get unbalanced, but it is possible to change it into a more harmonious balance through our thoughts and decisions, and it's also possible for another person, a healer, to rebalance it for us. When you allow a healer to do this, you will feel different, sometimes dramatically, sometimes subtly, but the most powerful instrument of change you have is your own conscious mind.

Nothing has more power over you and your life than that. It is as though all the cells in your body look to you as the boss of the factory. They work hard on the factory floor to do their job according to your instructions. You may have been sending down instructions on an unconscious level that are different from your conscious thoughts. Your emotional reactions generate instructions on the unconscious level. Your conscious thoughts tend to reflect your perception of logic and 'reality'. If your cells receive mixed messages, they can function differently from the way you think they should.

How you get in touch with the messages you have been sending yourself unconsciously is where we're going now. These are the methods and the experiences I want to share.

Chapter 5

Interlude – 'A Time Before You Were Born'

Imagine going back to a time before you were born, before you had any body or any connection to the desires and needs that stem from having a body. Imagine you are free from thought and emotion. You are pure consciousness, at one with God. Imagine residing in a heavenly state of peace, or visualize a peaceful resting place beside a springtime brook.

After an indeterminate time you hear God call: "Have I got a job for you!" Or, looking at it another way, a memory of unfinished business arises and your karma of leftover tasks and desires calls to you. This summons stimulates your thought forms (composed of air and ether) and brings on more memories. You get excited, which can be construed as nerve energy, and are no longer as restful. From a state of pure spirit you begin to spiral downward into denser matter.

You choose your parents and conception occurs. You are no longer as spacious as you once were. Although you have not yet identified yourself with this developing body, it becomes more dominant as cells multiply, a brain and a spinal cord develop. This embryo is already much heavier than the thoughts that created it.

You take both into the physical world and now you are much more restricted. Soon you start to build a self-image around this heavy elemental form because of the constant need for food, air and elimination. Bodily chemistry is cumbersome, compared to the being of pure spirit you were. You begin to connect to events outside yourself and identify yourself as this vehicle, as something other than pure spirit. Consider the implications.

Donald VanHowten[1]

Chapter 6

Rooting For Mother – *From Anxiety To Trust*

How we come into being is beyond knowing. We will never learn the answer with our rational faculties. Imagination can take us to the edge of thought, and each person's imagination will be their emotional truth. As we explore ourselves intuitively, we begin to lose our lack of trust in ourselves, and appreciate those ways in which we excel, which add up to our purpose, to the point of us. Yet we need our rational faculties to help us get there. Rationally we can perceive how very special the bond with mother is in the human experience. The body we are given to live with has some unique properties compared to other mammals.

I am watching a film of an elephant being born. After 22 months in her womb, the baby is finally ready to become a separate being. He lands safely on the ground in his caul, and his mother begins at once to prod and even kick him. She breaks the caul, so that quickly he stands up, while she washes its remnant from him with jets of water from her trunk. Perfectly formed after his long gestation, he staggers a little on unfamiliar legs, but in a matter of minutes he is ready to follow his mother into the bush. Still connected to her by his need for milk, safely hidden between the flanks of the other females of the herd, he can walk, drink and swim in their protective shadow, almost from the moment of his birth.

It strikes me how our human fragility at birth is so unlike other animals. We take a long time to develop the senses we need to survive. We can barely see, we cannot use our arms or legs. We cannot even lift our heads. We can smell and we can breathe and, once we are guided to the source of food, we can suck.

The first months of our life appear to be concerned with developing those important senses. Our mothers encourage them to develop in us for just the same reason that the elephant mother brutally pushes her baby to walk. She wants him to survive. We describe ourselves in biology books as having five senses: the sense of smell, taste, sight, touch and hearing. Most of us are blessed with those faculties and they are the ones we pay attention to because, just like the elephants, those 'outer' senses keep us safe in our environment. Quickly we learn to observe the outer skin of our surroundings so that we can distinguish between what is helpful to us and what is potentially harmful.

Yet, though we are born physically frail, we have been developing silently an inner capacity that gives us what we lack in outer strength. We have been learning, listening, reacting and remembering all through our time in the womb. The inner consciousness of a human being is already well developed at the time of our birth. We tend to forget that there is a lot more going on in a baby human than there appears to be. I remember a conversation with one of my daughters when she was about three years old. I made some remark that I'd made before and she said,

"Oh yes. That's what you used to say when you changed my nappy on the bathroom floor!"

I was shocked. When she was eight or nine months old, we lived in a tiny flat that had a carpeted bathroom, and I used to change her nappy on the bathroom floor. I would natter away to her as I did, as most mothers chatter to their babies, but she couldn't speak, so I never imagined that she could understand what I was saying, let alone remember what she heard and where she heard it!

Right away I began to understand that you cannot judge the internal senses of a human being by the exterior, and everything I have experienced since has taken me deeper and deeper into the extraordinary powers of the consciousness we humans possess.

My experiences with healing have been adventures in human consciousness. Every healing I do teaches me another facet of the extraordinary but purposeful patterns we trace in our lives, even when we are not aware of them. The information I receive from you when you ask for healing is an unspoken language that neither of us would see with our conscious minds. Yet it comes to me in silent conversation and appears as images, sounds and sensations on my internal camera.

I have come to expect and accept what I see as valid information, just as I would assess the height of a doorway before I step through it, so as not to bang my head. Yet, still, I offer my perceptions up with a question, because only you, the person who has asked for healing, knows how or whether these perceptions reflect your emotional experience.

Working with hundreds of human beings has taught me much about how we live and die, and what we need to change or balance in our lives to be happier. A long time ago, in my early days of working as a healer, Tim came to me for healing. Before we began, I asked him what he wanted to be different and better in his life. Tim said he didn't really like where he lived, but he wasn't sure where he would rather live. He didn't know either what kind of work he wanted to do. He was restless, unsettled and unhappy, and he wanted that to change.

Tim sat in a chair and closed his eyes while I began to look inside – something I can best describe as peering into an internal kaleidoscope. Down by his feet, I knelt on the floor and looked to see how his 'roots' connected with the earth. We all have roots, just like plants do. They are our individual connection to the planet that we live and die on. They speak of our connection to the physical elements we are made from: the carbon, the calcium, the iron and the silica. Everything that we are in our physical selves comes from the earth: our bodies, our clothes, our food, our houses, roads and cars. And when we are done, everything that we are in our physical selves goes back to the earth and is reformed in the planet.

When I looked for Tim's roots, all I could see was a stingray, floating its wide fins close to the seabed but hardly ever in contact with the rock and sand below. Absorbing the information, I set about changing the picture. I drained the sea (ha! the power of the imagination!), dug a hole for Tim in fertile soil on a riverbank, and planted his roots deep into this hole, waiting to see how he would grow. He grew, I remember, as a poplar tree, tall and strong, but pliable and resistant to the onslaughts of wind.

When I finished the healing, I asked Tim how he felt. He had some sensations in his legs and felt slightly sick and unbalanced, but that quickly passed. A bit uncertainly, I told him what I'd seen in his roots and asked what it meant to him.

"It's very strange," I told him. "I didn't have a sense of your connection to the earth at all at first. You were like a stingray, floating over the seabed but never touching it. Your root chakra affects the energy of your legs and feet, and your skeleton, the basic structure of your body, on a physical level. But all the chakras have a non-physical aspect as well. This one concerns your relationship with mother and its energy is shaped by your reactions to her. So, if there was this complete lack of connection, could you explain that?"

"I was adopted," Tim said quietly, feeling rising to his face, "and I never felt connected to my adoptive mother."

I understood. Tim's birth mother brought him into the world, and by the time he was born he had already perceived and remembered her thoughts and feelings, receiving them as precisely as the nourishment he absorbed from her blood while he was in the womb. His mother was his shelter, the source of survival for this fragile, defenceless being. Her reactions were immensely important to him. From the picture I received it seems likely that she decided to give him up for adoption early in the pregnancy, so that he was born with the feeling of having no root. Otherwise, the picture in his energy could have come from that early separation after birth, so that he felt he could only touch a safe haven, never rest or feel secure in it.

This mattered to Tim in his adult life because that relationship with his birth mother had a defining effect on his attitude to everything that meant security in his later life: job, money, home. Regardless of his talents or desires, he had had the expectation that nothing would give him the security he craved, and he had been restlessly pursuing alternative homes and jobs for most of his life.

As we root into the protective bubble of our mother's body for nourishment and growth, we absorb also the whole of her experience. Sometimes we react with sympathy and sometimes with alarm. That depends on our own individual story. Those of us who have siblings, or children of our own, know that each one of us is unique in our reactions and feelings, even when we share the same parents who have tried to treat us in the same way. Those initial reactions begin to shape us, just like a climbing plant begins to shape itself around a trellis.

Knowing this may explain a lot of things in your life. When you become conscious of the emotion that your unconscious body has stored for you, you understand very quickly how it has coloured your reactions to situations that touch on the same aspect of your life. Once you understand, over half the battle is won. It is as though your unconscious has been holding on to pain, emotional or physical, willing you to understand that what you experience is not an objective reality but a variable situation that can change when your emotional reaction changes. Once you understand, your conscious mind is free to take action. You become the boss of the factory again. You can effectively release old feelings, freeing you to aim towards a path you like better.

Sometimes this happens spontaneously. Susan is a woman in her early seventies who came to me and asked me if she could have 'half a massage'. She had been suffering from *plantar fasciitis* for a couple of years and despite all the treatments she had tried, the pain from her foot was stubbornly present, preventing her from enjoying her life. She wanted half a massage only, however, because she didn't think she could afford a full one.

Money is the language of security in our society. Some of us use it as energy to enable our life, allowing it to flow freely and trusting that we will have more as and when we need it. Others see it as a restraint, constantly fearing lack, holding back from enjoying the power of what they have now, for fear of the future. In this way money becomes a symbol of trust and self-belief. Looked at as a spiritual value, the way we choose to use or receive money becomes a currency that teaches us a lot about ourselves. As the writer Alfonso Vonscheidt put it:

Real wealth isn't about money. It's about access to resources. ... Money is a symbol of our confidence in our product, our service and ourselves. If you want to have more money in your life, for yourself or to help others, or both, then you have to make yourself more valuable in the eyes of other people. It won't be enough to provide valuable goods and services, or to be in the right place at the right time. You'll have to be more spiritual than that. You'll have to have more faith, more confidence in your own value as a provider or as a person.[1]

Whether or not you perceive what money you have as an enabling or a disabling force in your life is often closely linked to your emotional experience of security in those first years of your life. The more you trust the safety of your home, the more confidence you have naturally that the world will provide for your needs. The opposite is also true. If you don't feel able to enjoy the wealth of the earth that your birth has given you, you will never have 'enough' money. A sense of lack, mistrust and fear are products of not trusting the safety of your birth mother's love. The effect can be a lack of confidence in your own worth. Once that emotion is in place, experiences in your life repeatedly confirm that reality for you. But you can make a conscious change in that expectation when you feel ready, and marvel at its effects.

I didn't give Susan a lecture about the meaning of money, of course. Instead, I accepted her request and told her I would see what I could do for her in half an hour. As I was working, I felt the tension in her left leg, all the way up into the hip. I explained how the body doesn't make a distinction between emotional pain and physical strain. It expresses your deep feelings and manifests them as tension in the part of the body through which that feeling speaks.

"Judging by what your body is telling me, you have been feeling unsupported, emotionally and physically. Is that so?" I asked.

Immediately she burst into tears.

"My husband died three years ago. I've been telling everybody that I'm fine, that I can manage on my own. I've always felt so independent. But really I've been feeling so alone and afraid."

The tension in her leg relaxed. Feeling is healing. When my clients cry, I know we are clearing what we need to clear. After half an hour she got up from the massage table, and the *plantar fasciitis* was gone. Really.

It doesn't always happen like that. Some of us have to work a bit harder to clear mental habits that have been with us for as long as we can remember. Once we become aware of our pattern and our reason for it, however, we have all kinds of faculties at our disposal to change it for something we like better.

Sometimes we have to feel our way to our emotional truth, by inches. We remember some things with startling clarity, or we remember nothing. The impressions that shape the energy of our root chakra form initially between conception and the age of two or three, when we are most fragile, most dependent on our mother's protection and rooting for her support. Somewhere in that experience are incoherent, unexpressed feelings, none the less deeply felt for that. When we imagine ourselves as babies in our mothers' arms, those feelings come back to us and shape the pictures of our imagination. We find we can see and speak to our mothers in the eloquent internal world of our feeling and often that experience will help us to understand the decisions we have made since. This imaginative world is not an objective reality. It would not necessarily be agreed by our brother or sister, or even by our mother. But it is *our* reality. To find our way forward, we have to start by accepting what has been true for us.

The American yogi Ram Dass, once known as the academic sociologist, Richard Alpert, described the challenges we face in our lives as "the curriculum".[2] There is a lesson, he maintained, that we need to learn in our lives, and each time our consciousness takes form in life, our experiences reflect the lesson we need to learn. We cannot avoid it. It is 'the curriculum'. If we don't learn the lesson, we need to repeat it.

Diving into the inner energy of other human beings, at their invitation and with their consent, reveals more mysteries than the land under the sea. When Andrew came to me with severe back pain, I knew that there would be something that needed to be resolved in his root chakra. This centre is the densest energy in our body and affects its primary material structure, the skeleton. So, problems with the spine nearly always reflect an issue in the root chakra. I expected there would be an issue, but I didn't know what it was until I took a look at the inner picture.

Andrew's back pain was so severe that he had had surgery, twice. Despite that, the pain persisted, so that he could barely sit down. He was not working at that time. He said he had been forced to leave his job. I was not surprised, when I began the healing, to find pockets of anger, burning in different parts of his body. I could have detected those without connecting with the inner world. Anger causes inflammation in the body, and acute nerve pain and tenderness is often the result. Also, I knew, without looking, that the pain in his back was connected to tension over his situation at work, since this is the form security would take in his adult life. But I didn't know why the situation had arisen until I looked inside.

When I was healing Andrew's root chakra, a vivid picture came up before me. Down there in the ground, somewhere in the buried past, his roots portrayed him as a wounded soldier. I could see the red cross of a crusader on the tabard that covered his armour. It looked as if he had lost a part of his leg and he was lying on the ground with his fellow soldiers around him. They had made up their minds to leave him, as they could no longer carry him. He had received this decision with anger and a deep sense of betrayal. In the healing I sent angels to grow the severed leg again, picking this body from the ground so it could stand upright on its own two feet. Then I sent the roots deep into the earth so they could release all the material they had stored and take fresh nourishment from the energy of the earth for their future growth.

We finished the healing and I talked to Andrew about what I'd seen. The picture bore no relation to the urbane international banker I saw before me, so, somewhat hesitantly, I related the story of the wounded crusader I had seen in his roots. Slightly to my surprise, he showed instant recognition.

"Until I was six, I always wanted to be a priest."

The part he related to at once was the crusader fighting for a holy cause.

"But in the picture, you were being abandoned by your fellows. You had been a tight band, fighting together, and then they left you to die. That energetic picture in your root chakra would suggest that in your current life you have experienced a similar pattern – working with people and then feeling abandoned."

Andrew explained that he had faced this situation repeatedly in successive jobs, feeling forced out by colleagues who he had thought of as friends. I marvelled inwardly at the long reach of the energetic picture that had presented itself to me, reaching deep into past history. I had no conception, before I became a healer, about whether people carry a memory of a past life or not, or even about whether there has been one. I was familiar, of course, with the concept of reincarnation, but it had seemed to me merely theoretical. How can we know what we carry, when it is apparently beyond the reach of our functioning brain, beyond life itself? Yet here was an image that was instantly recognisable to the consciousness that carried it, that had had tangible practical effects on his life, even though he had no conscious memory of it in his lifetime! More extraordinary still, that image presented itself to some aspect of my consciousness in a form that I was able to relay back to him.

Over the years, the stories of people who have come to me for healing have expanded my understanding of human consciousness. I don't always see an image from a previous existence when I am healing. Sometimes I have the feeling I am working with a very young soul: beautiful, fresh, loving, and painfully sensitive. Yet, at other times, the pull of the past has been dragged into this life as a lesson that begs to be learned. This child is much older than the mother and takes on the role of caring for her even before he or she is born. As it happens, my mother and I had always known this to be true and it was openly acknowledged between us. She was the child, and she expected me to look after her.

This inner vision I share with someone being healed only matters because it corresponds to their external reality. Where two realities intersect there is enough information to create dynamic physical change. Many realities that create this kind of change were born in the realms of human imagination, deep intuition, the inner voice. Realities like acupuncture, the chakras themselves, or stories that express the truth of our humanity, whether *King Lear* or *Harry Potter*. When you learn to trust that inner voice in yourself, it will lead you further than you think possible, while helping you, nonetheless, to keep your feet on the ground in the present reality of your life.

Andrew and I talked about what he could do now to further the healing and change things for himself. The healing alone would present him with opportunities for a change in his perspective on his life. The information he received afterwards in dreams and memories would offer an invitation for him to pay attention to the feelings they evoked. He could begin by taking his imagination seriously and using it to dispel the pain and anger when it reared up in his body.

I guided Andrew in a technique I have found to send pain into the earth.

The planet can bear our pain much more easily than we tiny humans can. The planet, which gives us life, food, warmth, shelter and ultimately the oblivion of dark rest, is unmoved by our rage, our shame, our regret, guilt and fear. I showed him how to stand, barefoot if possible and outside, so he could feel his feet sink into the earth's surface, and when that fresh, direct feel on his skin was not possible, just to allow his imagination to put it there. When he was sure he could be alone and unchallenged, he was to speak out loud to the earth some words from his heart, asking her to take his pain, his fear, his anger, whatever it might be. Then with his eyes closed and his knees softened, so that he was standing loosely and relaxed, allow himself to feel where in his body this feeling he wished to let go of was lodged. It is always somewhere. You will always find a part where there is tension, even if you didn't know it was there, when you close your eyes and allow yourself to look inside. When the pain is found, I told Andrew to crumple it up like coloured paper left on the floor after a birthday party, and to take this crumpled ball of paper down through his right leg and foot into the surface he was standing on. I told him to imagine its journey through the layers of soil, the shifting rock, the underground streams and caverns, and finally, through the layers of molten magma to the white-hot fire at the centre of the planet where it would be entirely consumed. Then from the fire at the core of the planet, to take pure white heat and energy: to imagine it coming up like a spear of growth through the planet and travelling swiftly through the layers of earth until it touched the sole of the left foot. I told him to absorb this spear of white energy into the muscles, spine and skin, seeing it travel up through the trunk and legs until it filled the whole body and head, resting finally in the place where the crumpled piece of pain had been.

When you try this to resolve your pain, whether that is physical pain or anger, fear and panic, give yourself a minute to absorb the sensation of lightness that comes with allowing yourself to let the pain go and take up energy from the earth. Enjoy the full possibilities of that minute. Like Andrew, note the differences you can make to your body with the power of your mind. This technique works better than paracetamol.

I warned Andrew that if his intense pain recurred, he should observe what was happening in his life at that moment, and what he felt about it. Then he should go through the process I've just described to free himself of his reaction. At times of deep crisis, he might need to do this several times in a day, perhaps even ten or twenty times. Even so, this process would allow him to ride the storm, and release the pain, rather than reaching for oblivion, in the form of painkillers or alcohol or other drugs. Gradually, I told him, the sea will calm, and instead of feeling churned in rushing water, he would feel he was floating his boat calmly on the surface of the ocean.

I developed this technique to deal with my own pain which, in a troubled time of my life, seemed to back up inside me like an immense wall of water held by a cracking dam. It was unbearable to hold on to and terrifying to let it out. I remembered a Dutch children's story I had read once, about a little boy who stuck his finger in a hole in a dam that threatened to break and overwhelm his village. It seemed to me that if I could let the pain out slowly, in a trickle rather than a rush, like making a hole in a dam, I would lower the tension and survive the exodus. As I focused on my body and its physical pain, standing barefoot on the earth at the end of my garden, I could feel the tension leave me, drop by drop, and each time I did this little exercise, I would feel a little more energy, clarity and confidence.

One of the consequences of passing your pain into the earth in this way is that you become much more aware of how you react physically to emotional circumstances. You notice that you are a living exhibition of feelings. Understanding this brings you closer to your body, realising that its processes are sharing your experiences with you, reacting in a way that alerts you to what you find difficult, painful, or unacceptable. I noticed that as I began to release the pain and feel where in my body it had lodged, my body itself was nudging me towards understanding my feelings.

Knowing we can release pain helps us to move forward in our lives. How to move forward is another matter. The greatest inhibitor that prevents us from choosing to do what makes us happy is fear. Sometimes our fear is buried under layers of avoidance. We tell ourselves that what we want to do is impossible, or too expensive, or something we would have liked to do if we'd been born as someone else. All this while we are wasting time and opportunity, opening ourselves up to regret and resentment.

How do you know whether what you are facing is a crazy idea that could be harmful or something you need to carry through and experience in your life? In fact, you don't, until you know yourself better and learn to trust your intuition. The chances are that when an idea repeatedly returns to your mind, it is something you need to go through with. The more unfamiliar it is to the life you already know, the more you will fear it. If you are perpetually giving yourself reasons why you can't do this thing, then there is a good chance that you are unconsciously using avoidance to protect yourself. At the heart of avoidance is fear, so you owe it to yourself to explore that fear.

Overcoming Fear and Anxiety

Anxiety is a constant state of mind for some of us. We believe it is a particular event we need to worry about, but after that event is passed, there will be another, and then another. Transferred from one event in your life to another, anxiety is a sign that you are living in a state of fear that is depressing your energy and freedom. If this sounds familiar to you, then bear in mind that there is an instant fix that will calm you and help you get through the current situation. You need to put your body in contact with the ground for five or ten minutes. If it is possible, take off your shoes and walk barefoot on the earth, or lie down on the grass. If this is not possible, try to find a tree where you can lean your back against the trunk. Allow yourself to feel the sensations of activity in the trunk of the tree or in the ground under your body. Concentrate as hard as you can on the connection between your skin and the earth's skin or the plant's. The world around you is alive, and everything vibrates at a frequency that can harmonise with the natural frequency of your body's organs. The heart and the brain frequencies are low in their natural state. When you are tense, the frequency in your body rises. Plants are highly sensitive to sound and vibration. When you lie on the grass, or lean on a tree, you open yourself to harmony between your body and the plant body. Concentrate on this and you will feel the energy that is the currency of our world flow into you and give you strength.

If you have a busy mind, and find it hard to concentrate, see if you can listen instead to hear the plant tell you a story. Put your back against the trunk or hold a leaf in your hand and imagine what the plant has to say. You may be surprised how easy this is! You can do this even with an office plant on your desk, but trees are especially rewarding because they have a much longer life span than human beings. The chances are you will lean on a tree that was a youngster when Queen Victoria was on the throne, or when Jefferson was in the White House. The perspective the natural world affords you will calm you, physically and mentally, and then you can go back to considering the problem that had been making you anxious.

Fear is a reminder that feelings change the biological processes in our body. We are familiar with shaking legs, tight stomach, and short breath in the face of something that scares us. But when our fears are continuous or non-physical in form, we come to treat these reactions as 'normal' and learn to override or ignore such damaging alarm signals from our bodies.

Sooner or later you must move from overcoming momentary anxiety to facing your fear. Anxiety is a condition that overlies a fundamentally fearful perspective that can be changed when we address it. Once you look the demon in the eye it can be a beautiful teacher and guide.

The Tibetan Buddhist teacher Chogyam Trungpa was brought up in a monastery from the age of eighteen months because he was identified when a baby as the reincarnation of a tulku, a teacher whose enlightenment brings him back into human life to help others. He said that, as a child, he was always taught that he must run towards fear. One day, when he was about nine years old, he was visiting an outlying monastery in eastern Tibet with some older monks who were looking after him. The landscape of this vast open plain is dramatically arid, with no trees or bushes to mask the snow-laden mountain peaks that break starkly out of the horizon into the sky. The boy Trungpa and his fellow monks were not expected. The monastery they were visiting was protected by Tibetan hunting dogs: large, fierce animals which, that evening, had not been chained. In a pack, the dogs charged the strangers, snarling and foaming at the mouth. Trungpa's companions turned and ran, but the boy remembered the instruction that he must always run towards fear. As fast as his legs would carry him, he rushed towards the dogs, waving his arms and shouting. The dogs stopped, and they turned, and they ran back to their kennels, cowering.

If you can remember this story when you are aware of feeling fear, then fear can become your friend. You may not know that it is fear you feel. But your body knows. You will find that the possibilities you create in your imagination, thinking over the difficulties you will face, are experienced by your body as a real event. You can try this experiment.

Think of walking along a plank on the ground. The plank is about 24 cms/12 inches wide, and about 5 metres/15 feet long. It's wide enough for you to walk along comfortably, placing one foot in front of the other carefully, without falling over. With care you can walk along it easily. (Even if you have a disability you can do this in your mind! Such is the beauty of your imagination.)

Now imagine that the same plank is 10 metres off the ground. Nothing has changed in the width or the stability of the plank, only there is now a chasm underneath it, filled with rushing water. Even while sitting and just imagining this picture, you will begin to feel the changes in your body. Your stomach tightens, perhaps. Your legs feel weaker and your ankles shaky. Your breathing is light and shallow. Your arms reach for something to hold on to, but there is nothing.

All that has changed is your mental picture of what *might* happen. You might wobble and fall off, you might hit your head on the rocks below, or drown in the water. Your imagination will take you there as a physical reality. I have this reaction when I'm watching television! Sometimes I have to detach myself from the drama because I realise my body is physically in the scene.

Once when I took a group of people through this process, there was a woman who imagined the situation especially vividly. She saw the plank stretching out in front of her over the wild howling chasm and she felt, literally, unable to move, as though in a dream her body had turned to stone. Then, in her mind, she saw her little dog on the other side, trembling and alone. At once her feet unglued themselves from the ground and she was able to launch herself over the chasm to scoop up her precious dog and hold him. When you visit your fear in your mind, and put it in front of you in as much detail as you can muster, the thing that will take you through to the other side will appear for you. This woman was carried over fear by her tender heart. Her love of caring for a small dependent creature took her across the chasm.

For some, just the process of offering your vulnerability to unshakeable earth will allow new strength and clarity to dawn. You do not need to be ashamed of your weakness. We are all weak. In our lives we are constantly exchanging what is fragile and ready to be discarded for new strength and energy. That is the natural process. It happens in our bodies in the form of apoptosis. It happens in our minds as we accept our mistakes as lessons. A baby learning to walk falls over repeatedly. She doesn't dwell on her mistakes. She gets up again and pursues her desire until her body learns the trick of balance. She learns to translate desire into reality.

Your body is a vehicle, on a racing track or a river. Your anxieties are obstacles in the way. The British racing driver, Jackie Stewart, said:

Always look where you're going. Never look at the bend, or you will crash.

This is not the same thing as pretending the bend is not there. Acknowledging the bends and twists in the road will keep you on your toes and help you negotiate, but if you keep your eyes on your goal it will take you forward.

Grasp your invisible fears and aims as physical objects in your life and you will find your body has the mechanism to deal with them. Standing still from time to time, you can give your body roots into the earth to gain the strength and renewal from the earth's support. If you let your mind follow the roots to the end, you will find they go very deep indeed, into your energetic resonance with the past. Your individual roots go deeper than your mother, or her mother; into your personal spiritual root, as deep as the lives you have lived before and the experiences you have brought with you. To make sense of those you have to keep digging.

Chapter 7

Hunting Treasure In the Dark – *Seeking Spiritual Roots*

Beware lest you lose the substance by grasping at the shadow.
Aesop

About a year before my mother's final illness made it impossible for me to travel, I had been doing some digging for roots of my own – spiritual roots. I was drawn to India to find them. At the time I had no idea how close to my birth family's roots this search would bring me, but this curious interlacing between different races and cultures that forms the background to so many family stories emerged later.

Initially my search was inspired by a man from Mumbai. He had worried me and simultaneously sparked my curiosity. Sitting in my house in the English countryside one morning, I was surprised to get a message from a man in Mumbai saying that he wanted healing. He had stumbled across me because of the Internet, that extraordinary network that would have been magic to our grandparents, which dissolves geography instantaneously. Based on what he had found on my website, he asked if I could heal him. I thought he could do better.

"Look," I said, "most of my work comes from principles out of India. I work with energy in the body. There's no more detailed description of the way invisible energy works in the body than there is in Indian culture. Can't you just go around the corner and find somebody who can help you?"

"Do you know someone?" he asked. "I don't know where to go."

I didn't, but I was sure he would find something if he looked. I said,

"I do charge for healing you know. Have a think about it and come back to me if you really want to go ahead."

A few days later Karim got in touch with me again. He had arranged for his brother-in-law in Manchester to pay me as he was unable to send money out of India. I was impressed he had gone to such trouble. His confidence made me put aside my doubts and do the best for him I could.

When someone comes to me for healing, we discuss what they want to have healed and what those symptoms or their situation might imply in terms of the way the body uses energy. Then I sit them down in a chair and ask them to relax while I look for the picture of energy that they have been carrying. What I see inside doesn't bear much relation to my impression of the outside body, but nevertheless, in those days, I felt reassured by having a physical body in front of me in a chair. I knew that healing energy was not physical, in the sense of measurable by an instrument, so that remote healing was just as possible as being face to face with the person I was working with, but I was doubtful whether I had the capacity to heal at a distance of thousands of miles.

Even so I understood that the challenges you are presented with do not come by accident. Karim was inviting me to stretch beyond what I thought possible and each time this had happened in the past I had found that the limits I imagined had dissolved. I just needed to trust that this was something I could do. So we set up a time to 'meet' over the Internet.

We spoke briefly on Skype about what Karim wanted to have healed. His problem wasn't physical so much as practical. He was married with a young son and he needed to find a job. He had been made redundant and he needed to find another one. He also wanted to lose weight.

I did the healing as though he was sitting in front of me in a chair, asking the heavens to direct me to his energy. I thought a little prayer would help the situation along.

A very short time after, I felt that I was linking into a person whose energy pattern I could see clearly, and I set about shifting it into balance. Afterwards I spoke to him about what I had seen and the changes I had made. This conversation is always important. For the person being healed it is like having a conversation with their unconscious selves. Like dredging up objects from under the water line, I am presenting them with things they already know about themselves but have kept tucked away. Either they haven't seen them as important, or they are feelings they recognise that have never taken conscious form. If they have a 'dark secret', something they know but do not want to reveal, it rarely appears until they are ready to reveal it, unless it's directly connected to a physical condition that needs to be healed. Such is the power of our conscious minds. Our 'knowing' self directs and controls the whole orchestra of our being, but sometimes the information we need to move forward gets lost in the unconscious, 'below the water line'. When I give someone back these feelings, this information about themselves, they are in a position of power. They can reflect on feelings that have no value in their current lives, and decide to let them go, releasing the physical tensions that have been caused at the same time.

As always with healing, the situation Karim wanted healed reached far beyond the immediate effect of finding himself stuck at home without a job. It had to do with his relationship with his mother and home, and all of this needed to be brought to his attention as well as trusting the power of healing energy to make changes in the wonderfully subtle way in which it works.

This healing itself was a revelation to me. I was delighted that when I told Karim what I had seen while I was working in his energy, he recognised the situations I described as true descriptions of what he had experienced. It was clear that, somehow, his desire to be healed and my desire to give him healing had connected beyond the laws of time and geography.

Just by wishing to be there, this desire had acted like a satellite and bounced signals halfway across the world to make a bridge between us. I was awed by the magic, and even more pleased when, the next time Karim contacted me, he was calling from London. He was in the city travelling for his new job.

I have done many remote healings since that time, inspired by that event, and I have understood that the energy which is healed, the vital energy at the core of the human being I am working with, exists beyond the laws of time and space that manifest in our visible physical world.

Yet I found this experience troubling also. Karim's native country, India, is the source of so much ancient wisdom about how to maintain a balance between physical and spiritual energy in our lives, a wisdom that matters because it makes humans happier, healthier, more productive, creative and peaceful. India is a country that has plentiful written descriptions of its ancient cultural tradition, consisting of documents that have been preserved and taught from as far back as 900 years BCE. Although there are civilizations that date from much earlier than this, demonstrated in the caves of France and Spain, the fossils of Kenya, the rocks of Africa, the pyramids of South America and Egypt, the bronzes of China, the ancient culture of India was lived until it became documented, and as far as I knew, it had so far escaped destruction. Mumbai is the heart of India's rapid modernisation. I was shocked by the suggestion that the practice of that culture was more available in an English village that it appeared to be in Mumbai. Could it be that after centuries of survival the pressures of modern commercial society were killing off that culture in the land of its birth?

I wanted to explore the roots of ancient experience to give the work that I practised as a healer, constantly revealing new dimensions to me, some kind of continuity. I wanted the relationship that we all want with our mothers: the security of superior knowledge that I could trust and feel safe in, guidance and protection for my evolving soul. Was there, still, a living source, or many living sources of this kind of knowledge in a land that had inspired so much respected wisdom in the past? Could I make a personal connection with such a source?

Teaching from India encourages us to train the mind and the body in ways that respect the laws of physical space and time but also to comprehend our existence beyond them. The first written text in an Indo-European language that points to the depth and power of consciousness is the Rigveda, which dates back to sometime around one and half thousand years before Christ. About eight centuries later the Upanishads were compiled, both texts in Sanskrit. The philosophy they talk of is not a denial of the physical but an acknowledgement of the power of the spiritual energy within it.

Healing has no physical boundaries. Thought is not limited by time and space. On the contrary, it executes change in time and space. Ever since I first entered this magical space, I have wanted to delve deeper into it.

The ancient philosophies and practices of India are the best recorded explanations of how and why invisible energy works in the body, even though the perception of this energy is not only not unique to Indian culture, but seems universal before it was overlaid by modern forms of 'knowledge'. No other civilization has devoted so much time and respect to the practice of monitoring the internal energy that human beings can perceive or described so many techniques for cultivating and developing it to create a bridge with the energy of the visible world. No other society has produced, in living memory, so many masters of techniques that seem to make them capable of leaving their physical body and returning at will.

Sanskrit, like Arabic, is a language made up of root forms of words that give a single word multiple meanings. The Vedic scholars of India have devoted centuries to interpreting and explaining the true meaning of the original texts. The problem with such ancient and detailed teaching is that it becomes very complicated over time. Philosophical truths in the original get buried under different interpretations. Different schools with different rules grow and spread like mushrooms, all based on original Sanskrit texts whose meaning is quite impenetrable to any person born outside Indian culture but also to many within it. So where should I start to dig deeper?

The *idea* of India was important to me. The idea of India was cemented for me when I read, like millions of others, *The Autobiography of a Yogi* by Paramahansa Yogananda. In it, Yogananda describes his early 20th century upbringing in Bengal in the east of India, his longing to discover his spirit from an early age and his eventual relationship with an extraordinary teacher. According to his account, his master, Sri Yukteswar, was able to go beyond his physical body, so that on several occasions Yogananda saw him and spoke to him in one place while other people saw and spoke to him in another place miles away. The description of this exceptional ability is one of the reasons that the book has piqued so many people's curiosity since it was published in 1946. These are feats equivalent to the miracles attributed to Jesus and yet not separated from us by so many centuries of strife, politics and dogma. This relationship with the human body and with the human consciousness was something that Sri Yukteswar was not just demonstrating, but advocating and teaching. This is powerful for anyone interested in understanding the complex nature of being human, whatever their experience of spiritual teaching.

I had explored the Indian peninsula only once before. I was just out of university when I stayed in a clean white house near Mysore, with spacious rooms and airy high ceilings, shining terracotta tiles on the floor, visited by monkeys from the surrounding jungle. No window glass or doors separated us from the monkeys or the swathe of clipped grass that led to the bank of the river that swept around the property. A bath meant a dip in the river. I got used to keeping clean by scooping water with a little brass bowl from a big earthenware jar that was placed in the bathroom and filled with river water every morning. A separate building in the garden was a clinic by day. Mothers with babies, little children who had walked for miles, and a few men, would form a line every morning, waiting silently for a diagnosis and simple medicines like aspirin or free supplements of milk. I should perhaps have seen that their lives were hard, but the environment was lush, and they seemed so calm, that all I saw was a kind of magical beauty.

I found I had no words to describe India. Everything was so different from what I knew. Indians were gently amused by foreigners who didn't know how to eat with their hands, or who asked for eggs in the strictly vegetarian south, but never harsh enough to be openly disapproving. Passing a site where a new road was being made, the labourers were women wearing saris of glorious colours, carrying baskets of broken rock on their heads, elegantly lifted above their slim bodies as if they were bowls of flowers. In Kochi (then known as Cochin) I stayed in an elegant old hotel facing out over the endless ocean to the west. You could sit here on the wide veranda, on chairs built for bulky European ancestors, and watch the fishermen draw in their nets, stretched like gossamer umbrellas to catch the sea and the setting sun. It was quiet, simple, and beautiful. I was simultaneously dazzled, and hopelessly confused.

I realised much would have changed since the last time I went exploring in India. But I was barely prepared for just how much! Once again, I was completely surprised by what India threw at me.

I dithered over where to go for fear of finding a source that couldn't be trusted, but in the end, I decided to head for the east of India. I had never been there before, so there was less chance I would be disappointed by how much it had changed. I had heard extraordinary stories of temple dancing in Orissa

(Odisha) from the owner of the white house I had stayed with in my twenties, which had piqued my curiosity. But more importantly, there is an ashram in Puri in modern-day Odisha whose leader was taught by a teacher who was taught by Sri Yukteswar, the teacher of Paramahansa Yogananda, whose words I had found so inspiring. There is there a direct and living line of teaching that reaches back over a hundred and fifty years at least. This is clearly not an unbroken line stretching back to the Upanishads! But it dates back to a time before yoga became so fashionable in the West that it developed into a commercial commodity in the land of its birth. I wrote to the ashram and received an invitation to stay. I stopped dithering and booked my ticket.

Landing in Kolkata, I found a sea of human effort. The apparent struggle is to get somewhere, to be something, to have what is wanted, and yet so often it seems the effort is too much. No one paints the walls, repairs crumbling brickwork, cleans the streets, directs the traffic or takes care of the disabled. There are few beggars on the streets but the disabilities of those are startling. People who have lost their legs or been born without them manage to get around by hauling their bodies' weight with their arms, sometimes with the help of a little wooden board fitted with casters. Artificial limbs or wheelchairs are rare. Even without legs or eyes, you must find a way to survive. The bus conductors are kings of their buses, cramming as many passengers on their vehicle as the grinding engine will stand, and yet, as they hang from the ever-open doors, they pause and shield the old man who steps on as tenderly as if he were their own father. Taxi drivers are champions worthy of Formula 1 races, edging their way through a thick river of traffic, flowing erratically like stormy water. The clattering taxis weave their way between buses, trucks clouded in black smoke, motorbikes carrying whole families, cycle rickshaws, motor rickshaws, cows, dogs and pedestrians, stopping within inches of collision and finding a space to start moving again. Every space must be seized and fought for, on the pavement, in the bus, on the road and in life. Cars blare their horns even on an empty road as regularly as breathing, as though the horn itself gives power to the engine. Yet when a small child runs or an elderly woman creeps across the road, they slow and stop with a patience that suggests there is no such thing as time. Damage or death in this heaving mass is rare.

When a friend of mine visited Rajasthan she was alarmed by this cacophony of noise and traffic that now characterises every Indian town. She tried to negotiate her way through the city by scuttling nervously in the wake of her guide as he strode purposefully across the roads. This man never wavered as he made his way across, and she told herself this courage came from his warrior heritage. His name denoted him a tiger from the warrior clan of Rathore, and his long wavy hair and eaglelike gaze seemed to make him worthy of the name.

When he saw how she dived and darted to avoid the traffic, he told her.

"Stop! You must never run across busy roads in India. Walk in a straight line at the same speed so that drivers can judge how to avoid you. They are the water which flows round you."

India has always valued the holy waters that run through her veins, but in the 21st century the sacred rivers have become choked, polluted and depleted. Still blessed with vast tracts of fertile wilderness, India has nevertheless become a country of noisy, dirty, polluted cities, their ancient beauties hidden behind veils of smog and cords of traffic, like jewels lost in the mud.

Indians are generally proud of their prowess in working with the invisible that dominates all our lives: the World Wide Web. I had heard that cash machines were common in the country and the preferred way for foreigners to obtain Indian currency, which can't be bought outside the country. Kolkata

International Airport is unused to welcoming visitors from the West, however. Neither I, nor the French couple behind me, had much joy in trying to use our cards to obtain cash from the Punjab national bank ATM. So I changed money in a little booth where they gave me £50 worth of rupees in high denomination notes. I intended to change more later when I found an ATM that would accept my Mastercard. That would be a long wait!

A short time later I was rattling through the crowded river of traffic, my eyes streaming from the smog, wondering when the taxi I was in had last had windows you could close. The rest of the day I spent negotiating the curiously Victorian bureaucracy that still dominates public life in India. Every train, every bus in the country has a name, like a pet. And these trains and buses are run by competing individual companies. The timetables and advance booking information, punctuality and status of intercity trains are published in mind-blowing detail on the Internet. There are apps you can use to book your ticket by phone, and it is possible to buy your ticket in this way. Unless, of course, you're a foreigner.

For a foreigner to buy a ticket to travel to Odisha by train, as I wished to do, it is necessary to go to a special office in the centre of the city. I walked round and around one of the large old colonial buildings in what used to be the administrative and financial centre of the city, looking for the office I had been told it housed. I wondered whether my grandfather had also walked these streets, as he was sent out from England to work for a cotton company in Kolkata as soon as he left school. The business of the cotton company was so disengaged from European affairs that they would not let him go to fight in the First World War. Eventually, after his brother was killed, he resigned and joined up anyway. I reflected that the cotton company's delay probably saved his life and delivered mine.

Many of the old buildings, like the much vaunted 'Writers' Building', named after the many clerks who used to work in there dispensing the rules of British colonial administration, are quietly crumbling. Protected by sandbags, wire and sometimes a couple of soldiers, they are a testament to Indian rejection of the humiliation they felt under Britain's presumed 'ownership' of their country in the past. Like a cruel mother giving birth to her child, much of the infrastructure that makes India function in the modern age was built and created by British rulers, but that does not mean the child has forgiven the mother her cruelty. The 21st century is seen by many Indians as the age of revenge.

After stumbling between ribbons of street vendors on the pavements, past unmarked entrances that led into the bowels of the great old buildings, I was eventually guided through a small dark door by a former Railway Employee himself, dapper in a shiny Western suit and hat. Inside, I found rows of seats for the waiting tourists. An Irish photographer named Dave told me he loved Kolkata above all other Indian cities and came there every year for about six months. Otherwise I saw few Europeans. Most foreigners were travellers from neighbouring Bangladesh and seem to have a talent with something I quickly realised I lacked: Bengali. In this capital of eastern India, I mostly spoke to people in English and they would guess what I meant. They replied to me in Bengali, and I would guess what they meant. Generally, it worked.

I was told to take a number, fill in a form that required to know everything from my age and sex to my maiden name, and wait my turn. It was a procedure strongly reminiscent of applying for a passport in the old passport office in London. When my number was called, the attendant checked all the details of my form and we had a lengthy discussion about the position of the overnight berth I would take before I handed over the cost of the ticket in cash.

The ticket was cheap, relatively speaking. There are not many countries in which you can travel overnight in a train berth for the cost of taxi ride in town, so I went back to find my bed for the night with a certain sense of achievement, in spite of my exhaustion. The next day, I told myself, I would have to change some more money. Then I would be free to explore the city.

I woke the next morning to big changes happening in the world. Not just the world I had entered as a visitor, but the one I had come from. My hostess, Sonia, had switched on the television for the morning news. Returns were coming in from the US election, in a time zone twelve hours behind. To the obvious astonishment of the commentators on screen, Donald Trump was becoming the next president of the United States. While I was busy texting this extraordinary news to my children, Sonia was fixed on her morning paper.

"This news is going to have a much bigger effect on you than the new American president," she said. "This article says that from today, all large denomination rupee notes are illegal. Do you have any large notes?"

I checked my wallet.

"I have three 500 rupee notes (each one worth about six pounds). That's what I have left from the money I changed at the airport."

"You won't be able to use those. You'll have to go to the bank and change them. Do you have anything else?"

I had two small notes and some coppers, enough to buy a cheap supper at a market stall, but not enough to take the taxi rides I had spent my money on the day before.

Sonia told me that banks and ATMs would be closed all day and I was pleased. I hadn't come all this way to spend my first full day in the city in a bank. I would make do with what I had for the day, and deal with the money problem tomorrow. I wasn't worried, merely curious.

"Why has this happened?" I asked, wondering if in my haste to get ready to come away I had missed something. "Was it planned?"

"Nobody knew anything about it until this morning. It's

Narendra Modi, our Prime Minister."

Like the soon-to-be president of the United States, and the radical ex-President Chávez of Venezuela, the Indian Prime Minister is one of a breed of democratically elected politicians who know no compromise. Narendra Modi has made his way to the top of the Indian political system despite, or perhaps because of, his origins way outside it. He once worked as a tea wallah, selling tea up and down the Indian trains. In notoriously caste-ridden Indian society, it is astonishing for such a one to become Prime Minister. Committed to a deep pride in India's spiritual heritage, he is a devout Hindu, intolerant of others' practices. He thinks like a hunter and his surprise action was intended to catch people out: political opponents, corrupt officials, black market operators. It just happened to include all of India's burgeoning middle class, small businesses and, way down the pecking order, foreign tourists.

"Most people are not affected," said Sonia. "They don't have any money. But here in India it is normal that if you sell a property you declare only 60% of it as the selling price. The rest of the transaction is paid in cash. Those people will be hurting."

The social pressure to put aside money for a daughter's wedding, which will last for three days and devour huge amounts of cash, or a lavish funeral that will do the same, is a feature of Indian life. The newspaper said that people would have until 23rd December to deposit their old notes in a bank in exchange for new ones. Of course, in the process they would have to prove their identity and fill in a form explaining where the money had come from. Clearly there were going to be some interesting developments. But for the time being I was simply relieved that I could not do anything about my small pot of money until the next day and set out to explore the city. By bus.

Not many foreigners take the bus in Kolkata, and when you do it is a shock to discover that this journey costs thirty times less than the taxi fare. But that is the nature of survival in India.

Most people do not have any money, as Sonia had said, and now it was my privilege to be one of them.

I had sought this corner of India with an idea of looking for roots. Root energy is the point at which the non-physical becomes physical. Inevitably once something becomes physical it will also die and disintegrate. There is a fragility in our own root which frightens us. We prefer not to think about it and enjoy the day like butterflies. We shore ourselves up against the disintegration of the self with material protection. In modern societies the tool that we use to obtain protection and shelter is money. The money that we have is like captured energy. It should be an enabling force in our lives, but we tend to get so anxious about it, imagining that we are responsible for having obtained it and that once it is gone there will be no more, that it becomes a restriction. We tighten our hold on it and use it as a reason not to move forward into our desires.

Here I was, looking for the spiritual truth behind religious creations that supposedly grant the protection we seek in our lives, the multiple gods and goddesses who are revered in the religious pantheons in the Hindu and Buddhist traditions of the East. Would I find any emotional or energetic truth in all the noise and fury of modern-day Hindu practice? These are, after all, the traditions that have grown out of the philosophy that seems so clear and powerful in the ancient texts. I could not escape the irony of arriving in India and finding myself with no money from the very first day. It was as though God was laughing.

You are looking for spiritual truth, the Universe seemed to say, *Look! Spirituality today is all about the money. See what it looks like when you have none!*

Strangely, I found I was quite prepared to do that. Anyone who has ever been to India knows you are universally regarded as one of the rich and privileged from the moment you touch down at the airport. Which you are, by virtue of being able to fly to India. It can get tiresome having all this money. You have to make judgements all the time. How much money should you give and to whom? Do you have enough to give for all? What is the real value of what you need to buy, the price that it costs a local person or the price that you are being asked for? Should you haggle over amounts that you would consider insignificant at home? Being rich brings a burden of care alongside the freedom from fear about whether you have enough money to find something to eat, or somewhere to sleep. Knowing that I was not, for the time being, a cash cow, brought a sense of freedom all its own.

Eastern India, and Bengal in particular, has a long tradition of dedication to the archetypal spirit of the earth mother. Here, she is the Goddess Kali, a powerful creator and fearsome devourer, whose name is derived from the Sanskrit word for 'time': *kal*. Images of her show a terrifying open mouth, her tongue dripping with blood. Her neck is draped with a necklace of skulls and her skirt is a string of human forearms suspended around her waist. In one of her four hands she holds a monstrous black head which she has severed from its body with a scimitar in another hand. She stands forcefully on crushed bodies, and under her right foot, is a tiny white male body, curled in complete submission. This is the male principle, Shiva, the energy of creation, which can only enter the world of physical form by coming through the mother. The female gives form and destroys it. The male principle is the life within that form and beyond it.

In this region, Kali is honoured for her fecundity and begged for her favour to destroy fear and evil. Those monstrous beheaded creatures in her hands are the devils of fear that besiege us. On the dark moonless night that falls between October and November when the rest of India celebrates another aspect of the all-powerful earth, the Goddess Lakshmi, the bringer of wealth and good fortune, in Bengal, Assam and Odisha the households make effigies of the Goddess Kali and pray to her to extinguish their demons. Devotees fast all day and carry huge statues of her that belch smoke and fireworks along the streets. Well after midnight, they rest and break their fast.

In Kolkata, Kali has a famous temple, which is considered to be her home: the Kalighat. It draws pilgrims from all around who come to get a glimpse of her physical presence. They walk in barefoot, bringing newborn babies for blessing or private anxieties for cleansing, waiting in crushed queues for hours for their moment of 'darshan', the time when they will be face to face with her effigy, in the presence of the officiating priest. The moment of 'darshan', or presence, is the key point of the pilgrimage. For this they have made the journey, bought expensive offerings, sacrificed their shoes, queued in a melting press of others and offered their precious donation, to have these few seconds when they are face to face with the goddess. They must be ready with their prayer, utter it quickly, receive the priest's blessing, before they are hustled forward to leave room for the ones behind. This 'ghat' or temple is not just the house of the goddess. It is as though by coming here they have entered her body and are one with her great power.

My hostess in Kolkata expressed disgust when I said I was going to visit the temple.

"Ugh!" she shivered. "All those people and having to walk barefoot on the filthy ground. It's horrible!" She paused.

"But I have been there once," she confessed. "It was a few years ago when I was really down. I had all these problems with this house and no money. I didn't know where to turn. A friend of mine dragged me along there. When we got inside, she suddenly said, 'There! That's where the goddess' toe touched. Touch there and make your prayer!' I did it, and you know, things really got better after that. It was very strange... But I've never been there since."

With such a press of people in this temple, an industry has

grown up to deal with the crowds. The selling of offerings, the guarding of shoes, guiding and informing, all these are livelihoods. The management of the temple itself and the goddess' effigy, receiving, storing and disposing of the offerings, all these jobs are in the hands of the priest, his family and appointed representatives. Becoming a priest is not a matter of vocation in India. You must be born to it. The Brahmin caste, who traditionally have the knowledge of the ancient scriptures, are those who guard the temples. The care of such a famous temple as the Kalighat in Kolkata is so lucrative that the chance to officiate is reportedly auctioned to the highest bidder.

I was curious to see if I could detect some spiritual treasure in this place, gleaming through its reputation of murky backroom bargaining. The concept of Kali has been important for me. I have used this powerful image of the earth's strength and energy to divest myself of fear when I have faced something especially difficult. I have developed a meditation which is an effective way of walking through fear, as physical in my imagination as Chogyam Trungpa's facing down the dogs that chased him. I chant Kali's song, focusing my thoughts and feelings on a kind of internal 'darshan', where I unload my fears one by one as I approach a shadowy goddess down a long, dark tunnel in my mind. As I enter this tunnel, I name each fear that I've been holding, strip it from me and toss it into a brazier that burns at the side of the tunnel. I watch as each fear is destroyed, and move on, so that, finally, when I come into the shadowy presence of the earth's spirit, I am as naked and empty as a newborn baby. In this state, I kneel before her in my mind and ask for her natural blessing. I allow myself to receive the gift of the energy she manifests into my empty being. As I travel back along the tunnel towards the light of my daily self, I find in each flame that lights the tunnel another gift of light to replace the darkness that had enveloped me before.[1]

The physical changes I have made in my body and my life,

whether healing illnesses of my own or others', or changing relationships and circumstances, all come from imagined reality. Imagination has a powerful physical effect. It is the bridge between the physical and the 'not yet manifest' reality. Using your mind creatively fuses the physical with the non-physical. This fusion is the real meaning of 'tantra', meaning 'union with the absolute'. Such is the power of 'darshan', whether it involves a physical image or, as I prefer to work, an imagined one. I wondered whether I would see a breath of this power in Kalighat.

Tourists are, I knew, considered a particularly rich source of funds for the temple and one who stands out tall and blonde as I do had little chance of being an unnoticed observer. However, that morning the Indian Prime Minister himself had delivered me an unexpected suit of armour, behind which I discovered I could relax and observe unmolested for as long as I liked. When I left the Kolkata subway at Kalighat, I joined the file of people heading down the backstreets to what I guessed would be the entrance to the temple. As we filed through the outer gates I slipped off my plastic shoes and tucked them in my plastic bag. (It is forbidden to carry leather in the portals of the temple as the cow and her skin also are sacred.) Immediately a man emerged from the crowd by the door to offer to take me through a special entrance around the other side. As I began to follow him, he explained that it was usual to make a donation.

"I don't have any money," I said.

"Oh, you don't need much money. Just 500 or 1000 rupees." (This is actually one or two months' salary for many Indians.)

"No, you don't understand. I really don't have any money. Your Prime Minister took it all away from me this morning."

I turned away and my 'guide' did not pursue me. He knew what I'd said was true. At this moment, to be poor in India was a blessing. I wandered freely through the buildings of the temple, and I walked, almost unnoticed, up the steps of a covered platform where I could look down on to the core activity around the goddess herself.

The building where I stood, known as the Nat Mandir, was once used as a dance floor, where young girls would perform the sacred dance in front of the goddess. It's positioned so as to give an unobstructed view across into the building alongside. This is the open building known as the Jor Bangla, inside which the goddess sits at a lower level. She is the heart of the temple complex, and her home is known as the Garbhagriha.

There was no temple dancing that day. The atmosphere was more like a bus shelter. A few people were sitting on the floor, resting in the shade or rubbing their feet. One was sitting cross-legged facing the goddess, saying his prayers while he ran through the string of beads, the mala, in his fingers. In this pleasing oasis of calm, I stood by one of the pillars and watched the feverish activity in the temple heart before me.

Immediately in front of me but separated by a narrow alleyway that runs between the two buildings, were about five or six assistants of the temple treasurer. They were crouching and gossiping and laughing amongst themselves while clinging incongruously to ropes hanging from the ceiling. Holding on to these they could swing out over the crowd of pilgrims filing along the alleyway at my feet. Their job was to collect the donations the pilgrims brought and anoint heads with a mark of sandalwood paste in exchange. Tiny babies were brought to receive the blessing on their foreheads. A sober looking cluster of women from one family crushed together to receive the mark. A constant file of flashing saris, more women than men, crowded the alleyway while the donations were handed up to the treasurer's assistants. One man offered a 500 rupee note. Everyone laughed. The note was waved around and handed back to him. He found a 100 rupee note instead and that was accepted. Suddenly someone appeared with a crisp pink bank note. This was one of the new 2000 rupee notes that had been introduced to replace the 500 and 1000 rupee notes. Nobody had seen one before. Pilgrims were forgotten while the note was pored over and examined on both sides, passed from hand to hand before it was returned to its privileged bearer.

Behind this group, the pilgrims who were waiting for darshan filed on. Watching from the outside as I was, I could see them arrive on the threshold, pause before the officiating priest, and stare for a moment at the goddess before being hurried along by the priest's assistants. The goddess in the Kalighat is a black stone. She has three red eyes, the one in the centre of her forehead as large and imposing as the others the stone is inlaid with. She has a gold tongue protruding down as far as what would be her navel if she were not a creature of immaculate birth. She sits on a marble dais which is carved with the figure of her husband, Shiva, the male principle who she has crushed but not extinguished. Her neck is hung heavily with flowers and garlands and her head is crowned with cloth and flowers. The temple timetable is devoted to her needs. She is 'woken' in the morning, bathed and anointed. The temple is closed while she takes her breakfast and again later in the day when she rests. Evening visits are allowed up until the time she goes to bed, and then she is disrobed and allowed to remain in quiet until the next day. From my vantage point I could only see the top of her head, the priest and his assistants, and the devotees rushing through. I made my silent tribute to the goddess of the earth and turned away. This stone goddess was not the source of magic for me.

On my way back to the subway I met a young boy. I asked him if he had been in the temple. He shook his head.

"I'm a Christian," he smiled.

I nodded. *Yes*, I thought. *If I had grown up in India, I'm sure I would have been a practising Christian too. So peaceful.*

Chapter 8

Rediscovering Innocence – *Feelings Change Your Brain*

It takes a long time to become a child.
Pablo Picasso

A wasp buzzes in through my open doorway, disturbing my peace. I let it settle and crawl over my bare arm. I know it is exploring, like me, and when it finds I am not sugar, it will leave me. I look at this creature and remember how people flap and scatter when it approaches. Why would it sting me? Of course, it will sting me instinctively if it feels fear. The sort of fear I would feel if a giant was waving his arms and threatening to squash me. I think of my mother. As my mother approaches the end of her days, she is like this wasp. Fear eats her silent lonely hours in the night and in the morning, she stings, indiscriminately.

She has taken to quoting Shakespeare, the seven ages of man, as she hangs her head and contemplates her situation.

At first the infant,
mewling and puking in the nurse's arms,
And then the whining schoolboy...

She trails off, because her mind is on the last line. The lines she did not quote, could not recall, tell her a bitter story she does not want to know.

... Last scene of all,
That ends this strange eventful history
Is second childishness and mere oblivion
Sans teeth, sans eyes, sans taste, sans everything.

In this final chapter of her life, my mother is more childlike than ever. The instincts that have sustained her life force for nearly a hundred years are vigorous. She eats everything that is put in front of her, while in the past she might have been more discriminating. She enjoys the taste of food so much that, in the night, when there is no one and nothing to distract her from the pain she feels inside, she goes hunting for more. Every morning there is a trail of scattered sunflower seeds leading from the kitchen, pools of spilt milk on the hob, remnants of burnt porridge glued to the bottom of a saucepan. She denies having played any part in this. Someone else has made the porridge and eaten it. She even wonders why they need so much!

This person who roams around the house in the night, often wailing and calling for help, is someone she doesn't recognise. Her unconscious self is expressing itself in unacceptable ways, so she doesn't want to know. It is as though there is person A and person B and the link between them has been severed.

The instinct to eat comes from a deep part of our brain which has suffered no damage in my mother's case. It seems to be the connection between this unconscious instinct and her conscious mind which is broken.

My mother may have suffered brain damage, but many of us encounter a similar separation between our conscious selves and the deep power of our instinct. Sometimes in very simple ways. You read in a book that eating only protein and fat is guaranteed to make you lose weight and improve your health, so you decide that you will follow this regime. You plan it all out and decide when to start, thinking that it will be easy because you don't really eat bread, or cakes or fruit or whatever it might be. So, you begin. Out of nowhere comes this deep rebellion. You find yourself longing for chocolate, fantasising about the taste of an apple, envying other people's bread and potatoes, until soon you find yourself tucking into chips like a person who has been starved! You haven't been starving. You have been eating plenty. But you feel deprived because you haven't been eating what you want. Who or what is this person who is making you desire food that you never knew you cared about?

There is a point in the centre of the brain, just above the amygdala, that part of our brain where emotions are perceived, which is known as the *nucleus basalis*. This is the point of your brain where attention is focused. It records vital messages for the survival of your whole mechanism, receiving pleasure registering chemicals, serotonin and dopamine, from other parts of the brain, as well the activating chemical, noradrenaline, sending out messages to all parts of the body in the form of the neurotransmitter, acetylcholine.

Researchers are currently exploring its role in growth and learning or, alternatively, our physical and mental decline. They have shown that the brain synthesises a nerve growth factor which is released by neurons when we need them to coordinate to perform a specific activity. When we need to pay attention, this substance (called brain-derived neurotrophic factor or BDNF for short!) turns on the *nucleus basalis*. Once it is open, this part of our brain is capable of making new pathways and remembering them. Actions and reactions are forged here like lines on a map. They can be difficult to dislodge. To make new pathways that serve us better we need to pay full attention to our feeling, the emotion that prompted the pathway we established in the first place.[1]

The unconscious power of feeling permeates the body. It is intrinsic to the autonomic nervous system and accompanies every part of the nervous system that is linked to your conscious mind. The vital hidden autonomic system has all the power, so in a dying body, it is the last to lose its vigour. Think for example of something you do every day: run upstairs, get into bed, put a spoon in your mouth. All these actions have to be learned, and you learn them in a very interesting way. A baby doesn't know how to walk, or go upstairs without falling, but a baby has a strong desire to do so because the people she loves behave like this. They stand upright, they hold their own implements to eat, they run upstairs. Although this baby has no idea what to do and there are no instructions, she copies the bigger people she sees. She stretches her legs to stand up. She has no balance and she falls. She bangs her nose or her head and she cries with pain. But failure does not bother her. Desire is like a flowing river. She tries, she fails, she cries, she tries. Eventually she stands up and she staggers unaided across the room, to everyone's surprise and delight. Once the lesson is learned the instructions are passed to the autonomic nervous system. They become instinctive, part of the unconscious intelligence of the body.

The same is true for everything we learn in life. It is obvious to anyone who has a physical skill, like playing the piano, driving a car, swimming or typing on a keyboard. You remember the first painfully laborious lessons where you deliberately tried to give your fingers or your feet the right habit, by thinking about what you needed to do. You remember the frustration and the grinding despair of getting it wrong repeatedly. Perhaps you can remember these things if you try. But if you have persisted and mastered the art, it's probable that you never think about the painful business of teaching your body the process at all. You just let your fingers and feet fly while you think about something else. Imagine what it would be like if we had to think consciously about every muscle, bone and nerve involved in taking our body upstairs. The process would be so slow and complex, we would be exhausted by the second step. Yet when something doesn't work, when we have pain and difficulty, this is where we need to go back to.

Some skills that you have, you learn by a painstaking process of patience born of desire that comes from the unknown. Some skills you seem to find easy. They come naturally as though you were born with them. They take effort and persistence to perfect, but the initial steps seem to come ready made. Such is the genius of the body we live in. This unconscious autonomic system works hard for us day and night. Our unconscious selves are powerful and much cleverer than our conscious minds, although it is our conscious minds that are in charge: the kings or queens of our kingdom, or the bosses of the factory, if you prefer. This all works fine until, as sometimes happens, the boss loses touch with the workers.

This autonomic nervous system ranges all through the body and it is controlled deep in the brain, but all ancient traditions of wisdom, that predate the modern insistence on visible reality, give it a centre in the trunk of the body. This centre is the area a little below the navel, at the back of the lower abdomen, focused just in front of the spine. This area, called in Japanese the 'hara', is known by the Chinese as the lower *dantien*, by yogis as the sacral or *svadhisthana* chakra, which means 'one's own base'.

This is physically true. This part of our anatomy is the beginning of us: the area of the navel; the location of the generative organs in women and men, though the male organ hangs lower which has the function of keeping male sperm cool. It is the first pathway of our physical existence and the source of procreation of the species. It is the home, therefore, of the deep primordial instinct which is the quest for and the joy of sex. It is the area of the body that makes a deep and direct connection with the part of the brain that directs us towards this end.

Once we are here on this planet, the primary instinct for our survival is our appetite for food, and this instinct resides here too. Remember the feeling of having eaten a good meal, tasting just exactly what you wanted to taste, enjoying the process of eating it and the feeling of satisfaction afterwards. I'm not talking about eating too much, when your stomach feels stretched and bloated half an hour after you've eaten, but a meal that has been just right, just what you wanted, when you wanted it. You can lie back and relax with a feeling of comfort and calm. Naturally you put your hands on your belly, your lower abdomen, because that is the part of your body, remote though it is from your stomach, that radiates this satisfaction and comfort.

This is the meaning of instinct: a powerful desire that drives our whole organism, generating and coordinating chemicals in our body, without even reaching the level of conscious thought. It tells us what we like to eat, when we need to sleep, who we want to sleep with, wakes us up in the morning and tells us how we feel about the day.

This area of the body is all this but so much more. Like all parts of the body it has emotional resonances as well as physical functions. The Hawaiians call it 'the child' and they say it is the centre of the body's memory. It remembers every experience and emotional reaction you have ever had, like the hard drive of a computer. Anecdotal evidence suggests that there is a strong nerve connection between this part of the body and the limbic system in the brain which includes the *amygdala* and the *nucleus basalis*, responsible for feeling, attention and learning.

This energy in us is powerful, primordial, essential to our animal being, but it is not always easy for us to be aware of. Its language is sensual, emotional, and to us as adults it can seem wildly uncontained, overwhelming.

In northern France one morning, I sat on the wide, open beach, marvelling at the light and power reflected on the water in the bay from the early morning sun. The peace was shattered suddenly by a little boy who charged down the dunes. His face was bright with delight and he crowed his joy at top volume as he rushed towards the sea, waving a yellow plastic bucket in one hand and a red spade in the other. He sank to his knees and began to make a camp not far from me, where his mother joined him with other children. A second later I heard a piercing squeal of fury. I looked over to see the boy's face distorted in anger, hot tears all over his cheeks, throwing the yellow bucket away across the sand. His mother went to retrieve it and gradually the drama subsided and there was peace and happiness again.

This drama, moving from joy to despair in seconds, is part of all of us. It is there in my 95-year-old mother as she tries to negotiate the new reality of being a weak and dependent being. It's there in sophisticated middle-aged adults who proclaim that they are 'rational beings'. In small children between the ages of about 3 and 6, we expect to see swiftly changing extremes of emotion. This is the age of emotion, of exploring the power of our feelings. Equally we expect that children will not continue to behave like this. We teach them to 'master' their feelings and pretend. Small children are just short people, no less sensitive and aware than bigger people. What they experience so intensely, many of us have simply learned to conceal.

Our fundamental search in our lives is for love. We may look to receive love from other people, from spirit, or from animals, but searching for the sense of being loved is our core motivation. Just like a plant responds to light, human beings respond to love. As babies we are programmed to look for this love from our birth mother and father. Our experiences of the love we receive from them have a far-reaching impact on our lives.

I see this impact when I am healing. The energy of your root chakra reflects your response to your mother's way of being. This affects your ability to trust, or conversely, your tendency towards anxiety, fear, and insecurity. The energy of the sacral chakra reflects what you decide to do with those feelings. Some children learn very young that it isn't safe to express the way they feel. They learn to keep their emotions hidden. Perhaps they feel their parents' love and protection is threatened. Expressing their feelings would risk losing it altogether. Perhaps they are alone, or they understand that they are better rewarded for paying attention to other people's feelings than to their own. Sometimes, as the sensitive souls they are, they perceive their mother's suffering and decide not to burden her with their own childish troubles. Or they experience the powerful confusion of abuse from someone they love. Some children suffer trauma that is too painful to remember: death, loss, physical or sexual abuse are all too common. Trauma like this casts a long shadow.

You may have made a decision to keep your feelings locked in a dark subterranean chamber, at a point too far back in time for you to remember. As adults, we forget that we have been making important decisions about life from the moment of conception. Those decisions may have felt like good reactions at the time, but there comes a point when we need to reconsider whether we want our lives to be shaped by decisions made by our three-day-old, four-year-old or even seven-year-old selves. You are not obliged to stay within the imprint you sketched out early on, that you might have perceived as 'reality' with your childish eyes. There are plenty of other 'realities' out there which you might prefer. Your powerful conscious mind can release emotions that don't serve you, and change reactions. Yet so long as you remain unaware, those childish fears and agonies don't disappear. They are covered over by the layers of experience you build subsequently in your life, but they remain. They lurk under the surface in your unconscious and break into your adult life in unexpected ways.

Thomas was in his mid-fifties when his childhood experiences brought a dramatic change of heart. He was a tall man who wore a permanently anxious expression. He was a well-read medical academic who talked incessantly. He had a habit of looking at the floor when he was talking or looking away instead of at the person he was talking to, but he had a sudden sweet smile that was engaging and revealed his tender nature. With his wife and children in tow, he had moved across continents and countries and jobs many times in his life. He was constantly adding new professional attainments to his CV and worked hard to build a successful career that was nevertheless hampered by sudden changes in direction. His adult restlessness mirrored the disruption of his childhood. His birth mother died suddenly when he was two. His father was working abroad at the time and unable to get back to live with his son. The little boy was sent to live with first one relative, then another, before being sent to boarding school at the age of eight. His father was back in the country by this time but felt unable to look after a child on his own. So he lived by himself and visited his son at school on weekends, taking him out on visits to churches and tearooms in the English countryside.

A few years later the father married again and brought Thomas to live with his new wife and her three children. Thomas was now part of another family, and outwardly adapted well to his new family life, enjoying a companionable friendship with his step siblings. As an adult Thomas was energetic about keeping contact with his stepfamily, phoning regularly and swopping news and emails about the family's respective lives. He was also in close regular contact with his father. They had weekly phone conversations and Thomas relied on his father's advice and good sense, until his father began to lose his memory and could no longer hold a discussion. Thomas's stepmother and father were married for 45 years, and his stepmother cared for his father with great devotion during this last illness. Then Thomas's father died. Overnight, something like a torrent of fury seemed to freeze Thomas's body. He stopped talking to his stepfamily, refused their hospitality, only reluctantly attended his father's funeral, and rejected all attempts to share in honouring his father's life. He focused instead on collecting his inheritance, threatening his stepmother with eviction, and since that day, has refused contact with any of his stepfamily.

Above all else Thomas thought of himself as a rational man. He believed that all his actions and decisions were governed by logic, not at all by the emotional reactions of a small and frightened child. But his body had already expressed his deep discomfort with the experience of being uprooted from his mother's protection at such a tender age, and the underlying anxiety which prevented him from settling happily anywhere. He had developed bowel cancer, which he survived, about five years before his father's death. As soon as he inherited his father's money, he moved back to England to settle himself and his wife in a village he was completely unfamiliar with. But it was the village where his birth mother and father had once lived as man and wife, and here he began to settle down.

If you are overwhelmed by childish feelings, you are very unlikely to recognise them as such. The feelings are so deep that they colour all the reality you perceive. The feelings will appear to you as 'rational' arguments that justify the way you choose to behave.

But feelings lurk beyond rational thought. When my father died, I felt a kind of dull grief, followed by shock that in his will he left money unequally to his children. Yet although I brooded on this, I would not have been able to explain why it hurt so much. On the surface, it seemed like a reasonable decision on his part, and I dismissed it as such. It was only later, when I began to understand the resonance of feelings in the physical body, that I was able to connect with the small child in me that felt forever unfairly excluded from my father's love. I was able to see how this expressed itself in my recurrent nightmare about being mown down in the water by the prow of a huge ship. It was on a liner like this that my mother took me, as a two-year-old, away from my father's household in Indonesia. My brothers and I never lived with him again. For my optimistic, growing, conscious outward self, all of this was acceptable. It had to be. For my inward, emotional, childish self, it wasn't. When my father died, leaving what felt like a grade or exam mark for each of his children, my inner childish self felt this situation could never be resolved. I could never be as good as the others. From that moment on, I began to have acute headaches that I continued to ignore until they manifested as a brain tumour. Ultimately, my body forced me to pay attention.

Emotional tension within a physical body will radiate around you and affect the situations you experience. From my privileged position of helping people through trauma, where I act like a mirror to this energy inside, I have come to see this much more clearly and quickly than I ever saw it in myself. Extreme trauma is often hidden. It can express itself more easily in surrounding events than it can show itself to the person who carries the experience. Just as your physical body is a sounding board for your feelings and can nudge you towards taking conscious control of the situation, so events that affect you give you information that will do the same. There is, as they say, no such thing as coincidence. Look carefully at what you experience.

Deborah's mother died suddenly when she was six. Although she remembers a phone call after her mother died, she remembers nothing at all about her mother: no touch, no word, no situation in which they were together. She is grown up now and has her own family. When her eldest child was six, however, things started to go wrong with the stability she had worked so hard to build. Bear in mind that the relationship with mother affects your relationship with things that concern your security. In your adult life these are job, home, money. The house that Deborah and her husband had bought was found to have been leaking oil into the soil, creating pollution so severe that the whole house had to be razed to the ground and the soil removed and replaced. Meanwhile Deborah's husband was offered a promotion he felt he couldn't refuse but which terrified Deborah. The promotion entailed Deborah moving her precious family into an earthquake zone in Japan. After much anxiety, the family went to Japan, survived through earthquakes and flourished, despite the destruction of their home in England. Deborah found the events easier to cope with once she recognised their resonance with her own, deeply unspoken, fear of loss. In this way the events became like a reminder that this emotional issue is something she still needs to resolve. Our own children can be mirrors to the child within ourselves.

Indeed, children are the clue as to how we resolve these buried emotions in ourselves. We look at children playing, and we call them innocent. This doesn't mean that they are entirely good. We see their jealousy and their schemes, we see their obstinacy and will, we see their fury and feel their pain, but with all of that we see love so open and pure that we laugh at all the rest. Children are ourselves: human beings who have not learned how to cover their human feelings. Innocent doesn't mean good, or pure. It simply means open, not knowing. Later, we learn to be ashamed, conflicted, guilty, and we shut up the child within.

The childish energy of our sacral chakra is unrestrained. It means growth, joy, laughter, delight, wonder, hunger and sexual desire. In the innocent pursuit of all these things there is shock, pain, disappointment, disgust and fear. For as long as we have life we need to recognise we carry that engine of growth in our being: a fierce and powerful energy that gives us joy when it flows freely but which can get spoiled, just like a child, when it is allowed to dominate all other aspects of our intelligence.

The instinctive nature of the sacral chakra is one key part of our intelligence, and we have a lot to thank it for. When we recognise what it does for us, how it wakes us up in the morning, sends us to sleep at night, presents us with just the right taste for the food we crave, we can appreciate what it does for our living body and love that energy in ourselves, instead of trying to hide it away. When you sleep at night it is this part of your intelligence that is at play. Your conscious mind is resting. Your unconscious presents you with dreams, visions, and feelings, like toys from an old toy box you have stored away. This is the language of your unconscious. It rarely speaks in words, which are the language of the conscious mind. If you don't sleep at night, you may ask yourself why you would not want to get those old toys out of the toy box. If this is a new or temporary situation, are you going through something that reflects experience in your early childhood you haven't wanted to revisit?

One of the ways we use to cover up difficult emotions in our childish selves is to feed another aspect of sacral chakra energy. We seek to placate an angry child within by giving it sugar. Or we try literally to 'drown our sorrows' with drink that will numb us to the pain. If we have been especially good at covering or suppressing our feelings, this too can become an addiction. We consider we are 'in control' and refuse to feed ourselves, in conditions we call anorexia or bulimia, and then we are horrified by the power of the monstrous desire that rushes out when we open the lid of the toy box just a little. We slam the door shut and try desperately to regain control.

So powerful is the energy that the sacral chakra stores that it is not surprising that adult human society has devoted centuries of education to suppressing it. Suppressing this energy might seem to serve society but it doesn't serve the individual. Think of the way you might grow a garden. Every plant that grows in your garden space is thrusting up from the earth with energy converted into sap pulsing through its veins. This sap contains its life and its potential. It is the present and the future of the plant, that will allow it to take its form, to grow, to flower, to fruit, set seed and eventually to die when it has done its best. Who would not want this for themselves or anyone they love? You are a natural phenomenon, like any one of these plants. You can choose to be your favourite plant! The energy that pulses through your body is your birthright, a gift that came to you through your mother and father, but now it is all yours to play with. There may be some plants that overstep the boundaries the gardener has in mind. These will be cut or restrained, trained or even destroyed. The gardener is like our collective society, concerned with the overall view of the garden. But where would the gardener be without the individual vigour of the plants?

So your first responsibility as a human being is to yourself. Understanding what you hold and what you would like to let go of gives you the energy to keep growing and enjoying your growth. With this strength you give pleasure to those around you. You can release old pains and shame and make space for childish joy and pleasure which, as we all know, is engaging and infectious.

This process comes quite easily once you accept your significance, the importance of your being. You are a bundle of energy that has an effect on the world around you, just as you are affected by the surrounding world. You need to explore what is in that bundle. What is the silent voice within you? You can do this yourself in the process that we call meditation, a waking sleep that observes what we are without reacting.

Many, many methods of meditation have been taught throughout our human history. They all work, I believe. If you do them. Practising meditation is different from knowing about it as you may have experienced. We live in a rapidly changing world and we look for rapid results, which many of these methods do not seem to bring us. One practice I've been using for many years is not a traditional method, but it is highly effective in times of crisis and pain. It's a tool that I call 'targeted meditation'. When we try to achieve an 'empty mind' that so many meditation practices talk about, our devils and demons scream at us for attention. Our conscious minds are uncomfortable with the power of silent emptiness within which appears to have nothing to say, but which might say too much. If we have navigated to a place in our lives where we are happy and comfortable, why would we want to revisit old agonies that we have successfully overcome? It is only when they break into the present with their emotional or physical pain that we will even consider it. That is why pain is also a positive. We can embrace it as the engine of our growth. But first we need to recognise it for what it is.

The language of the unconscious is in the images and feelings lodged in our memory. When we have a strong emotional reaction to something, we need to find its root so that we can let it go. The root of our feelings will have begun to grow from the moment of our conception, but your conscious mind will not be able to go back that far. Perhaps you remember something of your childhood between the ages of about 3 and 6. Perhaps you will not be able to go back as far as that. Whatever your earliest memory is, give yourself some private space and go back to it.

Close your eyes and picture yourself as that child. Remember the feeling of the environment, perhaps the colour of the walls or the touch of the ground beneath you. Let yourself hear again the words you heard then or feel the reaction to those events in your heart. Picture the person who is saying those words or the people around you. Allow yourself now to say what you feel. Speak or scream it out loud if you need to. Say the things you never said at the time and then wait. Listen for the reaction that comes from the person you have said them to. Imagine that you are that person. Allow yourself to walk into their body and look back at the child that you were. Let them speak. Then walk back into your childish self again. If you have more to say, say it now. Don't hold back on your feelings. Only you are watching. Then listen again to what this person has to say. When you are done, and there is nothing left to say, allow the other person in your vision to float away. See them disappearing over the horizon like a helium-filled balloon, and consciously cut the string that binds you to them. This action frees you from something that has kept you confined. Let yourself come gently back into your present body, sitting alone in your space. Breathe smoothly and reflect on where you have been.

All through this process your conscious mind is watching, like a mother watching over her child. She has been understanding things she had never understood before: decisions the childish self made about the meaning of this experience, about how to behave to get love and how to avoid pain like this in the future. The conscious mind has observed it all and your conscious mind is now in a position, like any mother, to understand, forgive and love the child who has carried this feeling so long. We need to accept our guilt, our shame, our fear, allow it as we would allow it in any child that we love. We see this dark shadow, and, in our imaginations, we bury it in the earth, or throw it in the sea, or cast it off like an old coat. If you let yourself imagine this process clearly, you will feel physically different. Having seen, accepted, loved and discarded this old grief, you will soon feel lighter, freer, more joyous, enthusiastic and childish. Our emotions and passions are not bad. Nor are they good. They are what make us human. If you do not recognise your own, you can never understand them in others, and this understanding is the key to compassion and the power that is love.

In the final chapter of her life, my mother can no longer use this tool. She has kept busy all her life, urging her creative spirit into painting the dreams that bubble up inside her, delighted by the image without wanting ever to explore their emotional origin. Her conscious mind has urged her ever onward, rejecting or running away from pain. Now she is close to the end of the road and she can no longer run. The unfamiliar pain is so great that her brain refuses still to compute the situation. She takes refuge in amnesia. She could not now muster the mental strength to relieve her agony, even if she wanted to.

But in her old age, her childish energy is more powerful than ever. While other people take care of the mundane substance of life, preparing food, washing her, cleaning sheets or fixing broken taps, my mother is queen of her little kingdom. She imagines herself on top of the world and declares loudly that she doesn't need any help. Like a four-year-old who runs away from home, she finds the adults tedious.

Meanwhile, events around her reflect the vibrant nature of

her naked childish energy. As her body declines, so does her home. Hornets burrow into the wall directly behind where she lies in bed. They buzz hungrily around the lights she switches on during long sleepless nights. On her 95th birthday a sudden storm brings down a tree in her garden. A flash of lightning strikes through the electrical wiring so that her computer sends sparks into the living room. The electricity is unaffected. Even the computer still functions, and Internet signal comes to the house. But it no longer comes into my mother's computer. That connection is fried. Her links with the world we know are disappearing.

Chapter 9

Sex and Spirit

Sexuality is... the 'other face of God,' the dark side of the God image.
CG Jung[1]

"No sex? I'd rather die!" he said.

We were talking about a friend's choice to be celibate in order to further his spiritual development. After six years of this, our friend's wife left him. My husband simply could not understand how anyone could make the choice our friend had done, and it confirmed him in his conviction that all religious teachers are charlatans.

A man of few words, my husband, but gifted with an ability to occasionally express something profound in those few. In an absolute sense, of course, he is right. We would all die without sex. Sex is life itself. As a race we need it, just as, as individuals, we need food. But nothing causes more pain, more long-lasting damage, in body and mind, than our confusion about sex. And nothing brings us more joy, energy and fulfilment than sex and the children it generates. No one who seeks understanding in their life can avoid considering how they choose to integrate sex into it. Most of us assume that sex is separate from spiritual understanding, and of all the pain that is caused by sex, it often causes most damage when it crosses paths with spirituality. Yet in a fundamental way it *is* our spirituality. Everything we are and can experience exists through it.

We have consistently made sex into as much a problem as a pleasure. But this paradox cannot be resolved simply by turning our back on it. We have to face this monumental paradox among all the paradoxes of our existence. In the trilogy of novels by Philip Pullman known as *His Dark Materials*, angels are actors in the story. The last volume, *The Amber Spyglass*, features two angels who can see and understand what is happening on a far grander scale than the small humans they communicate with. But they have no arms and legs. They have no physical form, so they cannot take action to change the outcome of the story for the better. Only by communicating through the children who act and respond as their agents can they avert the effect of destructive intentions. I have always thought of human beings like this, blessed to have physical bodies that give us a vehicle to perform the good, or the bad and the ugly.

A fundamental teaching of Buddhism is that human birth is a precious opportunity. As humans we can learn more, come close to unity with energy that is all knowing, and achieve freedom from the pain that is inherent in our physical animal being. And you do not get that opportunity of birth except through sex, which should therefore be respected. The paradox is that our natural passion is also the source of pain, which we wish to avoid. Joy, optimism, delight, are natural, but so are greed, aggression, and fear. As our physical bodies grow and develop natural urges, we navigate between these two powerful forces in our lives: the instincts of our animal selves on one side and our understanding which seems to reach beyond the physical body, and therefore beyond pain, on the other. These extremes are like two banks of a river we will swim as long as we live. To navigate our lives as best we can, we need to learn to harmonise these paradoxical opposites, to find the spiritual in the physical so we can embrace the power of our spiritual being within our physical selves.

In the great sprawling city of Madras (Chennai) elephants wearing jewelled headdresses carried brightly dressed statues of Hindu goddesses along the main street amid rapturous crowds. People poured on to the streets, flashing saris of green, magenta, peacock blue or gold, and garlands of flowers, heads and noses smeared with sandalwood paste, the deafening noise backed by a cacophony of drums and cymbals. In the crowd was a tall European girl, her body jostled but able to see comfortably over the heads of most about her. She was transfixed by the elephant at the head of the procession, filled with a mixture of awe and pity. This magnificent animal, crowned with a sparkling red headpiece, looked like the embodiment of power, gliding steadily forward. Yet his headdress, with the effigy of the goddess perched on it, humbled him in service to her. At the temple gate the elephant stopped and knelt. His mahouts released the tottering goddess from his back, delivering her into the hands of six young Brahmin priests. The girl watched intently as they shouldered the goddess and carried her into the temple, unaware that now she herself was being watched. A hand touched her elbow. She turned to see a grinning Brahmin, wrapped in a saffron dhoti, sandalwood smeared untidily from his forehead down the length of his nose. He beckoned eagerly for her to follow him, walking a few paces and then turning, smiling to urge her to follow where he walked.

The Brahmin's smile was so eager and joyous she decided to trust and follow him. They slipped away from the commotion at the temple door around the side of the building. The temple was a stone square concealed under a monumental tapering dome, so laden with gaudily painted carvings of gods and goddesses that the whole edifice resembled a giant's birthday cake. An ebullient mass of sculpted spirits in action framed every entrance to the building. At one of these doors, the priest turned to gesture to the girl that she should take off her shoes. She slid them off and followed him into the shadows.

Stepping out of the sunlight, the darkness swathed her face. Her eyes adjusted to a cool stone chamber in front of her, its inner space gleaming softly in the light of oil lamps arranged in a wide square. She felt the smooth stone under her feet gratefully. The feel of stone, polished clean by endless bare feet before hers, was reassuring. Pillars separated the central area from the receding dark all around, supporting an open balcony that reached up into an atrium pierced by tiny openings. Beams of daylight shone on an object at the centre of the temple floor. Her guide stopped and pointed to it, indicating that she should pay attention.

The thick smell of incense misted the air. It took a while to make out the object, the cause of the raucous carnival that had brought her here, the point of the temple and its tumultuous roof. It stuck up out of the floor no more than twelve inches high, a simple lump carved out of black granite. Then she recognised the dark stone phallus known as a *lingam*, emerging from the centre of a wide granite basin. The stone was glistening in the soft light with sticky white coconut milk with which it was continually anointed. On the other side of the temple young Brahmins, dressed in saffron dhotis like her guide, were taking offerings of flowers and coconut, pressed into their hands by the worshippers. One after the other in an unbroken chain, they brought the flower garlands back to hang around the neck of the *lingam*. Then they would break the coconuts on the stone and pour the milk over its smooth round top, the milk trickling down and gradually filling the shallow basin underneath, where it drained through a lip carved into the rim for that purpose. Other young Brahmins hurried forward in a separate operation to gather the continual flow of offerings and carry them away into the dark recesses of the temple.

Looking on, the girl prickled with an uncomfortable sense of shock. The elaborate rituals around this naked phallic symbol made her suddenly conscious of her femininity, and, at once, she felt vulnerable. After a few minutes, she edged her way back towards the door and daylight, fumbling in her purse for a note to give her guide. Quickly she found her shoes and hurried away, grateful for the quiet empty backstreets of the city.

I was that European girl, shocked and puzzled by my first

glimpse of the underbelly of Hindu worship. The temples of southern and eastern India celebrate sexuality in exuberant form. For hundreds of years the female body has depicted the manifestation of divine energy. Religious carvings of the 9th century Chola dynasty are especially lavish in their celebration of glorious feminine shape. Temples are covered in sculptures that show the jewelled breasts and rounded hips of the goddess Parvati in all positions, sometimes wrapped around her consort Shiva, sometimes accentuated by the swaying moves of a dancer.

I had been in India learning the traditional art of Bharat Natyam, in which female dancers with bracelets of bells around their ankles stamp, sway, mime and sing the story of the delicious sexual union between Shiva, the active creative essence, and Parvati, who receives his essence and brings forth matter from her body. I failed to learn the Indian dance. Neither my hands, my feet, nor my voice, seemed able to master the subtle pounding rhythm of it, the guttural chesty tone. I blamed my ancestry which had viewed Indian culture at close quarters for years and, for the most part, rejected it. I had spent weeks living in a hut in a school in the desert, trying each day to teach my ankles and toes the moves that I saw children perform effortlessly. They also spent each day learning to sing, dance and play, some of them as young as six and far away from their families who they saw only once a year. Every day I was stunned by the beauty of their slight twisting forms, their dark eyes flashing, white teeth sparkling, as they performed the dances they'd learned to the deep moaning rhythm of the *veena*. Every day I felt large, white, solid, in contrast, so that by the time I reached Madras I'd decided my efforts to learn classical Indian dance were like a whale trying to learn to tap dance.

I understood, however, that the dance appears to be all about sex. One of the few Western women who claimed to be an accomplished Bharat Natyam performer told me she learned the dance in Orissa. This woman made her home in southern India, where she lived dependent on her Indian boyfriend, an aging and impoverished Maharajah. She was no longer the flashing exotic dancer she had been, but her story that she was trained in classical Indian dance so that she could initiate young Brahmins into sex was somehow believable.

The Brahmins are the highest Indian caste from which the priests are always drawn, although not all Brahmins are priests. Traditionally they are the teachers, the philosophers, the leaders of the people. The virginity of female brides of such a caste would be highly valued and fiercely protected, although many marriages take place when both parties are pre-pubescent. Once, the association between classical Indian dance and the sexual act was so universal that, for a while, under the disapproving gaze of British rule, the dance itself became disreputable. It was revived in the early 20th century by educated Bengalis seeking to rekindle national pride in Indian culture. Since then it has been taught as an art form, sanitised of its role as a kind of sexual foreplay.

The dark romance of ancient Orissa is now the modern state of Odisha in eastern India. It is the home of this continually attractive and perpetually baffling mix of sex and spirit. Deep in the heart of Odisha's hinterland is the almost ruined temple that celebrates sixty-four aspects of the feminine, the so-called *dakinis*, embodiments of all matter, carved into the stonework of its crumbled walls. The *Ranipur Jharial* in the Sambalpur region of Odisha was built in the 8th century at the height of the practice of tantra, when it was used as a place of initiation. These images testify to honouring the feminine as the root and form of matter, revered by Hindus, tribal shamans, and Buddhists in this area for centuries.

The mix of sex and spirit is easily misunderstood. Erotic imagery in Indian temples has perplexed and surprised people for centuries. Played out in dance and wonderful erotic sculptures, leads to misinterpretation of the original symbol of the *lingam* at the heart of the temple, according to yogi scholars of tantra. Paramahamsa Prajnananda, a yogi born and bred in Odisha, explains the spiritual view of the exuberant celebration of the female form in ancient Indian culture:

> *If seen only on the ordinary level of understanding, this image might seem to confirm so many of the longstanding misperceptions about Tantra as evidence of a practice that incorporates sexuality into worship. Nothing could be further from the truth. The form represents the highest spiritual attainment in the union of consciousness with God or the Absolute.*[2]

Tantra, which has become almost wholly associated with sex in the popular imagination of the West, is the art of seeking unity with the absolute through perceiving the force that interconnects the gross physical body, the mental body and the *causal* body. The causal body could also be described as the 'reason' why you're here on earth. The *lingam* honours the creative force of nature, personified as the Divine Mother, who hides at her core the negative magnetic force that attracts the positive charge of unformed energy. Deep understanding of this interconnection brings freedom, according to ancient Vedic philosophy, but naturally humans are mesmerised by the power of the physical.

The magical natural beauty of the landscape in Odisha inspires awe. The flashing blues of the peacock's tail, the fearsome slinking flash of native tigers, the deep greens of jungle trees whose leaves have provided water, medicine and plates for food, the rushing streams and the rolling edges of granite outcrops have inspired tributes to the Divine again and again. A tall white dome poking into the cloud that rolls off the mountain, a temple crafted in the style of King Ashok's reign, 900 years before, is a familiar sight.[3]

In Bhubaneswar, the commercial heart of the modern state,

there are said to be a thousand temples. They are now so overlaid with the noise and hurry of a city that few people know where they are. There are no signs to divert you from the flyovers, highways, buses, booths and screaming horns. Only when many people have been questioned and a few have answered do you find yourself wandering down ramshackle streets of houses with a sense that you are getting closer. And then suddenly you turn into a space where the scale and time has altered. The smooth stone paving and cluster of temple buildings carved from dark red sandstone is unlike any of the modern crust which almost swamps the site. There is space, and peace, and darkness also. Here the small chambers that lead one into another take you deeper and deeper into a silent place where lessons of any kind could be learned. Here are secret chambers where the tumbling of desire fulfilled and understanding realised would remain forever personal and secret. Here the walls are carved with all the richness of divine fertility manifest in the breasts and open hips of the goddesses who preside. This, you can believe, was a perfect space for a privileged young man and woman to discover the power and divinity in their own physical being through a slow and careful awareness of their sexual energy and the shattering of their selves at the point of union.

The chosen dancer came to such a chamber to wait for the chosen man. She would be wearing the traditional dancer's garments: trousers of gossamer fine chiffon, clasped at the waist and ankle, slit into strips so that glimpses of her brown legs poked through when she walked or danced; a necklace of heavy white scented flowers rolling down between her naked breasts and another woven into her black oiled hair; her head, wrists, and ankles wreathed in chains of little bells that tinkled when she moved. The sexual ritual demanded that the couple remain together in the dark chamber for three days and nights. They would sit in silent meditation for all of this time, not allowed to speak, nor to look at each other, and not to touch. Only then, by degrees, were they allowed to explore each other's bodies with their fingers. From the very first touch the experience was electric.

Such rules around sex have enhanced and sanctified the act into a celebration of the gift of energy that the human body expresses. It reveals the power of this energy when fused with another's, the expansion of communication and the shattering of limits. Ritual focuses the attention and intensifies experience. But it is rarely observed.

Today the ritual of the secret chamber is a thing of the past. Sex itself is more often ringed around with taboo or treated with shame or disrespect. The urgency of desire is snatched greedily by the strong, leaving the weak to take the consequences. Sex becomes ugly, abusive and damaging.

In Odisha, the Divine feminine is more honoured at the ritual of the October full moon, seen as a special time for women. The moon, which shines because it reflects the sun's light, is the symbol of the feminine that gives birth to life but is not the source of life itself. On the eve of the full moon in the coastal town of Puri, families and friends parade up and down the street late into the night, buying sweet treats, exploding firecrackers, preparing feasts. Then, in the hour before dawn, silent crowds of women, fresh in their best saris, glide towards the beach in the moonlight.

Down by the sea, hundreds congregate on the sand, the children in the family laughing and dancing around them. Each family group prepares a little boat made of a foot length of banana stem. They try to balance a candle on board, and light a stick of incense, with the picture, or the thought, of a lost loved one, honouring death as part of the continuous cycle of life. The oldest woman in the family hitches up her sari and staggers into the waves on bowlegs, curved by decades of squatting, holding the fragile offering high above the water. Often, she is helped by a gleeful grandson, jumping and laughing and shouting instructions at his old granny. She tries to send the little boat sailing on the waves, launching it as far as possible before it is overwhelmed by the ocean and returns in a crumpled heap to the beach. She will stay in the sea, muttering a silent prayer, allowing the water to lap around her waist, before being helped to clamber out. The thought is there. The mother moon has been asked for her care and assistance and takes this prayer with her as she fades in the rising sun.

All around, Hindu temples celebrate the feminine spirit at this time of year, drawing thousands of female pilgrims who wait squeezed among the crowd to have their dreams and desires honoured by the goddess. The Hindu priests are the guardians and interpreters of this process. Non-Hindus are no longer allowed into Hindu temples. The inner temple I was once led into is now shrouded in mystery.

But in a sanctified spot up in the hills, I watched from outside the railings as pilgrims came to give their offerings to the goddess in a holy river. The river water has been diverted into the temple complex, flowing into a brightly painted pool. The water in the blue pool is now alive under the white walls with splashes of vibrant orange where clouds of marigolds float. Offerings have been arriving all day because the priest is there at this auspicious moment to receive prayers and interpret the response.

A woman in a sky-blue sari steps forward, slipping the money she has brought into the hand of the Brahmin protecting the entrance to the pool. She utters her wish to the presiding priest who squats over the holy river water. He nods, taking fruit and flowers from her hands. She wants a baby. She wants the goddess' power to make her pregnant. Either she has not fallen pregnant or she has not brought a baby to term. The priest ushers her down into the water, and she descends slowly through the film of coconut juice that now covers the pool, her sari billowing as the water rises above her waist. She glides through the pool to face the priest again and takes a flat brass dish from his hands. On a signal from him, she dives into the water, rising again a few moments later with the brass dish full of water and sand that she has gathered from the bottom. She hands the dish to the priest. He swirls the water around in the dish, gazing intently at the sand formation in the bottom, scrying the wisdom of the moon goddess. He empties the dish and hands it back to the woman in blue, indicating she should go down again. She dives three times and hands the dish to the priest. Then he gives her a prediction, and she bows her head before climbing out of the pool.

I cannot hear or understand what the priest says to her. It feels as though I have torn a curtain and entered a private world, for I can feel, even at the distance of twenty yards, how the woman in blue is moved and uplifted by the experience. It seems clear that the guidance she has received will help her to relax and trust her body to conceive. The priest's activity is the remnant of ancient shamanistic rituals which are in tune with the rhythm of nature, even though they are hemmed about with the conventions of society's religious rules which have turned the process into a commodity that is sold by a privileged few.

This land resonates everywhere with a human hymn to the power and blessing of nature's power. Further and further up into the hills of Odisha are tribes that live by their own rules. Here the power between male and female has a balance it has lost in the mainstream society of the lowlands. The men are tall, moustached, and broad shouldered, but the women appear in the marketplace with little sabres to pin back their hair. The knives are not mere decorations. These sabres can cut fruit and penetrate flesh with equal effect. The women laugh at strangers openly, challenging anyone to underestimate them, sometimes dragging on huge hand-rolled cigars.

Here too they praise the earth goddess at the time of the new moon in October, but they do not allow temples and gates and guardians to get in their way. Their temple is a tree. A special tree among the forest's many. In the hills, I chance on a ritual playing out.

The tribe beckons me forward to sit with them while their leader sings their prayers. She has hitched her sari to leave her bony brown calves exposed and free to dance. She stamps her bare feet on the ground and swings from side to side to side before a makeshift shrine at the base of the chosen tree. Her hair is grizzled and her face is drawn in concentration on an inner power while she sings a chant of gratitude to the earth, cradling on her head a cockerel who seems content to stay there, soothed by the rhythm of her swinging body. Beside her two women also sing and dance, one with a bow and arrow, another with a spear. Three young men stand beating drums, giving the women energy for their dance, which will last all day until the sun sets. I look around me. My companions seated on the ground are mostly women and children. This is a festival of fertility, a time to celebrate feminine creation.

The shaman stops singing, turns around to her audience and laughs. The cockerel wriggles on her head and she slaps it down, but she looks suddenly shy, gentle, as if asking her audience whether they are bored yet. Should she continue? After a minute or two the drums start up again, and the woman launches into another song. This time she takes the bow and arrow and draws it so the arrow points high up into the branches of the tree. She releases the tension on the bow and hands it back to her companion. Then she takes the spear from the other's hands and beats its base into the ground. The power of nature is also the inevitability of death.

As if he knows it, the cockerel has emerged from his trance and tries to struggle free, but she takes him by his bound legs and swings him around her head while she sings. The time is fast approaching when his blood will bring the ritual to a close. This precious sacrifice will demonstrate the tribe's devotion to the power of the earth. That devotion will bring them the earth's rich rewards.

I feel as though the poor trussed cockerel is our sacrifice, everywhere. We dance a brief time on the surface of the earth praying that her astonishing power will yield us mercy. All our rituals have some element of this prayer. I leave before the blood is spilled, squeamish about the cockerel's fate. But the women's chants stay with me for a long time. Their ritual, which makes a temple out of a tree, a spiritual leader out of a village grandmother, is a highway for every human being to follow. These practices invite everyone to join in the breathing, the chanting, the dancing, the fasting and the feasting to experience the joy of being alive. Through this joy you discover the spiritual power that lodges inside your own animal physicality. You can learn to trust your authority and your wisdom, by witnessing and working with the wisdom of your body.

The divine feminine is this incarnation of matter. For thousands of years, the recognition of this energy in matter was manifest in the gods and goddesses worshipped by humans to express it. This way we have sought to harness external energy and harmonise with nature. Shamanistic schools of spirituality, from the first people of Australia to the Hawaiians to the Druids, have found God in this energy. The measurement of matter by its fixed physical properties, at the beginning of scientific study, gradually desensitised us to its unmeasurable, invisible properties. Laymen learned to disregard the power of the invisible, to our cost. For at least the last hundred years or so, however, it is the quest to measure these hitherto invisible properties which have formed the frontiers of physics.

Matter is the reflection of Divine energy just as the shining moon is the reflection of the sun. The Hawaiians' most powerful goddess is Pele who creates earth and fertility from the belching fire of her volcano. Matter is not God, but God is the primal energy that enables matter and therefore inhabits all. This understanding is fundamental to Hinduism and Buddhism too. 'God is in the hedge at the bottom of the garden,' as the Zen Buddhists say. The word God or the Divine doesn't refer to an entity. It is light, vibration, sound. So, like the sun's light on the moon, it can only be known by us through our experience of the physical. We can see it in the tree, in the cockerel, in the hedge at the bottom of the garden. But the way we are able to discover it is through contemplating the complex bundle of physical, emotional and mental tensions that is ourselves.

I look at spirituality this way, as something that each of us is led to discover through the richness of living our human life in all its aspects. In time it becomes clear how the physical life we experience is a long lesson in the value of our spiritual being. The more we learn about our spiritual selves, the smoother and sweeter our physical experience becomes. But many schools of spirituality have turned their back on human physical desires as distractions that get in the way of spiritual energy. Whether Catholic Christian, Hindu acharya, or Buddhist monk, the teaching rejects the energy that comes from alternating fasting and feasting and advocates permanent fasting. Of course, this cannot apply permanently to food, so it is applied to that other fundamental human desire: sex.

In the last few hundred years most religions have taught abstinence for the serious spiritual seeker. A common yogic teaching is that the seminal energy that fuels human life in the form of appetite for food and sex can be diverted by a trained and dedicated person to rise up the spine and give the experience of oneness with formless primal energy. The senses through which we experience life are connected only to our physical experience, not our spiritual being. To understand our spiritual being we need to turn off our physical senses.

Perhaps this is the basis of the monastic tradition that is a feature of Buddhism, Islam and Christianity. Yet the Tibetan

Buddhist teacher Lama Chime Rinpoche maintains that the reason for a monastic or a convent experience for someone who wants to develop their spiritual understanding is simply that it's easier. Without the distractions of family relationships and others' emotional needs, you can concentrate entirely on understanding your own humanity and its role in the universe. Intense relationships with others never go away of course. They will always be part of our human experience, and I believe they can be the mirror that helps us understand ourselves.

One feature of the monastic tradition is that it has made it seem as though understanding yourself as a spiritual being is only available to monks, nuns and priests who must broker your connection with the power of the Divine. That cannot be true. The energy that we call God is in everything and everywhere, so every being has an opportunity to witness themselves as a part of that energy, with all the experience of love and authority this entails. A bigger problem arises from the fact that the nuns, monks and priests are human with natural instincts like the rest of us. Since time immemorial, the rule of abstinence has been as often honoured in the exception as in the observance.

Something that is prohibited but cannot be resisted leads to deceit, hypocrisy, and manipulation. The misuse of sexual desires has drawn a dark curtain over many pure-hearted attempts to understand our spiritual nature. Religious institutions of all faiths have hidden lies and abuse, which are the enemy of spiritual clarity, for the sake of encouraging people to deny that part of themselves which is physical. Prohibition has a tendency to intensify desire. When the rule of abstinence is broken, the value of all the spiritual teaching comes tumbling down amid pain, tears and recrimination.

When I worked in China in 1983, I used to hear stories of the Cultural Revolution that the nation had lived through from my colleagues. The Cultural Revolution was propagated by Mao's government in the 1960s to break and humiliate everything that had been valued by the traditional 'bourgeois Chinese society', from teachers to temples. Maoist Communism was the new religion and it had an interest in dislodging people's reverence for the Buddhist teaching of the past. This had worked spectacularly well for many, including one of my colleagues. She told me how her family lived opposite an important temple in Beijing. When the Cultural Revolution began, the temples were closed, and all the monks and nuns had to leave. My colleague remembered watching the procession of people being driven out of the temple. First came the monks. Then a procession of nuns, and behind these came their children. She said a monk and a nun lived next door to her after their exile from the temple as a couple with their children. They put away their robes, grew their hair and took secular jobs. Then came the end of Maoism. China cautiously opened its doors and began to welcome tourists who wanted to see traditional Chinese culture. The old monks and nuns were swiftly recruited again. They retrieved the robes and went back to sit in their temples as tourist guides.

In practice, the 'divine feminine' has more often felt like the exploitation of women. Even in this century where new technology has allowed women to show that intellectual and emotional strength can be equal to physical strength, women find themselves used to satisfy hidden sexual desires. The damage for anyone, male or female, who has been manipulated in this way is not so much the act of sex itself but the feelings of betrayal and guilt it leaves behind. The confusion of love and shame can lead to a burden of self-loathing which is toxic in its physical and mental effects. Many powerful male spiritual teachers from every school of spirituality have abused the trust of students in this way.

When she reaches for spiritual guidance from an enlightened being who 'knows' the answers, she gets a kiss. She wants to be guided by superior wisdom that she has not yet found in herself. He is led by the instincts of his body to find the release of his spirit that comes with the climax of physical power. Suddenly, she realises with a shock that she herself is apparently the embodiment of the Divine feminine. Is she flattered, or betrayed?

The ideal picture of tantric sex is complete communication in a physical form, in which each experiences self as one with the other. This is a place of bodiless union, where physical matter appears without boundaries. Two people must explore together in an equally voluntary act of participation. It cannot happen when the partnership is unbalanced by a perception of power on one side and submission on another.

Does the teacher's sexual appetite invalidate everything he has to teach about developing spiritual strength? No. At this moment he is guided by his animal nature. The wisdom of spirit may be something he has access to at other times. She does not need to throw the message out with the messenger. Only to be clear that even the most enlightened teacher is also a human being, subject to the laws of animal existence. A spiritual teacher can show you many different paths to uncover your divinity, but you must be the judge of the experience. Beware of teachers who do not lead you to greater trust and love of your own being. The wisdom you need is within.

The sexual act brings with it vulnerability. For women, the added complication of carrying a baby gives it the significance of a potentially life-changing action. Naturally, this vulnerability is for both parties, but especially for women this means that for centuries it has been ringed about with fear. We are afraid of being naked, as defenceless as children, and we grow afraid of our own feelings and desires. Sometimes there is good reason for those desires to be contained. Indulging them might be damaging to someone else. Yet our instinctive desire is also the energy of our growth, our joy and vigour, and we may have nothing to fear from it but the fear of feeling itself.

Fear stops us looking at those dark feelings that have

arisen from our reaction to what we have experienced. To heal ourselves, we have to reach deep into those feelings, explore them, allow them to be, see ourselves and others in them, before we send them on their way. Feelings, acknowledged, pass away, like every material thing. Feelings, hidden, stay fresh and active in the body as though concealed in a deep freezer. To grow, we need to let the most vulnerable part of ourselves tell us its secret.

Many people stay with the impulses of their physical needs, and don't see any greater purpose in their lives than fulfilling these until they die. You don't need to move beyond your physical body. It has energy and intelligence of its own without our human questing for other dimensions of existence. But humans are odd creatures. Our rapid curious minds are constantly searching our environment for form and meaning, distracting us from the deep instincts that we are born with which less curious creatures use to navigate their physical existence. Arctic terns have been shown to navigate with pinpoint accuracy over thousands of miles through storms and turbulence by using their sense of smell. Elephants have been shown to communicate with fellow herd members hundreds of miles away through their auditory sensitivity to vibrations in the earth. Whales can hear the high-pitched call of their fellows' song through oceans thousands of miles across. And when animals come to die, they do so with an acceptance of the end that is calm and painfully beautiful to watch. Everyone who observes animals closely, whether domestic or wild, has this experience, of learning the wisdom inherent in unconscious being. But humans cannot live like this. While we may develop many of their instinctive abilities in ourselves and allow them to teach us to extend ourselves, our minds are made for problem solving – a process which generates almost as many problems as it solves!

When we are pushed to extremes, it is the relationship

between our animal instincts and our conscious minds that can lead us through monumental barriers to ensure our survival. What we see in animals we can learn to respect in ourselves. We learn to nurture the animal instincts of our bodies' unity with all the life of the planet we live on.

After 58 days lost in the Atlantic in a raft, sailor Steven Callahan is starved and despairing. He has used all his skills and ingenuity to distil fresh water and hunt the dorados that cluster around his raft to keep himself alive. Increasingly, as he weakens, he finds that he has to give his body commands that it is reluctant to obey. It is as though his rational self, his conscious mind, is in charge of a mutinous crew, and only discipline from the 'Captain', the rational mind, will keep the crew in line. The survival of all depends on how much he can make 'them', his instincts, obey 'him', his reasoning self. As his isolation and desperation grows, after so many days drifting slowly westwards in his raft, he spears another of the fish that cluster around him and will keep him alive. With admiration and regret he watches her die:

Lifted up, she glints in the sun. Her body pulses. She curls her head toward her tail, left side, right side, left, right, faster and faster. My delicate lance sways to her rhythm. What a magnificent animal.... Again I am provided with a buffer against starvation. Again I am saddened by the loss of a companion. More and more I feel that these creatures exude a spirit that dwarfs mine. I don't know how to explain it rationally – perhaps that's the point. I don't think that these fish reflect or think as we do, their intelligence is of a different kind. While I cogitate about truth and meaning, they find them in their immediate and intense connection to life – in bodysurfing down huge waves, in chasing flying fish, in fighting for life on the end of my spear. I have often thought that my instincts were the tools that allowed me to survive so that my 'higher functions' could continue. Now I am finding that it is more the other way around.

It is my ability to reason that keeps command and allows me to survive, and the things that I am surviving for are the things that I want by instinct: life, companionship, comfort, play. The dorados have all of that here, now. How I wish I could become what I eat.[4]

Once we accept that our animal nature is intelligent, it begins to yield us information in a thousand small ways, just as close observation of any animal does. How can we enjoy the pleasure it brings without the suffering that it so often entails? We can learn to value it and balance it with our conscious attention. Once we do that, the area of our energy known as the sacral yields up its secrets in a profoundly interesting way.

Chapter 10

Under the Armour

You're everywhere and nowhere, baby. That's where it's at.
Jeff Beck

We are sitting at the table, a family group. We have just finished lunch and the conversation has turned to a project one of us has. We are swopping ideas about the best way to achieve the effect desired. My mother is with us, sitting in a rocking chair that we have pushed to the table. She has eaten a good lunch, gazing intently at the food which she has chased round the plate with a delicate silver fork. But the plate is empty soon enough. Now, engrossed in our imaginings of how we would each achieve the desired result for the project we're discussing, we have forgotten her. We are talking about cost, constructions, techniques and durability. Suddenly her voice cuts across the table.

"This is when I realise you are all grown up and I am not!"

We laugh, loving the absurdity of our 95-year-old mother, grandmother and great-grandmother becoming the child again. But she is a child with a difference. She is a child who remembers the trappings of knowledge, reputation, skills and projects knitted around her like a sheath. Just yesterday it was there and now it is falling from her, crumbling away with the strength of her body. Behind the sheath she is still there. She is content. She is happy to be looked after by those she loves and now, perhaps for the first time she can remember, she shines the light of her love on them with open gratitude, uncluttered by her will, her expectations, her fears or her disappointments. Dependency brings its own delights.

In her delight she delights her carers too, drawing from them a willing energy to help her that is love. We feel blessed by this reversal in our power: her children and grandchildren do all they can to make her happy and comfortable and we are grateful, in our turn, to have this opportunity.

This is the love that children draw from us. If we are lucky, we are born into this love. Lucky or unlucky, the love of our birth mother and father is what we want to feel, and the way those two express love is the way we learn what it looks like. That is the starting point of our life's journey. It is where the dice has thrown us on the board game of life, as it were, or where the lessons and omissions of past experiences have led us to begin. The moves we make bring us pain or pleasure as we journey towards the satisfaction of discovering love that is and creates absolute harmony, infinite creativity. Paradoxically, pain is part of the harmony of that love. Just as you cannot perceive light without the shadow, you cannot have action without reaction, you cannot have form without dissolution, you cannot have life without death.

The birth of a child is like an explosion of love. When my first child was born this feeling took me completely by surprise. I remember such a feeling of connection with the soul of my child. I remember my astonishment at finding this piece of me was somehow external to my body. I remember treasuring the grace of her perfect formation, wondering at the wrinkles on tiny toes, miraculous colours in the eyes, creases behind the knees and the wonderful smooth elastic skin. I remember understanding how precious every child is. I felt that every parent must feel the need to protect the jewel that nature has given them.

Children grow quickly into what their parents offer. While still in the womb a foetus smiles and responds to its mother. Inspired by this feeling of love, I wondered about the different kinds of education all these beloved babies would have. Even those born in the same hospital and at the same time as my baby would seem like different people by the time they were ten years old. They would have different accents, a different understanding of wealth, different expectations of themselves and their lives in the future. When I went back to work at my job as a radio producer at the BBC, I made a documentary in which I explored three kinds of schools in the area where all these various children might be educated. There was a state school with a very good reputation, the sort that parents move for in order to be able to send their children to, or lie about their address! There was a state school with a very poor reputation, a cavernous set of buildings for hundreds of children that was known at the time as a 'sink' school. There was also an expensive private school with a uniform and strict discipline, that taught boys from 4 years old to 13. It was the head of this private school who brought home to me the decisive factor in making these babies into the kind of people they appear to be.

"When the parents bring their child to this school aged 4," he said, "all they want is for little Johnny to be happy. By the time little Johnny is 10, however, their definition of happiness is little Johnny passing the common entrance exam (for the next school)."

It is we, with all our frailties, insecurities, self-protection, fears and love, who are decisive in shaping our children, until they are grown enough to shed their parental ties and explore in their own way how they want to live. We admire their childish joys and insight, the spirit and the vision they are born with, but we soon set about schooling it out of them. Of course, we don't do this deliberately. Consciously or unconsciously we teach them to conform to the values of the society we know because we love them. A child who does not conform faces a hard battle confronting strangers, at school, at work and in life. So, gradually, we give them an armoury of our beliefs so they can protect themselves and function in society as we know it.

They start with the armour of our own habitual reality. Our caste, our race, our tribe will all be familiar and loved by them as they love us, and they learn to define themselves in relation to it. This self-definition is the energy of the solar plexus: the individual self, or the ego. It is not who we are, but it is often who we think we are.

Solar plexus energy develops initially between the ages of around 6 and 9 years old. This is the time when we learn to see ourselves as an individual in a group that is larger than our birth family. We go to school and hang our coat on a peg that has our name on it. It becomes our personal territory. We begin to understand ideas like competition and sharing. We begin to identify ourselves with what we possess and generally we feel we are making progress into a future that stretches endlessly before us.

For some of us this period is a discovery of our strengths. We find we can read or calculate sums faster than our peers and for doing this we receive praise from our teachers and untold admiration from our parents. We begin to perceive that our ability to use logic is a badge of honour with almost everyone we meet. This logic is the weapon that has apparently built our culture. In developed societies there is little to remind us of the power of other kinds of intelligence that we possess. In discovering our mental strength at this age, we may be inclined to leave behind any painful sense of childish vulnerability we experienced before this time. Fear and loneliness are locked away inside. We learn to cover up our personal tastes, disregard our emotions, learning to ignore also the information they give us about what brings us joy.

For many, this age is painful. We measure ourselves against others and we find ourselves wanting. Perhaps we have learned to be receptive and quiet in our birth family, and we have not yet built defences against louder, stronger classmates. Individuals whose confidence is built on imposing their will on others may seek us out, finding us easy targets, and cause lasting damage to our self-confidence. Stung by criticisms from teachers and peers, we add them to our store of self-imposed limitations. Just as a mirror seems to show the shape of us, so others' comments seem to outline what we cannot see ourselves. We build these comments into our record of information that defines who we are, whether we understand them or not. We all do it. *I can't sing. I don't run fast. I'm hopeless at maths.* We talk to ourselves in the tone that the adults use around us.

I had a grandmother who I spent a lot of time with at this age. I was pretty sure she loved me, but she had a confusing way of showing it. She had two pet names for me which she used to her delight and my despair. One was 'Rats' tails'. I understood this one well enough. It was my hair. No matter how I brushed and combed it, it was fine and straight and fell in a way that never matched up to the soft flowing locks my grandmother felt I should have. But it was hair. The name annoyed me, but I didn't much care. Her other 'pet name' bit deep, however. This name was 'Mrs Smug'. As I began to speak, she would stop me in my tracks with this somehow deeply insulting put-down. She enjoyed the joke and shared her wit liberally, so that, once it took root, the entire family joined in a chorus of 'Mrs Smug', successfully shutting me down. It was painful because it was so puzzling. I didn't know what 'smug' meant, but it sounded bad, like 'slug'. As for 'Mrs', well, I was the youngest in the family, so that confused me fully. Memories are a kaleidoscope of emotional highs and lows. In all of us the lows are deeply scored. Being 'Mrs Smug' haunted me for many years until finally one day I asked my elder brother why the family called me that.

"You always seemed to know things you weren't supposed to know," he said.

Now that, once it was explained, was not too bad. I could have told them that children are just short people. They have eyes and ears, memory and intelligence, just like bigger people. If you don't want them to know something, then you don't talk about it in their presence. You cannot accuse them of being 'smug', overly pleased with their inner knowledge, as I now understood, because they know what you don't want them to know. As the smallest child and the only girl, I was ever present and easily overlooked. My grandmother's 'pet name' for me expressed her irritation at her own mistake. Later, I even understood it as a back-handed compliment. As a small child, I was aware of truths that adults chose to ignore. There is always another side to the negative.

The comments and criticisms we hear around us build our way of looking at ourselves into an inner dialogue which comes automatically into play. We use it to protect ourselves in the way the adults in our lives sought to protect us from harm and disappointment. At times of stress we hear that dialogue loud and clear. Perhaps we are trying something new. We say, *You'll never do it.* Or we may hear, *If at first you don't succeed, try, try and try again.* This voice of our self is what the Hawaiians call the 'mother'. It is our conscious mind, that drives us forward on the wings of our will, or holds us back, discouraging us with grim views of the pain involved in future failure.

The inner voice carries the weight of our culture as well as the influence of family members. One of the workshops I teach is designed to show us how to respond to this inner voice instead of just treating it as the smooth sound of unquestioned reality. If we catch what we are saying to ourselves in a critical situation we can listen and refute it. We can come up with a different chant that suits us better. In one of the exercises during this workshop everyone writes their inner response to a personal problem on a little piece of paper and throws it into the centre of the room. Then we take up the papers and read out the responses to the whole group for consideration, to see if we can determine one that would be more helpful.

I have led this workshop in the UK and in the Czech Republic, and I have been struck by the different tone of the responses in general. In the UK, the majority of the inner voices are self-critical. When people start to read out other people's self-talk, they are reading phrases like: "You are weak." "You must try harder." "You make the same mistake over and over. Don't you ever learn?!" "Don't be such a baby!" "I'm going to make a fool of myself."

In the Czech Republic, the collective responses had a much gentler, more compassionate tone. The self-talk I was hearing sounded with phrases like, "Have another go. You'll succeed in the end." "Find someone to help you with this." "You can learn whatever you want to if you take your time." I could speculate for hours about why this should be. Perhaps it was that in the Czech Republic they had all grown up under communism where they had no individual freedom, but a lot of mutual support. The English public school system has instilled a 'stiff upper lip' into British culture, reminding us that we need to be self-reliant to push through emotional difficulties and get on with it. Neither one is necessarily better than the other. It depends, of course, on what kind of society you want to have, and your attitude to society starts with your attitude to yourself.

It's possible that the participants in my Czech workshop had more recently taken on board the Hawaiian notion of the relationship between different parts of your consciousness, so that they felt inclined to apply it to themselves. The Hawaiian tradition divides a person's consciousness into three aspects which they call the 'child', the 'mother' and the 'father'. These divisions were conceived long ago as a way to explain how human beings function but they correspond to the labels made famous by Carl Jung in the early 20th century as the id (the unconscious, the impulses that are common to all human beings: this is the Hawaiian's child), the ego (the conscious mind, our sense of self and individuality: this is the Hawaiian's mother), and the superego (this is the Hawaiian's father which we'll talk more about later). If you see your logical 'self' personified as the 'mother', and your emotional 'self' personified as the 'child', as Hawaiian culture does, then it is easier to be gentle with yourself, behaving just as you would to any child you love.

It comes down to your experience of persuasion. Most parents try everything from punishment to delayed gratification and bribery to manage their own toddlers. I certainly did, with varying results. But the trick that worked when everything else failed was to put myself on the same level as my wild little one and appeal to her intelligence and love.

My youngest daughter hated to be confined. Supermarket shopping was a nightmare. If I tried to put her in the supermarket trolley seat, which her elder sister had loved, she would wriggle and squirm and scream until I took her out of it. As soon as I took her out of the trolley seat, she was off, running down the aisles on the smooth open floors until she was completely out of sight. Once, as I was coming to the check-out till with a full shopping trolley, I let go of her hand for a minute and she flew out between the tills, out of the automatic doors and into the car park. I abandoned the shopping, leapt over the till barriers and retrieved her just in time. After that I resorted to 'reins', so that she could walk freely but still not stray from my side. As soon as I put them on her, she sat on the floor. That way we could neither walk, nor shop. At last, in desperation, I squatted down to her level and asked her to help me. Checking on my list what was unbreakable and stored on the lower shelves, I said I needed her to fetch it for me. Immediately she responded, with pleasure and pride. Shopping became a collective experience and her will and energy worked for me, not against me.

The relationship between our own emotional selves, the seat of our childish joys, and our conscious minds is very similar. As a logical grown-up we may make very sensible decisions for ourselves. We may decide that we need to study a certain subject in order to further our career, only there never seems to be 'time' to study it and in the time we manage to set aside we are overwhelmed by torpor or illness. Perhaps we decide to put an exercise regime in place, and we have a similar response. Exhaustion or injury keeps getting in the way. Or we have a habit that we can see is harming ourselves and the people we love. We want to break this habit. We put a new regime in place. We have researched it, considered it and prepared ourselves for this new regime. For a few days we follow it perfectly. We are perfect. We feel better and we know this is a better way to live. Then from somewhere, sneaking in through a tiny lapse of concentration, comes our naughty child, testing the boundaries, breaking the rules, just this once. Before we know where we are, we are overwhelmed. A craving for chocolate cake or wine, sex or drugs has taken us over, sweeping everything before it. We indulge it fiercely, greedily, because we know it is wrong. It is not what we want to want. Finally, we are exhausted, crushed. Our intelligent conscious mind lies in tatters before the steamroller of our animal instincts.

What are we to do in situations like this, where our intention cannot withstand the tide of wilful energy that seems to bubble up inside us unbidden? We have to understand that we will never crush that energy, and we don't want to. This energy of our unconscious selves has intelligence of its own, knowing how to take us upstairs, allow us to sleep, run or sit down in a chair. It has memory that may not yet be accessible to our conscious mind, to our 'Mother' self which has been battling to get on in life, to survive and to succeed. 'She' has willingly packed away uncomfortable emotions like shame, guilt and jealousy, or loneliness and fear.

Food and sex, essential to our growth and survival, are the domain of the child. Intense feelings belong to the child. They make us vulnerable. The 'mother' has found a distraction in activity, a way to forget that she ever felt like this. 'She' keeps us safe by pretending these dark places don't exist. 'She' does not recognise this childish fragile person as herself. But the unconscious self, the 'child' does not forget. The child retains the memory until the mother can listen and take its burden away. The 'child' has a power that is the vital seat of our energy, but when it is suppressed, this power can be brutal. Your 'child' will not be swept under the carpet or ignored, no matter how you try.

The energy of this unconscious self manifests in the symptoms of disease that people experience. It is the silent language of the body.

However, our conscious logical mind, the 'mother', has enormous power to get us out of a difficult situation. We are often unaware of the power of our conscious mind and don't put it to good use. It is our 'keen intelligence', the energy of our thoughts, our words, our self-talk and our decisions. It can influence the whole physiological function of your body, but you do not often get better just because you want to. Something has to change. You need to put your will to get better to intelligent use, recognising as a start, the power of emotional factors that may have made you ill in the first place. Your clever conscious mind needs to engage with what is already there and move forward by negotiation.

My experience of healing has taught me that the body doesn't distinguish between your physical and your non-physical experience. Take, for example, the pancreas, whose physical function in the body is to help digest carbohydrates, fats and protein and to release insulin to maintain steady levels of blood sugar. If you don't have these, you will die. If you don't secrete the hormone to digest them you will die without additional insulin. People who lack this hormone have trouble absorbing sweetness from life. That sweetness may take the form of love in relationships.

Celia married for a second time late in life after many years of widowhood. As a widow she had run a farm and brought up her children on her own. Her new husband had social status which conferred a title on her, and he was besotted with her, which had perhaps flattered her into feeling this would be a good move for her later years. He wrote her poems which he was delighted with and recited to everyone. He cuddled her in bed to the point where she could not sleep but he could not sleep without her there. And they went everywhere together. He was in his eighties but showed no decrease in passion. Some years into this marriage, she found she was suffering from pancreatic cancer. The language of her body seemed to say that an excess of indigestible sweetness after so many years of independence and freedom was, quite literally, killing her. I pointed this out to her when suddenly she needed healing. She grimly acknowledged the truth of it but felt trapped in this situation, quite unable to walk away from it or modify her husband's cloying behaviour. The cancer spread rapidly and, sadly, she died within months.

On the other hand, Debbie came to me with diabetes type II. When we did a healing, it was clear that as soon as Debbie had anything good in her life, she passed it on to someone else, whether her children and husband, or her mother or siblings. It had become a pattern for her not to take anything for herself and she had recently developed diabetes.

"Everybody needs a *little* bit of ego," I said. "If you give everything away you wilt like a plant that takes no nutrients. Without taking nourishment from the soil, how can it grow, flower and fruit, giving delight to everyone else? You have to learn to be healthily selfish, or you have nothing to give."

She recognised herself in this and took another way of thinking on board. She continued to be a devoted mother and daughter, but with subtle changes she made time for herself, and her diabetes cleared up. It is perpetually astonishing to me how powerful your conscious mind can be once it has understood the message your unconscious mind is delivering. You cannot outrun disease in every case, sadly, but understanding brings peace at the very minimum. Sometimes it delivers instant healing.

More often, as in my case, healing is a process, a gradual relearning of a different way of being that is reflected in the diminution and eventual disappearance of symptoms.

You can look upon the body as a machine, and in some ways, this is quite a useful analogy. When your mother and father come together, whatever they do right or wrong, they give you an exquisite car to drive and the key. This body is your vehicle, complete with sophisticated engineering that is beyond human powers of invention. It is responsive in minute and subtle ways to its driver's wish, and, moreover, it's the only vehicle that you as the driver can be sure of having. You can't swap it for another. If you park your vehicle, get out and admire a vehicle parked next door, considering it a better make or a nicer colour or not dented or chipped as yours appears to be, your own vehicle won't work for you. Your only option is to get in the driver's seat and drive it where you want to go, making the very best of what you've got. Then your machine shows itself to be responsive, malleable, continually adapting, and capable of unexpected renewal and recovery.

Our medical system treats our bodies like machines without a driver. Cure for symptoms consists in surgery or pharmaceutical drugs to alter them. This state of affairs is not surprising since the human experience that presents itself to doctors is so infinitely varied that it cannot be systematised. The responses of our bodies are as individual as we are ourselves. Surgery and drugs can correct the immediate problem and save a life. Yet we know that this is not enough for us to feel well and happy. Some surgeries and drugs make symptoms disappear in the short term and other symptoms appear in the long term. Some make more symptoms appear without correcting the original problem. Some correct the original problem but where there is an unresolved emotional situation underlying the condition then another symptom is likely to appear, in my experience.

We can only aim for health and happiness by being the person within the machine and taking responsibility for the symptoms that manifest. Assuming responsibility does not mean that we are at fault, or to blame for what goes wrong in our body. The bold claims of modern medicine seem to provide us with a cure-all cushion so that some people find it very hard to accept the connection between the emotional frailties we all have and things that 'go wrong' in our bodies. In the local doctor's surgery one bleak January day, a woman I knew slightly was talking to a neighbour. This woman was denouncing one of the doctors in the practice.

"I won't see him anymore," she declared loudly. "If they give me an appointment with him, I ask for someone else."

He was one of the most experienced doctors in the practice, so we asked her what the problem was.

"He tried to suggest that this pain in my leg, the one I've had to have surgery for, had something to do with the death of my friend!" she exclaimed in disgust. "When he said that, I just turned on my heel and walked out! And I haven't been back to him since."

Even when doctors' experience teaches them that the emotional state of the patient plays a decisive role in their condition, it can sometimes to be hard to convey that without destroying their trust, especially when conventional medicine appears to have no tools for managing feeling.

Assuming responsibility for our problem is a question of following the chain of cause and effect backwards from the language of the symptom to its original cause without blame or recrimination. The consequences of feeling are logical even if feelings themselves are not.

Suzi came to me in her seventies because she had been having problems with her digestion. I discovered that this was a chronic condition. She had had stomach cancer twice, and in the end, surgeons had removed her entire stomach, fashioning a small substitute out of the duodenum, so that she could eat very little, but enough to keep her alive. Nevertheless, she suffered a lot of pain and discomfort in her 'stomach', so she wanted to explore a healing approach.

I related in my earlier book how when I came to heal Suzi's roots, to see how she was connected in terms of security and safety in her life, the initial picture I saw was flashes of fire, explosions and burning villages. I changed the picture to one of peaceful nature, the roots of a tree planted deep within fertile earth, but after the healing I explained what I had seen and asked her if it meant anything to her.

"I was born in northern China, during the Sino-Japanese War," she said. "My father was a Japanese soldier in Manchuria, the Japanese colony in China, but when I was three the Japanese were driven out by the Russians who were fighting on the Chinese side. My family was forced to flee, hiding all the time from the Russian soldiers. If a child cried because he was hungry or tired, he would give all the refugees away. So if he cried, he would be shot."

Suzi's body, her unconscious memory, the child that was developing both literally and figuratively at that time, never forgot that it was dangerous to feel hungry, and her stomach was under strict instructions not to express that feeling. And there was a reluctance to express any other personal pain or fear, all of it concentrated in the stomach, which eventually developed cancerous tumours beyond the control of conventional medicine.

If she had made this connection at the time of her first illness, would it have made a difference? It could have. It might have been possible for her to acknowledge the child's fear and self-denial in her and, with an adult's compassion for that child's experience, release the feelings that had accrued on top of it since that time and come to seem like 'reality' to her. What we experience and our reaction to it can seem like the only possible way of seeing the world until we allow ourselves 'not to know' and imagine a different experience of reality. Once she accepted the relationship between her emotional make-up and the physical problems she was experiencing, then it might have been possible for her to imagine accepting her physical needs and her right to satisfy them. She might have been able to visualise her stomach gratefully releasing bitterness, hunger and fear and exchanging it for a sense of satisfaction and fullness. She might have been able to thank the cancer cells for pointing out to her that she could live her life in a more satisfying way and not continue to deny herself what she secretly wanted. By repeatedly sending herself love and imagining the fresh creation of healthy cells in her body, releasing the cancer cells, she might have been able to heal herself in a more subtle way than the surgery was able to achieve, a way with lasting results and the promise of new health.

Chapter 11

Finding Intelligent Life

I believe alien life is quite common in the universe, although intelligent life less so. Some say it has yet to appear on Planet Earth.
Stephen Hawking

In the early part of the 21st century the Indian government was making a concerted effort to bring tribesmen into the mainstream of public life. Many tribes, like those in Odisha, come down from their villages to town on market days to sell their produce, but disappear into the hillside jungle once market day is done. They are not registered by any civil or medical authority and have nothing to do with the mainstream of Indian society. Still, in order to interact on market day, they must have money. So the Indian government offered inducements for them to set up bank accounts. Bank managers were encouraged to interview a succession of suspicious and reluctant tribesmen in a bid to persuade them to put their money in a bank. One of these bank managers was interviewing a prospective tribal customer in a village near Puri in Odisha. The interview was the reverse of what he expected. The tribesman came in, sat down opposite him, and silently gazed at his face. Then he spoke.

"You are wise and strong," he told the bank manager. "You will look after my money skilfully and keep it safe."

The bank manager was astonished.

"I try to be those things you say I am," he said. "Certainly, if you give your money to this bank, I will keep it safe for you and give it to you when you need it. That is what I was going to say to you. But tell me why you say what you do about me, since we have never met before."

"Well you would not expect me to give my money to just

anybody," the tribesman answered. "So when I came to see you, I needed to assess your nature. Your nature is in your face. You have the face of a leopard, so you have the characteristics of that animal."

What neither of these men knew then was that in November 2016 the democratically elected Prime Minister of India would suddenly make any money the tribesman had *not* given to the bank illegal. He was forced to walk the 20 miles to the bank again with his 500 rupee notes and hand them over to the bank manager so that eventually he could receive legal 2000 rupee notes instead. But it is unlikely that the tribesman ever cast his vote in the Prime Minister's election. Without being able to study him at close quarters, he would not have known who to vote for.

Although these men grew up within fifty miles of each other, their education about how to measure reality was so different that to each of them the other's world seemed like a kind of magic. They both had the capacity to know what the other knew, but they used different aspects of their intelligence. The intelligence we call 'rational' is not the only way of knowing, or even a superior way of knowing. Like other ways of knowing, it is a useful one. But it is incomplete.

Generally, in modern society, we learn how to train our brains for rational deduction, and we do not learn how to use other aspects of our intelligence. Yet if we can embrace the other ways we have of 'knowing' and learn to use the whole of our intelligence, we do no harm to our rational faculties. In addition to the information that our rational minds can deliver us, there is *so* much more to be discovered!

To understand how this works in practice, we need to look at what different aspects of our intelligence are for. We know we have the ability to be logical, and many people would regard this as the chief aspect of their intelligence. If such and such is the case, then this result must follow.

This is the substance of most subjects on which we are examined during our formal education. Very little attention is given to the way in which we establish the initial facts from which our deductions are made. Far more to the logic of the deductions themselves.

Healers associate this logical aspect of our mind with the solar plexus. The energy centred here is primarily concerned with safekeeping the physical animal that is our individual self. It is energy associated with the eyes, the skin and the muscles. Staying alert, looking outwards for potential threats to our individual selves, or opportunities, it rapidly calculates the appropriate response. We look to measure how far away a car is when we cross the road, or how fast it is travelling. Instant decisions that start with the eyes, in most cases, send information to the unconscious or autonomic intelligence that activates our muscles, telling us to run or stroll across the road at our leisure.

In actual fact, the perception and the physical reaction take place in our brain. The retina of the eye is simply the receptor for information that our brain interprets, measuring it according to other information we have previously retained. We make thousands of calculations like this all the time we are awake, so this aspect of our energy is also associated with the frequency of brainwaves that is active when we are making them. They are not the most powerful of the brainwaves in living human brains, nor even the earliest to be scientifically measured, but they are the most obvious in the way we relate to each other and the way each of us relates to the world around us. These so-called Beta waves are involved in the exercise of logic, argument (even when the argument is not logical!), speech and response.

In order to act, however, we need rely on the intelligence that is innate in our physical bodies. The neurons in our brain need to pass an electrical response to the neurons that activate our muscles and hormones. We tend to ignore this reaction because it is automatic, or unconscious, but this hugely powerful aspect of our intelligence usually responds to something that we have *decided*. We take it for granted, believing that our decisions put us in control.

Most of us encounter times in our life when we feel we are not in control, regardless of our decisions. I have already likened the overwhelming impulse to eat when we decide to go on a diet, or the impossibility of bringing ourselves to do something we have chosen to do, to the actions of a rebellious child, refusing to obey its parent. There is no doubt that the child needs its parent. Our unconscious intelligence needs our logical mind to lead it in order to ensure survival. This relationship between two aspects of mind was so beautifully described by the sailor Steven Callahan as his senses were heightened by weeks of starvation. As he grew weaker, his conscious mind had to *take charge* of the autonomic or unconscious aspects of his body's functions, because this was the only way he could summon the energy to live.

In normal circumstances, we tend to allow the childish brilliance of our unconscious energy to prompt us unchallenged. Its complexity far outshines our conscious thinking. We go along with its dictates, following its daily pleasures: eating, sleeping, mating, moving. But if we feel unsafe at a fundamental level, we often try to resolve this by taking conscious control of our unconscious instinct. The less safe we feel, the more our conscious mind likes to take control and wishes to supress instinctive urges. We give ourselves rules to conform to. The rules, whether they relate to food or sex, are not what make us happy or comfortable, but what we think we ought to do to conform socially and feel safe as a result. Already there is a tension building up between two powerful aspects of our intelligence.

When our instinct comes into conflict with our wishes, the unconscious expresses itself through a physical reaction in the body. Suddenly we are unable to sleep, or we have no energy, or our digestion causes us pain.

If there is a problem, then we need to pay attention with the full scrutiny of our conscious minds. This turns out to be not as easy as it sounds. Unconscious patterns and reactions have been moulded into our brains. It is possible to change them. Many recent experiments have shown that our brains respond by circumventing the normal connections of our neurons when we make a conscious effort to use our body in a different way, either because of injury, abnormality at birth or because we want to learn a new skill. But this needs careful conscious effort and repeated instruction.[1]

In the murky depths of our unconscious lie all our hidden secrets. Often it is not the *outer* world we are fighting with, but our *inner* world. It takes our bodies, and our body's language, to show us what is going on. This process is going on all the time. We are accustomed to overriding the tension it generates until that tension becomes intolerable and may express itself in our immune system going haywire, unable to fight off an intangible threat.

Robert's story is an example of how this works. He called me because he was suffering from aggressive melanoma, a skin cancer that was spreading to his internal organs, and he wanted to learn about healing. I told him that the skin represents the face he presents to the world, and the disease would have manifested at a time that was significant in that regard. He said that he had just retired as a headmaster when it was diagnosed. He had loved his job and run a successful school. I agreed that there could be an issue powerful enough to spark a potentially fatal condition if he didn't feel that life was worth living *unless* he was headmaster of a school. Was that the only value he saw in himself? I heard a loud sigh of despair on the other end of the phone. He told me that he was born with a big birthmark across his face. He described it as being particularly ugly, hairy and obtrusive, so that people could not bear to look at him. I had no judgement on this. What was important was that this was how it seemed to him. He explained there was no way to disguise this birthmark, since it covered his eyes and nose, so he had worked hard to become somebody that people would look up to. He became important because of his position in society. Without that position, he felt, deep down, that he was worthless. And this unconscious feeling that he had no value outside his job because of his outer covering, his skin, began to manifest in a skin disease that was killing him once he was forced to retire.

Sadly, I never got to meet Robert. When he spoke to me the melanoma had already invaded his brain, and he died before he could travel south from his home in Scotland.

As I write I find my right ear is blocked. I have had an irritating infection in my right ear for several months but now it is growing acute. I am left-handed so my right side represents my emotional or inner self. It is the 'yin' to my left side's 'yang'. So I listen now: the problem has become painful.

"My ear is blocked. I can't hear properly on that side." That is my 'inner' self. What is my inner self saying that I don't want to hear?

As soon as I ask the question the answer comes tumbling out. It has been saying, for months:

"When this business of looking after my mother is over, I will be old and grey and my life will be over." And it is saying, *"My mother is so admired. She has so many friends who love her. I will never be good enough. I will never be as good as her."*

I am shocked to hear myself. I know these feelings are true. I recognise them. But my conscious mind ignores them. My conscious mind refuses to listen. Meanwhile, a part of my mind thinks she knows how the future will be, and, thinking she knows, she keeps telling me so, her quiet voice like a bass note in my life's symphony.

Your unconscious voice is not always right in what it has

to say. Sometimes it can help you with the strength and pure-hearted candour of a child. Sometimes it will be stuck in a point of view you conceived as a three or four-year-old. But, right or wrong, your unconscious has a voice you do well to listen to.

I remember the diagnosis of my brain tumour. At first the doctors seemed so certain:

"You have a brain tumour and we will have to cut it out."

My conscious mind was frozen with terror. My subconscious mind came to my aid. She is stubborn, rebellious, determined – just like my mother in fact. Quietly at first, and then louder and louder, my inner voice said:

"Well, if it's all over, you'd better finish the book you're writing while you can. Get on with it."

I did. I spent every waking day working on the book, regardless of my physical state. Then, most importantly, she said:

"There's no point wishing the doctors would behave differently. This is your head and you have to sort this out."

I listened. I began, with help and guidance from healers along the way, to explore the relationship between my body's expression and my inner feelings. Coincidentally, you might say, the doctors became less certain. They decided against surgery. They seemed not to know what they were dealing with or how it would turn out. They seemed to be unable to explore further without doing me greater harm. They could only guess at future developments, which they certainly were not going to share with me, so they settled for, "Let's wait and see."

This also was a blessing, although I found it deeply frustrating. It gave me time to explore what I had not known about myself, to change my understanding of what was possible, to open my mind to the possibility of a future for myself different from the self-critical bass note that had been a constant theme of my inner voice until then. I *forgave* myself, and curiously this meant forgiving everyone else in my story. I even started to *love* myself, because of course, when they were threatened, my eyesight, my head and my life were, and are, deeply precious to me.

I am lucky too that the doctors did not tell me that this tumour was certainly going to kill me. I have seen plenty of evidence that this so-called *nocebo* can have a powerful effect. The words of the medical authority lurking in the patient's subconscious sometimes wake up a voracious energy that feeds on the person's unhappiness before the diagnosis.[2]

There has been much more research to show that *placebo*, when a medical authority administers something with no active ingredients promising that it will improve the patient's condition, is very effective medicine. So much so that the placebo is often taken into account in randomized controlled trials for new drug treatments. This procedure starts by giving placebo to all the subjects chosen for the trial, to rule out those who respond to placebo. Those who get better with the fake pill alone are eliminated from the trial and half the remaining group will be given the drug that is on trial while the other half continues on placebo. If more than fifty per cent of those taking the drug see their symptoms improve, then the drug is deemed to be a success. However, this doesn't take into account the first group who responded to placebo. If their response was taken into account, then the result might be: "40% improved with this new drug. 60% got better with a sugar pill."

I see something like this has happened with my mother. She has become a fierce junkie in her old age. At night-time she has been roaming her domain looking for drugs that will knock her out. Her preferred drug is a sleeping pill that is given her on prescription. All the time she's been taking this drug, I've seen her grow more and more nocturnal, rattling around in the kitchen at 2 or 4am, making herself porridge and hot milk. She has been taking her sleeping pill regularly in the evening, and then another in the middle of the night, growing angry and aggressive with anyone who tries to stop her. Only in the morning, when daylight comes around, have the soporific effects of the pills seemed to kick in.

Her doctors know these pills do not work for her. They, like me, have been treated to a lament that she cannot sleep for decades now. When she grows frail, these night-time cooking marathons are a real problem. She runs the water and forgets to turn it off. She turns on the gas and forgets to light it. She pours herself milk and crashes to the floor while carrying it back to her bed. I spend most of one night reading the side effects of all the pills she has been prescribed. Of course, by the morning, I am thoroughly spooked. None of them seem to have the desired effect, and chiefly, above all, we both long for sleep. She cannot be left alone in this state and whoever is with her must spend the night tussling with her over how many pills she can take.

In the morning I phone the doctor, begging him to find something that will help her sleep. He pronounces the name of her old favourite. But I tell him it seems to have the opposite of the desired effect on her.

"You know it doesn't work," I say, "and the more she takes of it, the more aggressive and anxious she becomes. The guidance now is that it should only be given for six weeks. How long has she been taking it?"

"Twenty years."

I am speechless.

"There are a lot of old people like her, convinced that this drug gives them what they desire," explains the doctor. "They insist on having it even though it doesn't seem to work. It's a big problem. I have one in my own family."

"Can't you just give her a sugar pill, a placebo, so she doesn't know?"

"Unfortunately, that's illegal. I'm not allowed to do that."

My mother turns out to be resistant to all tranquillisers, from the most common to those reserved for hard cases. She swallows them all together, over the counter herbal remedies or medically prescribed. She downs valerian pills with her sleeping tablet and washes it down with morphine. They all have effects, but unfortunately not the effect she desires: a good, restful night's sleep. We even resort in the end to something known as the 'velvet cosh', apparently commonly used in prisons. I feel like a murderer when I give it to her. I needn't have worried. It has no effect.

Of course, I know what is really troubling my mother, the real reason why she can't sleep. At night, the party's over. There is no one to perform to and nothing to distract her from the deep and terrifying darkness of the next chapter facing her. She does not want to die, and she doesn't know how to do it, but it seems likely that her time has come. She keeps asking me how to do it. She *talks* about it often. But talking is quite different from the haunting terror of the void. At night it is this *feeling* that inhabits her subconscious that overwhelms her. If her conscious mind allows her to sleep, she might never wake up. Her resistance to this possibility is proving to be stronger than almost any drug so far invented. She keeps it at bay by concentrating on physical sensations like eating and drinking.

So here I am, writing, with the impact of this maternal drama resonating in me. Currently, it seems to be making itself felt in my right ear. Does 'listening' to my inner voice make any difference? Do my symptoms disappear instantly? This has never been my experience, although I have seen it happen in other people. I ask my doctor to have a look at it and she tells me I have 'otitis externa', probably caused by getting water trapped in my ear when swimming, and she gives me a spray to apply containing a little bit of antibacterial to clear up the infection. I muse on the fact that the other ear has been equally immersed in water, yet is unaffected, but say nothing because the doctor doesn't have time for me to complicate her life. I apply the medicine, which works for about a week until the problem comes back again.

I am grateful that 'listening to my ear' gives me real information that I know reflects my emotional truth. Now that I recognise the negative impact of the inner conversation I have been nursing I can use my conscious mind to encourage myself to see things differently, to start to apply remedies that will help me recover my energy and optimism. Months later, my view of my situation has changed, and the condition clears up by itself.

I have learned that I am most often wrong in my prognostications about the future when I see it as negative. The present me, predicting the likely result of one action or another, can only evaluate it by my present knowledge. I cannot take into account the effect of new growth, new understanding. How many people have you heard say that the illness which threatened to kill them was the best thing that happened to them? I would certainly say that. In spite of all the pain and suffering, the discoveries that you make about your strength, depth, and abilities, are full of power and wonder. The 'me' that is telling me I will be old and grey when I no longer have to look after my mother is stuck in the past. It does not take into account the unexpected sweetness I have discovered in the love between us in the process of her becoming completely dependent on me. A sweetness of mutual care that is stronger than life itself and will stay with me for ever. I could never have known the power of this if I had not been through the experience of caring for her.

When my inner voice speaks of the future in a positive light, it is often proved right. It seems to have the ability to know things before I have realised them. Through the ultimately successful process of encouraging my brain tumour to disappear, I had many, many days of anxiety and despair. But when I went deep into the language of dreams or meditation, I began to discover a brighter landscape and, with it, a conviction that I would eventually recover. This grew steadily stronger, to the extent that when I saw the slightest hint on the images from the MRI scan that the tumour was altering, I was jubilant. My family thought I was mad to feel so confident about a slight indentation on the upper surface of the tumour. I did indeed keep on working with myself to remove it, but deep down I knew that the tide had turned, and I knew why.

I do not know the future, but I have learned that my future depends on me. It is not 'out there', written in the stars. *I* am written in the stars. But I have choice. I am a conscious being, in motion. My future depends on how I, influenced by millions of others, choose to act in the present. I cannot know my future unless and until I know absolutely my present, and that includes my past. So potentially it is also true, paradoxically, that no one knows my future better than me.

Often, when things go wrong for us, they go wrong at this level of our energy: at the level of our minds telling us an unwelcome story about the way things are and the way they will be. The person we perceive as ourselves, our conscious minds, thinks he knows the future, or mistakes the way he perceives reality in the present as the only possible reality.

This energy of our solar plexus is potentially the power of our individual freedom, but so often it is the limiter of it. We look outwards for causes of our difficulties, clouding our vision with blame and anger, and do not take control of what we *can* control: ourselves. We focus our attention so intently on the external that we lose sight of our inner power altogether. Our conscious minds think they are cleverer than they are, and we tie ourselves in knots with them.

Our minds can be our greatest tool or potentially our greatest enemy. Sri Yukteswar, the sage who taught Paramahansa Yogananda, the influential author of *The Autobiography of a Yogi*, expressed this forcefully. Speaking about a beautiful and clever young disciple, he perceived a flaw in his outlook.

Keen intelligence is two-edged. It may be used constructively or destructively, like a knife, either to cut the boil of ignorance or to

138

decapitate oneself. Intelligence is rightly guided only after the mind has acknowledged the inescapability of spiritual love.[3]

We are not taught this way in most societies in the world today. We pursue outer success very effectively, through wealth, appearance and construction, but we only learn to use the power of our inner or complete intelligence when pain or disaster strikes. It is a paradox, of course, but we only begin to discover our power and potential and use it constructively when humility dawns. Thinking that you know ties you in knots. Knowing that you don't know, frees you.

The world we inhabit is constantly giving us information. Information is a tool to work with and we thrive when we live our experience in this way. If you put this understanding into practice, you can begin to perceive its power.

Take a situation that makes you angry for instance. Anger is information. You are angry because someone has treated you badly, and perhaps you have nursed this anger for decades, feeling unable to speak out about it. The anger has grown more and more potent over time, like brandy distilled from wine, and it has shaped your view of this person and reality. Whenever you meet this person, the same reactions occur.

The struggle you are having with this person is like a tug of war. Your anger makes you think about them. A lot! Far more than you would choose to. Perhaps they think about you all the time, but you don't know that. You have no power over their thoughts. But thinking about them so much ties you together by an invisible cord, what the Hawaiians would call 'aka'. It's a tug of war where you are tied together by the thread of your feeling. You hold on to one end of a rope of anger that is attached to another person.

Suppose you were to let go of your end of the rope? We all know how satisfying that would be! Someone who is your oppressor, however much you may also love them, would fall sprawling on the ground! You would be vindicated and victorious. But how could you do this? You are not having a physical war. All this struggle is in your thoughts. You need to find something in yourself to let go.

This is how you can do it. Settle yourself down in private and focus your mind on the thing this person does or says, or has done in the past, that makes you so angry. Concentrate on it hard. Then ask yourself, "What is it in me that makes this person act in this terrible way?" Give yourself a little time and something will bubble up. You will always find an answer. Keep asking yourself until the answer appears.

When you do find the answer, then see if you can let that thing in yourself go. See how it feels to try to detach it from you. Is it easy to imagine it floating free, disappearing over the hills, or does it cling to you when you try to throw it away? If it clings, perhaps there is another feeling behind it. Can you find that feeling and let *that* go? When this is done, imagine yourself disconnecting the cord that ties you to the other person in your scene. Let them float away.

When you feel anger rising up in you, treat it like an opportunity to try this out. I have never known it fail. Anger is useful information about yourself. Treating anger like this creates harmony out of discord, simply because anger must have two sides for fuel. Harmony allows situations to flow into change, like cohering sound waves. This little exercise will have a real impact on the world around you and you will notice that it also changes the way others perceive you. You may even find yourself looking for things that make you angry!

Lauren was being badly bullied at school. She was only thirteen when she came to me and the bullying was so bad it made her reluctant to go to school at all. I asked her to close her eyes and showed her how to relax her body. Then I asked her to picture her chief tormentor in her mind, right there in the room with us, and tell me how she felt.

"I'm expecting her to make some comment," she said.

"What are you feeling most unsure of in yourself?"

"I think I'm fat," she whispered. "I wish I was thin like some of my friends."

"This girl who is tormenting you, is she thin?" I asked.

"No," Lauren responded, surprised, as though she'd never really noticed before. "She's big. Not thin at all."

"If you could be anyone you wanted to be, would you want to be her?"

"No fear. I'd want to be like my friend Lizzie. She's pretty and everybody likes her."

"Would you like to have Lizzie's parents?"

"No-o." She laughs. "I'd want my mum and dad."

"Would you want to get Lizzie's exam results?"

"No! She's rubbish at maths."

"So if you could be anyone you wanted to be, she would have your parents, do your work at school. How would she be different from you?"

"Ummm. Just me, with a bit more confidence."

"When you think of the girl who bullies you, do you see anything like you in her?"

"Well she's a bit heavy."

"What about schoolwork? What about friends?"

"No she doesn't really have any friends. And I get better marks than her."

"That must be hard for her. Do you think she feels bad about herself?"

"Maybe. I've never really thought about it."

"If you think about it now, do you think she feels like you do sometimes."

"Mnn. Yes. A bit."

"Do you think you could feel sorry for her?"

"I'm feeling a bit sorry for her right now."

"Does that change the way you expect her to talk to you."

"Yes. She doesn't want to say anything. It's like she can't."

"Do you think you can let go of the bit of you that feels bad about the way you look, just for now? Do you think you could imagine it's like a magnet you could take out of you and throw away?"

"Okay," says Lauren, "I can do that."

"Good. Now imagine there is a rope connecting you with this girl. Take a big imaginary pair of scissors and cut the rope. Let her drift away over the trees and the hills. Can you do that?"

We pause.

"Yes, I can do that." Cutting the rope and letting the girl float away with it is real to Lauren.

After a while, I bring her back into her body and ask her how she feels.

"Lighter. Taller."

"Do you think you could do this again by yourself, if you're feeling oppressed? You might need to do it a few times."

She smiles. A beautiful sweetness lights up her face. "Yes, I think so."

I know this is going to work for Lauren. I know because it has worked time and again for me and dozens of others. Yes, I still get angry. I still catch myself thinking this is someone else's fault and if only they could behave reasonably like me, then there would no problem! But I have seen so many times how my anger is a reaction in me that is a way of defending those parts of myself that I don't want to see. In private, I can allow myself to explore, to see those things, and choose to let them go. If I can successfully release them, though I may have to try over and over again, I know for certain that the relationship that has caused me so much anger and pain will change.

Why does this work and how do I know for sure? Because I am part of the ever-wheeling, mutating river of energy that we call life. The only aspect of this experience that I have real power over is my own: the thoughts and feelings that lurk in my mind and make up my being and action. When I choose to focus on those thoughts and feelings and use different aspects of my intelligence to change them, I change the reality I experience, as surely as letting go of the rope in a tug of war.

Our inner selves can be very different from the person we appear to be on the surface. None of Robert's pupils or staff, not even his wife, would have guessed the way he felt about himself as a result of the birthmark on his face. Of course, that childish sense of inadequacy is something he had fought hard to put behind him all his life. But his *body* didn't forget. His inner senses, controlling the functioning of chemicals and cells within his body, also recorded and remembered feelings he preferred to put behind him. As our conscious mind is primarily concerned with keeping us safe, directing the show, it is often unwilling to listen to dissenting voices that appear to be outside its control.

This is what happens at first when people sit down to meditate. You decide you must have some peace in your life, space to make considered decisions about what you really want. Meditation is easy. You sit down. You close your eyes, because the eyes looking outward are conditioned to look for distractions in order to make sure you are safe. So you close them and listen to what is going on inside. You are breathing. How are you breathing? Is it long and steady? Short and uneven? For a short while this occupies your attention. Perhaps you manage to change your breath rhythm, even it out, make it longer, deeper. You start to relax, feel better even. Then you find you are thinking about something really important, something you have to do. You forget about your breathing but perhaps you realise after a minute or two that the rhythm has changed. You go back to the rhythm you were trying to achieve earlier, but another thought intrudes, and another. It has become positively painful to sit still where you are. Your inner voice is yelling at you about all these things that need your attention. You have no time to look for inner peace. You are *bored*! Perhaps you'll just go to your laptop and google a solution. Then you'll have answers and you'll be back in control. You come to believe that you *cannot* meditate. Inner peace and strength are for other people. You will continue facing the battles in your life in the same old way. You are trapped.

You are trapped only because your logical mind refuses to accept two opposite truths exist at the same time: the logical and the emotional, the physical and the non-physical, the yin and the yang, the inner and the outer. There is no light without dark, no life without death. Paradox, which dazzles and confuses our conscious intelligence, is the essence of our lives. Anything that becomes matter must dissolve. A truth we prefer to forget. The whole of life is a knife edge between two opposites.

If suffering or curiosity leads you to persist in exploring your inner world, this is what you find. Your external senses show you how to act in the outer world. Your rational mind is like your mother trying to keep you safe in an unfamiliar setting. But without your inner world you are no one. Your inner world acts in a completely different way. Logic is not the chief here. The controlling aspect is feeling. Since this aspect of our intelligence is common to all living beings it does not speak in verbal language but acts through the body. As human beings, we are conscious of it because of what we *feel*. But feeling can be overwhelming. The very fact that it has no logic, no beginning and no visible end, is frightening.

We try to put feelings into words because when we do, our intellect gives us the impression of control. Speaking about our feelings can give us the sense we can master them and send unpleasant ones away. Sometimes this works. We no longer hide the feeling inside where it grows in intensity and influence over our physical bodies, but present it to the outer world, through the medium of verbal intelligence, and as it emerges into the shared space of our world it disperses and dissipates, like a gas released into air.

Generally, this doesn't work if we don't allow ourselves to feel it first. The only way to disperse the feeling is to visit it, to sit with it like an adult beside a child's sick bed and watch how it has coloured your whole view of reality. You have the capacity to do this. Your being is complex enough to feel a feeling you may have thought you left behind as a child, with all the intensity of the contents of a freshly opened tin. You may cry or shout and this will shock you. At the same time, from a comfortable distance, you will find you can review the decisions you made in reaction to that feeling. You can do this through the medium of your imagination. Your mind is the mother *and* the sick child. As a wise and loving mother to yourself, you can now make a decision that is in your better interests.

To see things in a different way, you need to watch what you feel, without comment or control, until you understand how, and why you chose to react to circumstances in this way. A feeling creates powerful physical consequences. Letting it go has an equally powerful physical reaction. Everything that you are today is the result of choices you have made in the past. Some of them may have been conscious. Many of them were unconscious, guided by feeling. The more you explore your inner world, without judgement, without fear, the more you begin to understand that those choices you have made influenced you and everything you touch. When you review your emotional reactions from the safe distance of your adult experience, it is possible to see other points of view that escaped you at the time of your first visceral reaction. This vision will soften your emotional reaction, allow you to discard it, and leave the way open for a different outlook to guide you forward.

Your emotions are motivated by physical laws because these are the framework of the body they defend. Any threat to your life or body reminds you how precious your physical existence on this planet is. But the mind travels easily beyond physical laws, as we all know from our dreams and fantasies. Your mind can be a subtle tool for exploring your physical body. To get the most out of the body you have, you need to look under the bonnet and see what's there, especially if there is a problem.

At the level of the solar plexus we struggle to keep an open mind to experience we don't understand. It is hard for our rational minds, rooted in measuring the physical, to give up control. We feel vulnerable with knowledge that is different from what we have allowed ourselves to know. That vulnerability can be especially painful when we have valued our power. For some, not knowing is too much. They would rather be right than alive.

For hundreds of years we have been pursuing scientific measurement of the physical world, while taking our own perception of it for granted. We have no instruments to measure perception, so it cannot be scientific, but this does not mean it isn't real. The electrons at the heart of atoms in physical objects move around performing a dance around the nucleus. The pattern and the energy of the dance can change depending on the circumstances and how the object is viewed. We know this. Great scientists, like Albert Einstein, speaking here, have known this.

Imagination is more important than knowledge. For knowledge is limited, whereas imagination embraces the entire world, stimulating progress, giving birth to evolution. It is, strictly speaking, a real factor in scientific research.[4]

Yet still we crave a fixed reality. A fixed reality seems safe, while, in fact, it's the opposite of life itself.

Knowledge is a paradox. Our native curiosity leads us to explore the unknown and in so doing we learn more. Our instinct to remain safe tells us not to go beyond what is known, so we fix 'knowledge' at the limits of what we have discovered to be true or what we can prove to be true with the instruments we have so far discovered. The more we think we know, the less we discover. If you can allow yourself to approach a problem, internal or external, with an open mind, you will be surprised at what you can find out.

A couple of years ago I found myself hounded by the 'scientific' world in a way that reminded me how frightened some people are by an open mind. I had been asked to give healing to a man in his forties who had been diagnosed with an aggressively cancerous brain tumour. The cancer was grade 4 and this man had already had two operations at the Hospital of Neurology and Nervous Diseases in London's Queens Square, in an attempt to remove the tumour from his brain. The surgeons told him that, unfortunately, they had been unable to remove the cancer and there was nothing more they could do for him, so they sent him home. That was when his wife called me to ask for help.

I went to see him and did the healing more in a spirit of hope than expectation. I acknowledge that I can only do my best and what my best efforts achieve is beyond my control. But the healing went well and he rang me next day to express his thanks and say that he was walking better. I heard nothing more for about a year. Then out of the blue someone with the same name popped up in my message feed on Facebook. I got in touch.

Soon I was sitting in his house, having a meal with him and his wife, celebrating the fact that the results of his latest scan showed that the cancer had gone. The hospital doctors asked him what he had done. He attributed his recovery to healing, and to the course of homeopathy he had undertaken with a homeopath from his native Delhi soon afterwards. He was so enthusiastic about this treatment that he wrote about his experience and posted it on Twitter. I was delighted for him and shared the story.

Immediately I was bombarded with angry and abusive

tweets from all kinds of people who knew nothing about either of us but regarded themselves as defenders of medical truth that we had transgressed. I made the mistake of trying to reason with them that this was one person's experience in a vital matter and should therefore be listened to. This fanned the flames of their anger even more. I was accused of all kinds of fraudulent behaviour, dangerously misleading the vulnerable and undermining scientific medicine.

I know better now. The episode reminded me of one of Martin Brofman's sayings, the man from who I learned so much about the power of healing:

Never try to give healing to someone who doesn't want to be healed. It's like trying to teach a pig how to whistle. It's a waste of energy and it annoys the pig.

We know that energy comes before matter. We don't know how to make energy, only how to combine the elements. We don't know how to destroy it either, only divide it into its component parts: vibration, light, sound. And often we don't know how to measure or define it. Especially when that energy comes from the most potent and central part of our organism, without which we cannot function: our heart.

Chapter 12

The Heart of the Matter

Wisdom tells me I am nothing. Love tells me I am everything.
Between these two my life flows.
Nisargadatta Maharaj

Dr Ornish is an American doctor in the private sector who concluded that somehow, despite his best intentions, he was taking his patients into a confusing labyrinth of surgeries and medications which didn't do what he intended. Instead of feeling better, they ended up feeling worse. His patients suffered from high blood pressure and consequent damage to the heart. It was normal for these patients to eventually undergo open heart surgery. Surgery, of any kind, can take a long time to recover from, even if the surgeon achieves the desired outcome and the damaged organ or body part begins to function again as it should. If you have had surgery, you will know that your whole body and mind react to the shock of the surgeon's 'invasion' and carry the impact for a long time after the immediate wound is healed, sending ramifications to other parts of the body. To avoid this, Dr Ornish began to work in a non-invasive way with patients suffering from heart disease, teaching them, effectively, to help themselves.

He taught physical exercises, breathing practices, relaxation and meditation techniques, and put them on a low meat, low sugar diet with plenty of fruit and vegetables. The patients got better. In fact, they got so much better that heart surgery was no longer necessary. Dr Ornish became so convinced of the benefits of this programme that he wanted it to be available to all Americans, whether they had the money to pay for private health care or not. This, he decided, entailed getting his programme accepted as a valid treatment by the American federal health insurance programme, Medicare. He thought, correctly, that once the programme was approved by Medicare then it would be accepted and paid for by all the American health insurance companies. So he set about gathering the detailed evidence he needed to persuade the Medicare board that his 'non-medical' programme was medically effective. Patients were taught in a carefully controlled way, regularly attending a support group for eight weeks, and then the results were followed up at six monthly intervals. Eventually, Dr Ornish gathered enough evidence to present to Medicare and get his programme approved. It took him sixteen years.

As part of the process of getting the medical board's approval, he was asked to produce certification from an independent medical body that his treatment would not be harmful to older patients. He was incredulous.

"You mean you want me to prove to you that breathing, relaxation and moderate exercise are less harmful than open heart surgery? Surely you can't be serious?"

"We are."

So Dr Ornish did a control test with two groups: the ones who had surgery, compared with those who had followed his programme alone, to demonstrate that the outcomes were better in the long term for those who followed his programme. They were, and Medicare approved his programme in 2010 and it is now taught in over twenty American states.

But in the course of the controlled monitoring of outcomes something emerged that Dr Ornish had overlooked. When people were taught the exercises and the diet programme alone, they did not often thrive. When they were obliged to take part in a group to learn the programme and follow it up through a closely-monitored support group, the treatment was highly effective. Their symptoms diminished or disappeared without medication and they pronounced themselves happy with their lives.

It became clear that the essential ingredient in changing their lives was… the support group. These people who had heart disease and high blood pressure had an underlying problem in common: loneliness. Their hearts were suffering from lack of love.[1]

We come into the world looking for love. We seek it all the time, unconsciously, just like a plant looks for light. Love is the feeling that gives us energy and confidence to express ourselves. Love is this and so much more that it takes a lifetime to explore. It is so natural to us that we often forget how essential it is and think we can manage without it. We use all kinds of other things to express it: money; power; security; responsibility through our work, but everything we do is rewarding only if it makes us feel loved.

Yet in the battle for survival which we begin to undertake from the day we are conceived, there is so much that gets in the way of love! We feel fear, vulnerability, hunger, passion, hurt, anger, jealousy. There is also the conviction we are saddled with as soon as we come into the world. This is the conviction that we are separate, because our physical bodies and minds have autonomy. We can make choices. We have 'free will', something Christian theologians in the past have likened to 'knowledge'.

The serpent that spoke to Eve when she bit into the forbidden fruit is the emblem of the curiosity of the human mind. The disaster, the expulsion from Paradise that ensued, is knowledge, the fruit of curiosity. So many of us know this story. It was fed to us in our infancy so that it is an intrinsic part of the way we see the world. Adam and Eve, the mother and father of the human form, were instructed by God to enjoy themselves in the Paradise he had given them. They had complete freedom to do anything they wished, except one thing: the fruit of one special tree was forbidden. They did not know why, only that it would mean expulsion from Paradise. Eve, the mother of human form, was curious about this one forbidden thing. The serpent, her mind, called on her to explore, to discover more. When she tasted the fruit, and shared it with Adam, they discovered the freedom to use their minds in a way that is beyond the reach of the animal kingdom. With this freedom, they discovered also shame, guilt, self-recrimination and misery: the end of innocence.

As a child, no one ever bothered to explain the meaning of this story to me. Perhaps they didn't see it as I do. I enjoyed the fantasy of this perfect safe place, endowed with the riches of all the fruit and foliage of the earth, the beautiful forms and glittering colour of the animals, birds and insects that live amongst them, which man and woman enjoy. Indeed, it seemed to be where I lived.

Paradise is the Arabic word for a garden or park. The word implies protection, boundaries that keep danger out, so that if you live in Paradise you can relax into a state of total trust, and all your needs will be taken care of. Perhaps my elders understood that as a human being with a human mind, inevitably, I would soon fall out of Paradise. Did they imagine that I was already outside it half the time, feeling weak, fearing loss, angry about injustice and rejection, because I was born human? More likely they never thought about it.

The innocence of total faith, of unquestioning devotion to the infinite energy we call God, has all but disappeared from our society, if it ever existed. We scarcely value the power of faith enough to explore its power. Yet, in times of trouble, people crave the power of superhuman energy. It's hard to trust the power of the immaterial energy that surrounds us, and which we form part of, when our minds are attuned to the information our senses give us about physical form. It's hard for our minds to comprehend that we are part of the void, the indescribable space that is 99.9% of atoms within us and also constitutes the entire universe.[2] Our external senses serve the need of preserving our body so we can have the experience of being aware of this energy we are part of. Often it is the decline of physical strength that leads to revelation about the nature of life itself.

When we accept our limitations and allow ourselves to enjoy our being despite them, our lives grow richer. Anyone who has ever experienced serious illness knows how intensely we begin to appreciate being in our bodies when that happens. Any improvement in our physical state is infinitely more precious than gold or diamonds. The things we surround ourselves with are nothing compared to the beauty of being. When the health of our bodies is challenged, no physical object has any comparable value any longer.

One evening my mother asked me if I would like some chocolate. I said no. She smiled and flung out her thin right arm in an expansive arc as she was inclined to do, in a simulation of energy.

"She's an angel!" she sang happily to the retreating form of the carer I had hired to help, now on her way to fetch chocolate to complete the meal my mother had just enjoyed so much. "Angels don't eat chocolate!"

Actually, I was too exhausted and stressed to eat anything at all, but my mother had captured a truth as she so often did. While her body's strength fled from her, she was intensely indulging every physical sensation she could manage: the sweet subtlety of the taste of different foods, the comfort and pleasure of chewing and swallowing, the exquisite sensation of another hand's gentle touch, stroking or massaging her skin. Even the sensation of emptying her bladder was delightful to her. Other physical sensations were slipping away. She could no longer see or hear so well, and moving her body was an effort she would contemplate for many minutes, sometimes hours, before she forced herself into action. But the truth was that when she'd been active on the physical plane, she'd had much less time for love, either for loving her own physical being or to see others with love. When her physical powers declined, she began to feel the precious beauty in what remained to her and look at the world with an open love I had never seen before.

All her life she had been fearful of exactly what had now happened: of losing her power and independence. She had fought to assert and express herself in the way she chose, from childhood onwards. She fought her mother, fought her nanny, who left apparently because she was such an angry child, dominated her sister and ultimately everyone else who was beguiled by her vibrant creative charm. She drove herself to capture the beauty of the world she loved through her vision, embodying her imagination in photographs, paintings, etchings and books.

Her love expressed itself like a butterfly hunter. She would seek to capture what she loved and pin it down. I grew up trying to evade this capture, seeking freedom which I presumed would come with the distance I could put between us when I was old enough to travel. My elder brothers did the same. The eldest flew furthest and settled in Australia. The next developed a taste for spiritual retreats, in which he would be out of reach for years at a time. He burrowed into the non-physical world his imagination connects him to, emerging only to eat enough to keep his body functioning and to paint the colours of his glorious vision, ultimately making his home in Spain. I flew to America, to China, to India and France, but when I paused to make a home and bring up children, I settled close to my mother's reach.

Her fading strength in her 95th year brought with it this new experience of dependence. In reality, of course, she had been dependent on the love of others all her life, but she had never seen with such clarity how much she needed them. Now she needed help to wash, help to prepare food, help to keep warm, help to walk, help, in fact, merely to live this precious life which was slipping away from her.

She responded with shining gratitude which she spread around her like morning sunshine. The beam of her love fell especially brightly on me, because she was aware that I was giving or enabling this help so that she could live the last chapter of her life the way she wanted to. She didn't want to be dependent, naturally, but since she found that she was, she was happy for me to take care of her body and her beloved home so that she could stay in its shelter until her last breath.

I was surprised to find a new experience of love in the relationship between us. She began to praise me openly, to tell me how much she trusted and admired me, and her words were reflected in continual unspoken understanding between us. The more she loved so openly, the more I wanted to do for her. The more I did for her, the more the barriers of a lifetime dissolved to take us to a place beyond our physical bodies, a place of love, where communication and understanding continues even though she has now left her body behind.

A body in decline is far from the beauty of the human form in Paradise: the greed of an endless appetite for food, incontinence and mess, swollen skin with suppurating wounds leaching blood and pus, a chaotic nervous system wracked with pain. Decay of the physical form is an ugly process. But as my mother's body failed, she looked beyond the physical she had always attached so much importance to and saw the beauty of a different reality in everyone: the reality of love.

Coincidentally, perhaps, during this period of caring for my mother I was reading the biography of Chogyam Trungpa, the famous and influential teacher of Tibetan Buddhism in the West. I had never met him, and I know I would have avoided him if I had had the opportunity to do so, out of disapproval or fear of being trapped by his wild ways. But now I wanted to understand the apparent contradiction between his actions and his teaching.

Chogyam Trungpa was admired for his brilliance and the clarity of his exposition in the many books he wrote. He had a profound effect on many students, especially in the USA where he made his home. One of them, Pema Chodron, who has herself had a profound influence on many, said after he died:

> I would say now that maybe my understanding has gone deeper and it feels more to the point to say I don't know. I don't know what he was doing. I know he changed my life. But I don't know who he was.[3]

The difficulty in understanding a life like Chogyam's is that, while he was deeply committed to teaching Buddhism, many of his actions contradicted every single moral truth about what is 'good' about a spiritual perspective on life. Although he was brought up as a monk in Tibet, once he reached the West, he apparently indulged in every physical sensation to excess. After studying at Oxford University, he went to Scotland with a fellow monk, Akong Rinpoche, to found a Tibetan Buddhist Centre at Eskdalemuir that is now well known as Samye Ling. Not long afterwards he eloped to America with a sixteen-year-old girl who became his wife. He was alcoholic, promiscuous, and even imperious, while inspiring devotion from many followers. In the USA he founded several centres and ultimately created a kind of spiritual army complete with uniforms and discipline that is completely at odds with most people's idea of spiritual freedom.

While in Scotland, another event had a decisive effect on him. He crashed his motorbike and, although he survived, he remained partially paralysed for the rest of his life. This meant that he was heavily dependent on other people to help him every day. Washing, dressing, travelling, all needed support from others. And yet he lived a life of apparently ceaseless energy, travelling all over the world, dictating new ideas at 3am, and putting them into practice. In the process he created many books, many teachers, artworks, schools of instruction, securely rooting and spreading the influence of his understanding of Buddhist teaching in the relatively short life that he had. Looking after him was entirely unpredictable but the people who did so found such love in devoting themselves to his needs that they never resented the cost to their own energy and rest. Dependence, taken and given with love, opens the heart, and the power of an open heart is immeasurable.

We tend to live locked up in our sense of ourselves as separate from others most of the time. We stay in what a healer would call the energy of the solar plexus chakra. We look after our own safety, our own point of view, expressing our love for others only within those limits. When we look around us, we make judgements, assuming that we are in a position to judge, and that we are not that which we do not like. We see the outside of things, and believe we understand the invisible aspects of them. We judge others by the standards with which we judge ourselves.

Shock in our lives can shatter those judgements. Unexpected events leave us floundering, unsure of our ground, and the perceived truths of a lifetime can begin to dissolve. We may discover love somewhere we never thought we would find it, and it appears because the ordinary social communication we are used to is no longer good enough for our needs. As we begin to look inside ourselves for the causes of these unexpected events, we discover that we are more powerful than we imagined. Our judgements can have a powerful negative effect as well as a powerful positive one. When we begin to shed them, some of our self-defensive layers dissolve. Into an open mind we allow the energy of open love.

I believe the power of love to perceive, to create and effect change, to communicate and to transfer energy, is the whole purpose of exploring beyond the limits of the physical reality we know. The power of love is what every spiritual practice is urging us to discover. The philosopher Gurdjieff noted that when people move from perceiving the world through the solar plexus chakra, the sphere of logical, intellectual judgements and clear separation between one individual and another, to perceiving the world through the heart, this shift is often accompanied by turbulent events in their lives.

So what does it mean to perceive the world through love? I remember clearly what it means *not* to perceive it that way, to see it through the lens of the solar plexus. I remember my first entry into a healing workshop. I was carrying with me the burden of my illness. The drama of the diagnosis and its effects on my life were on my mind night and day. I sat down in a room of about forty people. At once my mind began to place everyone and everything. I decided who it would be most congenial to sit next to, considered who I had most in common with and who I felt quite different from. I considered that some people were on 'my wavelength' and others not. My critical faculties were in overdrive in this unfamiliar situation, especially because I felt so vulnerable.

Over the course of the next few days I found I did not need my familiar critical faculties. I was asked to respond to situations without 'editing' them or judging them in my mind. This was an uncomfortable place for me. I felt more and more vulnerable. Yet I also began to perceive that some part of my being spoke another language than the one I was used to. Once I allowed myself to do without familiar judgements, I found I could 'see' and understand the emotional energy of a stranger, and effect a change in that sphere. It was a wonderland, like nothing I had ever experienced before. As I continued to work closely with different people during the course, all strangers to me, I was continually astonished at how often it felt like the picture of their emotional energy was a mirror of my own. In every healing I gave I was learning something that was useful to me, just as much as in the healings I received. By the end of the course I began to loosen the locks of judgement that I had unconsciously been using to suppress aspects of my own being.

It was a great period of expansion and discovery. But it wasn't easy. In the ensuing months I crashed my car twice. I experienced a powerful rejection from a publisher I had been writing for, my daughter became ill and my husband was diagnosed with bladder cancer. I stopped sleeping and struggled like a drowning woman to make sense of it all. Yet in all those months I never lost the understanding I had glimpsed that there was a different way of perceiving the world than the one I was familiar with. I tried to remind myself to lose the familiar judgements, and as I did so, problems began to be resolved and difficulties melted.

Today, in daily life I ricochet back and forth between familiar judgements and those led by the heart. Sometimes the familiar sense is all I need. I use my eyes to measure the height of a door before I walk through it, or the solidarity of a chair before I sit down. And I remind myself when I'm driving that I'm in charge of a powerful machine to which I need to pay full attention! And sometimes familiar judgements still get in the way.

My husband was badly frightened by the diagnosis of bladder cancer. Strangely, because it is a relatively unusual cancer, a colleague of his had been given the same diagnosis shortly before, so when my husband saw blood in his pee he went straight to the doctor. Somewhat reluctantly, he allowed me to give him healing. When I did, however, it felt like trying to pour rain through a plastic sheet. I persisted, and saw areas I wanted to clear, but he grew restless, and I brought the process to a close.

There was no talk afterwards, no discussion. Just my intention to heal him. But I am too close to him. When we finished, there were things I wanted to draw his attention to, feelings he could resolve if he allowed himself to think about them, but he was uncomfortable. He began to whistle. Long experience has taught me that whistling is my husband's language for:

There's something important going on but I really don't want to know.

I decided it was best to let him deal with the cancer in his own way. He went into hospital to have the tumour removed, neither of us knowing the extent of it or whether it had penetrated the bladder wall.

After the surgery, he called me from his hospital bed.

"They've taken the tumour out of the bladder but I'm in so much pain that they think it might have spread to the kidney. They're going to take me down to do a scan."

I put down the phone and went for a walk. Suddenly the whole black picture that my husband had been creating through weeks of anxiety seemed to overwhelm me. He had always denigrated exercise and 'healthy' activities. It was part of his cynical, rebellious charm. He had persisted in smoking for years, although he had long since been relegated to smoking only outside the house. As soon as he was diagnosed, however, he was in a fever of anxiety, naturally. He began to have a presentiment that there was something more seriously wrong with him than the tests had so far revealed. Could this emergency scan that the doctors had called for now be it? As I thrashed around the field, I found I was angry.

"This is so typical of you!" I yelled to the poor imaginary version of my husband in my head. "You're so pig-headed you think you're in control and now you're going to go and die and leave me with the kids. What am I going to tell them!?"

About halfway round the field I stopped. I remembered I can be a healer. Why was I losing myself in this black fantasy that had not even happened? Healers use their mental energy to build the desired outcome, not to reinforce the undesirable. Deliberately I pushed all these dark thoughts from my mind, mentally turning 180 degrees, and ushered in only positive thoughts for the rest of the walk. As soon as I got home, I sat down and sent healing to my husband remotely. Slowly I sifted and rebalanced all the areas of his energy as I perceived them, understanding his situation in the process.

Half an hour after I had finished, the phone rang again. It was my husband.

"The scan was clear. There's no damage to the kidney. They think the pain is just gas, perhaps a reaction to the anaesthetic or the painkiller. It was a small tumour and they think they've got it all out."

The next day I went to collect him. I was determined to care for him when he needed me with as much attention as he complained I lavished on other people. He was already dressed, sitting impatiently on the side of his bed when I reached the ward. His bag was packed, and only very reluctantly did he allow me to carry it for him. We reached the car park and I went to open the passenger door to let him into the front seat. I looked at my car, appalled. It had a flat tyre. My role as the caring wife collapsed abruptly in a joint effort to change the tyre in the hospital car park!

It can be hard to help some people because they do not dare to be helpless. Despite all my pleas, he refused to sit and watch me change the tyre by myself, even though he had just had surgery. He insisted on using his weight to lever the jack and loosen the nuts on the wheel, so that by the time we got in the car to drive away, I was humbled with guilt that I had put him through this instead of steering him comfortably from his hospital bed to one where he could recover at home. I relieved my guilt by telling him what the remote healing I'd done had shown me.

I had cleared and cleared the bladder and the kidney, and when I went back to check that kidney, I seemed to find a hard shell inside that I needed to clear also. Inside the hard shell was a soft middle. It seemed like his anger at being born a man and having to appear to be tough when he's gentle and thoughtful and that's all he wants to be. And as I realised this, I realised something else.

"You know I did this healing on you and I realised something about us as a couple that is important for me," I said. "Who else in my life have I loved and felt very close to but found it difficult to communicate with?"

Poor man! He was a prisoner in my car listening in a post-operative stupor to my ramblings about emotional depths that he would rather have avoided. But even in his semi-drugged state he knew the answer.

"Your father," he said, not missing a beat.

We made it home. My husband consented to drinking the herb tea I prescribed for him (small flowered willow herb) and in the ten years since he was diagnosed has only had to return once for a minor surgical operation about six months after the first. Otherwise all the tests have shown him to be clear of the cancer. Bladder cancer is notorious for reappearing in different parts of the bladder, so his outcome has been exceptionally good. His colleague, who was diagnosed at the same time, sadly died.

You've probably guessed by now that my husband and I are very different in character. Yet we have been together for more than 30 years. Our differences are not always easy to navigate but while they are extreme in some senses, I think the fundamental understanding that love matters most has kept us together. Our relationship seems to me a little bit like the unity of opposites encapsulated in the yin yang symbol. Where the light wanes, the dark quickly grows to full strength. And when the dark diminishes, the light swells and shines in balance.

I understood this one day when we went to a biographical play about the writer Quentin Crisp, openly homosexual long before homosexuality was legal in Britain. My husband has always admired Crisp's witty observations on a society he felt excluded from. As an old man Crisp went to live in New York, where he continued to write his truth with the same level of bold detachment. As we listened to Crisp's speeches, it sounded to me as though he could have been quoting the Buddha. His view of God for instance:

I am unable to believe in a God susceptible to prayer as petition. It does not seem to me sufficiently humble to imagine whatever force keeps the planets turning in the heavens is going to stop whatever it's doing to give me a bicycle with three speeds.

But if God is the universe that encloses the universe, or if God is the cell within the cell, or if God is the cause behind the cause, then this I accept absolutely. And if prayer is a way of aligning your body with the forces that flow through the universe, then prayer I accept.[4]

I don't think the Dalai Lama would put it any differently. Quentin Crisp goes on to pinpoint that this conception of God, "the cell within the cell", celebrates the potential of each of us.

There is a worrying aspect about the idea of God. Like witchcraft, or the science of the zodiac or any of these other things, the burden is placed elsewhere. This is what I don't like. You see, to me, you are the heroes of this hour... You used to live an easy, lying down life in the sea, but your curiosity and your courage prompted you to lift your head out of the sea and grasp this fierce element in which we live. They are sitting on Mars, with their little green arms folded, saying "We can be reasonably certain there is no life on Earth because there the atmosphere is oxygen, which is so harsh that it corrupts metal."[4]

It's easy to think of ourselves as loving beings until we look at our relationships with members of our own family. It's a curious fact that the people we love most are the ones that generate the most anger and hostility in us. It's interesting to ask why that should be so. The obvious answer is that these relationships are the ones we can't avoid. If a neighbour, or a stranger, upsets us we can ignore them and forget about our differences. Friendships we can allow to fade away. In our own family, whether the one we're born into or one we have made after falling in love, we cannot avoid conflict. Sometimes we react by running away. Then we have learned nothing. The situation will repeat itself in other relationships in our lives because we've refused to learn what that conflict shows us about ourselves. It's only when we accept that we are part of the cause because of the choices we've made that we have a chance of resolving the conflict by choosing to act differently, even if that means walking away.

Carl Jung once said:

Everything that irritates us about others can lead us to an understanding of ourselves.[5]

You can look at any conflict that comes your way like a mirror that reflects something back at you that it would be handy to know. The next time you're angry with a loved one, remember what it is in them that attracted you in the first place. Exploring a relationship you have consciously chosen to enter into helps you to understand what love means for you. This is the true meaning of 'relationship': a relative space into which you fit with someone else because of your joint search for love.

You will understand it better if you look at your relationships with those you have not consciously chosen: your birth family. Your relationship with your father will help you to see what you look for from men in your life. Your relationship with your mother and the relationship between those two will likewise have formed the basis of what you expect, in terms of security and in terms of the support, or otherwise, that a long-term relationship brings.

The more you know about what love means for you, the more likely you are to find the space in which you feel you can touch it. Finding a space where you live in what feels like love makes you happy. This happiness gives you strength, both mental and physical, and you can use this strength to share your love with your environment: the people, the plants, the places. In this space you blossom like a flower and your fragrance attracts others.

Once you begin to explore the world around you through love rather than judgement you begin to perceive a wavelength that apparently has no limits. It is a wave of perception and understanding that communicates beyond physical barriers and encapsulates a unity that defies our logical brains. When you perceive your world from this level, you cease to see yourself as a drop, and become part of the ocean.

You've probably heard people talk in this way about love. You may also have experienced this wave of communication that it generates. Even so it can be much more difficult to experience it in your daily life! The minutiae of your immediate relationships is the microcosm you navigate to experience your existence within the macrocosm.

When Barbara came to me for healing she had lymphoma, a cancer that had begun in her bone marrow and spread to her liver. Her doctors had told her it would likely be fatal within two years, or six months from the time I met her! I explained to her that the symptoms of her body told a story of tension between her experience of love and that of security, something to do with home, money or job.

"The white blood cells are your immune system, connected with the root chakra, because they are generated in the bone marrow, and the skeleton is your fundamental structure. It's connected with the part of your awareness concerned with security, which would be formed initially through your relationship with your mother, but in your adult life this has to do with other forms of security: job, money, home. But the condition is connected with your experience of love since the T cells which fight infection are generated in the thymus gland in the region of the heart, and the B cells are generated just below that in the spleen, which is in the solar plexus region. And the blood itself is pumped around your body by the heart which sends it to all your cells and back again every twenty to thirty seconds. So, from a healing point of view, this condition is related to emotional tension about your confidence in being loved, especially in the context of relationships at home."

Barbara agreed that this resonated with her and we talked briefly about the power of perceiving the world around you through the lens of love. She seized on this enthusiastically. It was natural to her.

"I went to a lecture once where this man was talking about that," she said. "He was talking about how you could get outside yourself by looking at things through love. And I thought when I heard him, 'I do that all the time!' I just think, 'Love, Love, Love'."

She flapped her hands towards her face as though she was fanning a sweet smell in from the air.

"And then I can be up on the ceiling outside my body seeing everything from there."

The problem, as it turned out, was not seeing beyond her body, but living inside it. Even though she had been diagnosed more than eighteen months ago, this woman still had not told her husband and son that she was ill! Abstracting herself from her body and her home was natural to her. Her potentially fatal condition indicated that she would rather be outside her body than at home in it.

Our families, whether the ones we are born into or the ones we have chosen to make, are the launchpad for us to begin the journey of discovery of love in our lives. Our bodies are the vehicle. We find the way to go by looking closely at how we react to our most immediate relationships. They will show us what love means to us and give us the opportunity to choose whether to look for a different expression of love. This is your evolution and the opportunity your life gives you to learn.

The heart chakra 'develops', in healing terms, between the ages of around 9 to 12. By the time we reach this age we have made certain decisions about how we want to be in reaction to how much love we are rewarded with for our way of being.

We are programmed to love our birth mothers and fathers, regardless of who takes care of us from birth. I do not know if this connection is buried in our genes, but I have seen it again and again in healing, and in my own experience. Regardless of how we are treated by our birth parents, whether we are given away by our mothers, or have never known our birth fathers, theirs is the love we seek in our lives and their actions have a profound impact on our unconscious choices when we look for love in a relationship.

Our birth parents have already shown us 'what love is'. Perhaps we had a father who loved us and yet was inclined to violent anger. Love becomes something to be desired and feared in equal measure, not a place of comfort and security. Perhaps we had a mother who became angry or ill when we were upset or naughty. Love becomes something intermittent. We can only preserve love by suppressing our own feelings and behaving as we feel we should. Perhaps we only felt approval when we did well at school. We learn to associate success by society's standards with the comfort and security of love.

If this sounds simplistic, it is because it is that simple. Human beings love to love and be loved. When we are able to see love around us, and feel united with our surroundings by love, we are happy. It is not obvious to us because we take love for granted like the air we breathe. And, like the air we breathe, we feel it intensely when it is not there. But most of the time our minds are busy blinding us with knowledge, just like they do in the myth of Adam and Eve.

By the time we reach around 9 years old we are pre-pubescent. Our sexuality is developing, and we begin to look around us for models of loving relationships. We look at the relationship between our mother and father and draw our own conclusions about how love will feel when we are adults, and what it will look like. Our adult relationships are very likely to reflect the conclusions that we drew at this age, until we become aware of our reactions and look for other ways of finding and expressing love. Whatever we decide, the energy of love is the catalyst for the whole human world.

When a man and a woman fall in love, they tend to produce children. These are not the only circumstances through which children come into the world, but it is and always has been the vast majority. Babies are defenceless and need protection, which necessitates creating a shelter and providing food. The most efficient shelters and production of food come from settled farming, so these shelters cluster together for mutual aid and security, and they need roads and transport to connect the settlements. The settlements eventually have to be provided with food. Some people do one job, others specialise in another, and you get towns and a trading economy. Meanwhile some people will fall in love with an idea. They do not pursue this idea for money or security, although they may hope for these things, but out of a passion for the idea they envisage. This passion takes over their lives and often swallows their fortune until eventually something is produced that ultimately changes all our lives: ships; aeroplanes; the jet engine; computers; the Internet. These ideas, children of passion, begin to change the structures of the society we have created and changing social norms exert their pressure over all of us as individuals.

As society continually evolves there is conflict between the old and the new standards. Some people value the old forms above the emerging new ones and disagreements can be violent.

Violence breeds more violence. The growth and the turbulence generated by humans in the world is fuelled by feeling. Our perception of the world as individuals vacillates between fear and love. Love brings security and confidence, hope and power. Fear is the anticipation of its dark opposite. So is it possible to encourage the positive light of love in your life to dispel the darkness of fear?

Chapter 13

Heart Medicine

The 'divine soul' is like butter in the cream, the oil in a sesame seed.
Svetashvatara Upanishad[1]

A sixteen-year-old boy was speaking before a huge crowd in Bodhgaya, the place in India where the Buddha is supposed to have found enlightenment while sitting under a banyan tree. That Buddha moment was about 2500 years before but the ripples from it are still being felt. The sixteen-year-old's life was in many ways a consequence of it. He was born a nomad in the plains of eastern Tibet. His parents thought him unusually gifted and, when he was four, they sent him to the local monastery to be taught the Tibetan version of the truths the Buddha had realised. When the boy was seven, he told his family they should move to the next valley, which they agreed to do. In that valley they met a delegation of monks on horseback searching for the incarnation of the seventeenth Karmapa, the new head of their lineage, according to instructions left in a letter by the sixteenth Karmapa who had died two years before. The monks recognised the new Karmapa, the new head of their Kagyu school of Buddhism, in this little boy.

For the next seven years the boy was carefully taught the practices and philosophy that had evolved in Tibet since the Buddha's time, to prepare him to be a spiritual teacher and leader in his own lifetime. But the political landscape of the region in the twentieth century dictated that these teachings would no longer be confined to other monks. They would no longer even be confined to Tibet. In the boy's time, the teachings would spread around the world, and the language that would carry them so far was English. Born in a country that is claimed by China, the boy had spent some time in Beijing, but, by the age of fourteen, it seemed to him that he would never be able to teach the spiritual message of his lineage with freedom while he lived in Tibet. So, in 2000, pretending he was going on a spiritual retreat, he followed in the footsteps of the Dalai Lama, and all the older generation of Tibetan teachers who had fled their homeland on foot, and secretly crossed the border into India.

A couple of years later he found himself addressing this large crowd in Bodhgaya. Whatever he felt on seeing such a huge crowd gathered for him, there is no doubt about the excitement of the many Westerners among them on seeing this latest spiritual 'jewel' to emerge from Tibet. Western reverence for the exotic magic of unknown Tibet is something earlier Tibetan teachers, like Chogyam Trungpa, had tried hard to dispel. Yet on this occasion, fourteen years after Chogyam Trungpa's death, the sixteen-year-old fresh from Tibet was drawing crowds who had travelled halfway across the world to see him, listening to him with rapt attention. Among them was my mother.

Earlier, she and her group of Western Tibetan Buddhist companions, followers of Lama Chime Rinpoche, had met the young Karmapa and shaken his hand. When he heard that she was an artist he had asked her to draw him a horse. Hastily she had produced a drawing, not at all certain that she was doing justice either to the horse or the Karmapa. Now here she was, squeezed into her seat, perched high above the young monk on the stage, straining to hear him speak and follow his interpreter. She was already 79, and although she would never have admitted it, the long train journeys and a stay in the spartan surroundings of a Tibetan monastery in Sikkim were taking their toll. It's hard to say whether this had anything to do with what happened next, but for my mother this was one of the most powerful, and also terrifying, experiences of her life.

As the young monk swept his eyes across the crowd, she

suddenly felt as though he was gazing directly at her. At the same time, an intense feeling of detachment gripped her. She was hovering above the crowd, above her own body, part of the air that surrounded them and yet part of her body and everyone else's also. The strange sensation overwhelmed her. She struggled to get out of the hall, away from the noise and the crush, hoping to find her way again in the open air. The unfamiliar feeling stayed with her when she got outside. She described it to me as a sensation of vastness, of being a tiny particle lost in an immense ocean, as though she was lost in the void.

I knew what she meant. I had a similar experience once in Hawaii. I was learning the Hawaiian breath ritual, the Ha breath, under the careful supervision of Harry Uhane Jim and his wife, Sila. We had been shown how to breathe, deliberately panting short breaths that take in a maximum amount of oxygen and increase the alkalinity of the blood. This state of being induces a kind of waking dream, an altered reality which exists in your head alone but has the palpable reality of a movie in which you are led along by the story. It is similar to a trip induced by consuming plants that are high in alkaloids, but it comes from the way you use your breath alone. The story you experience is from you and for you at the same time. For me it has the qualities of both a prophecy and a mirror, and I have used and taught this ritual many times since to answer questions and point the way forward.

But this was the first time for me, and I was nervous. Very quickly the pulse and the rhythm of the breathing overtook me, and I was immersed in the journey. I felt myself emerging from a cave like a diaphanous blue creature and encountering at once a dark star-spangled wizard who directed me toward the forest. In the forest I wound my way downriver between the trees, listening to the calls of the native people there and learning and imitating their songs. But my journey was always onward, drawn downriver toward the great, open sea. Eventually I felt myself emerge from the forest and a sensation of openness overwhelmed me. It seemed there was neither sky above nor ground beneath my feet. I was weightless and floating, but there was no joy in it. I was in a blank sightless void. There was no substance, no barrier, no being. I struggled, full of fear, to get out of this emptiness. I seemed to encounter a barrier, like a skin, beyond which, perhaps, there was something, and I threw myself at the edges, like a goldfish trying to escape its bowl. But, try as I might, I could not break through. I felt lost, aimless and constrained at the same time. Then, just as I felt I would never escape from this hopeless being, Sila touched me. A feeling of love infused me like the sunshine of day. The blank fog of fear was transformed into a bright light of love that illuminated this space and shone through me. This love, I knew, was all for me, although I did not know its source. It filled and carried every cell of my being. I felt connected, significant, seen by something great that united me with all there is. The touch of another had passed this on through me like the flame of an Olympic torch. I have never forgotten it.

I have never forgotten either the lesson it showed me: that the difference between fear and love is everything, and yet it can dissolve in a heartbeat. They are almost together. Extreme fear induces extreme openness. The openness itself is what you need to experience the love which you are part of and the creative principle of the universe.

Prior to this experience I had never really thought of it like that. Afterwards I realised that I had never really felt loved. Not like this. It was not that people had not expressed their love, or that I had been in any way unfortunate. I had enjoyed the bounties of natural abundance in the form of food and beauty around me and received care that had given me shelter, education and health, but it seemed I had never really allowed love to penetrate. It was only when I felt the naked vulnerability of an open heart and, at the same time, the deep reassuring confidence of existing in an indestructible way, that I could say that I had experienced what love means and know that I am loved.

Vedic scriptures and Buddhists teach that the void is the only ultimate reality. Everything else is imagination, or, if you like, the picture of solidity our minds create because we cannot function in a world that appears as the micro-physical reality. The physical world we live in is very sparsely populated by measurable matter, when perceived at a nano microscopic level. So whether our information comes from Buddhist teachers or the frontier of physical science, we know that we live between two realities: the one where we are solid and our bodies obey the macro-physical laws of gravity and friction, and one where we have almost no substance. At this level of perception, everything is in motion, constantly fluid, and physical barriers have no meaning. Our minds are capable of crossing between these two realities.

The bridge that allows us to cross 'out' of our bodies, as it were, is our perception of universal love. This perception is a sensation, as palpable as the feeling of sun on your back or fire in your belly when it happens to you. It comes unpredictably, even unbidden, because it is a physical understanding beyond the reach of the conscious mind. When it arrives, it is strong enough to reassure your frightened human soul that it is safe to leave its concern for your body aside. But, unless you are prepared for this sensation, natural concern for the safety of your body will swiftly return. Then you can feel dangerously unbalanced and disoriented.

It is best to be prepared for this feeling with as much understanding as you can muster. This is the reason that people study teachings by enlightened individuals who are familiar with both their physical and non-physical being. My mother was taken by surprise. She had not been expecting this unfamiliar sensation of vastness and weightlessness, and it terrified her. She thought she was losing her mind or her body, or both. There was no human touch to reassure her, to reach through her fear, as there was for me, and naturally enough she quickly closed the door. She ate and drank something, and the physical sensations brought her back to the familiar feeling of being her individual self. She never forgot this experience, but because it ended bleakly in this way, she was reluctant ever to explore so far again.

The yogis say the sensation occurs when energy stored at the base of the spine rises suddenly to the brain. The channels this energy flows along are not physical. In your normal daily activity, your breath emerges predominantly from either the right or the left nostril. You can test this by holding the pad of your thumb under one nostril after the other while you breathe steadily and see which side is dominant now. The flow changes thirteen times in twenty-four hours, approximately every one hour fifty minutes. The channel on the left reflects the internal activity of the body, your autonomic functions, and its attributes are introspective, imaginative, receptive, depressive. It is the yin aspect of your energy and the yogis call it the *ida*. The attributes connected with the right-hand channel are extrovert, creative, aggressive, dominating. It is called the *pingala*. A physical constriction in one side or another will correspond to an imbalance in your habitual way of being. Perhaps you recognise a tendency to lean more to one of these ways of being than another in yourself. You may be interested to explore how this corresponds to the way your breath emerges from your nostrils and the times of day when you feel best.

Occasionally, the energy stored at the base of the spine, according to yogic anatomy, rises through the central channel known as the *sushumna*, the energy that normally flows through the *ida* or the *pingala* fusing together. This is such a powerful sensation that it is described as a moment of great opportunity, but also of immense vulnerability. If it is to work in your favour it is better to be prepared.

Sometimes this happens to people after an intense period of 'consciousness raising' activity: kundalini yoga; shamanic dancing; prolonged meditation or even LSD. Experiencing the power of these practices over your body when you are unprepared mentally for what that can feel like can knock you severely off balance. A friend felt something similar after a couple of weeks of intensive meditation in an Indian ashram. Quite suddenly she had the sensation of light emanating from everything. She had a surge of triumph in feeling that she had made it. She could see invisible energy and she thought, *I am enlightened.* There is no reason why she should not have seen this energy or recognised the light in everything. There is no law that says you must meditate for decades in order to achieve this perspective. But she had no experience to help her deal with the low when this feeling wore off. Instead of feeling that she had glimpsed things as they really are, she now felt disconnected and isolated, incapable of managing anything practical in ordinary life which no longer made sense to her. The fear and isolation stayed with her far longer than the momentary invincibility of her visionary 'high'. She became mistrustful of her own mind, so that she felt divided not just from her environment, but from herself.

The paradox is that love unites us with everything and then we are nothing in relation to the vastness of everything we perceive. So long as we perceive this unity, we are part of something immensely powerful that carries us like a floating cloud carries a drop of rain. Nothing can harm or dislodge us. If we return to our usual physical perception and see ourselves as separate in our physical body, then, combined with this sense of the vast power around us, we can feel exceptionally small, weak, and isolated. It is like finding ourselves unexpectedly able to balance on a tightrope and then looking down at the earth below and remembering gravity. We fall. It is possible to walk the tightrope and stay balanced, but we need to train our bodies and our minds to stay focused, continually making the choice to look up and remember our potential.

In all things there is a balance to be found – the point of balance midway between two opposites. At this midway point there is no contradiction, only unity between opposite truths. This is the place of the heart: in the centre of the body between the physical and the non-physical. It's the organ that pumps blood around our bodies and sustains our physical being, and the place where we feel passion that ignites our wish to be joined with the non-physical. It's the region where the lungs can affect everything that happens in the physical body through their ability to modulate and interact with the invisible air.

Entering the perspective of the heart chakra implies a balance where you, in all your weakness and strength, are part of the nature of all there is, flying in the endless cycle of birth and death that is matter. No part of you is 'wrong'. The essence of you is right. Because the essence of you is the same as that of other beings, coming from love and flourishing through love. When you look at your world in this way, familiar judgements and barriers dissolve. And since it is the 'others' who we judge and measure in our daily view of life, you will learn more from working with a teacher and experiencing new things in the company of other people than you will from sitting alone in the private cave of your meditations.

You have a key that opens the door to your heart, and all its understanding. It is a key that allows you to be yourself and yet be open to everything around you. That key is your breath and the way you use it. The doorway from the sense of yourself as an individual to the sense of being part of the universal is the way you breathe. The ancient yogis made a detailed study of the way breath works in our bodies and how to use it to train our minds and bodies to focus with the precision and power of a laser beam. Their 'anatomy' of the breath offers a map to work with, just as the Vedic map of the chakras offers a physical map of the way energy works within us.

It's quite likely you've experienced this phenomenon of energy from the *ida* and the *pingala* rising together up your spine along the *sushumna* channel spontaneously. When you've been absorbed in a creative thought, or after a prolonged fast or physical exertion, or perhaps after a period of intensive meditation, you may have felt it without knowing what is happening. You feel a powerful sense of invincibility followed by crashing down to earth. Our bodies need to feel grounded and the fear of instability often expresses itself as pain.

When I learned this anatomy of breath I recognised the phenomenon. Before my brain tumour was diagnosed, I used to get sudden, intensely debilitating headaches. These headaches would pitch me to the floor as though I'd been struck on the back of the head with an axe, and then it would be several days, or sometimes weeks, before I could find a position that I could be in without pain. Eventually, after the tumour had been detected, my consultant suspected that the pain was caused by blood vessels from the tumour bursting in the brain. The bleed would be felt by me only at the base of my skull, because you have no nerve endings in the brain. That was the physical anatomical explanation. After several of these attacks, however, I began to reflect on how curious it was that I would always be feeling particularly positive and creative immediately before one happened. I would be walking along the road with my head full of ideas about something I wanted to do and plans for how I was going to do it, a surge of energy running through my veins. Literally. And then came the crushing physical reaction which completely disabled me.

This doesn't mean that a surge of creative energy can't be sustained, of course. In the circumstances I was in at the time, my body was pushing me towards a more sustainable path, which I was lucky enough to discover. I had been overburdening myself with desires and ambitions while ignoring the internal workings of the 'me' that was going to do these things. I was unbalanced towards the yang, *pingala* side. It was as though the energy of my thoughts, sweeping my breath with them, was surging through my spinal channel but detecting a critical weakness on the yin or inner side. As these invisible channels travel up the spine, the left and the right cross at every major chakra, merging as they enter the brain at the level of the brow. When the tumour was detected, it was found to be, not surprisingly, on the right-hand side of my pituitary, behind my right eye, just where the *ida* emerges in a final sweep before uniting with the *pingala* and *sushumna* behind the third eye.

A sensitivity to the way your breath works in your body can unleash sustainable creative energy. This can do much more for you than the occasional uncontrolled high. The energy of the breath extends far beyond the physical limits of the lungs. This is obvious because the blood has to carry the energising oxygen to every cell in your body. The power of your mind to influence the way the energy is used in your body is not so obvious, although this power is used by nearly all sports people and in every school of inner development since time immemorial.

In the same way, if you want to reach a part of the universe, whether that's internal or external, you have to put your mind there. And where you put your mind, the energy follows.

To increase the power of your effective energy, you need to boost your concentration and you can do this by getting the habit of focusing on your breath alone. You watch the breath coming in, keeping it steady and smooth, and you watch the breath going out, letting it flow out for exactly the same time as the incoming breath. Then you do it again. And again. Your mind will calm and settle. Other thoughts will come in and, if you remind yourself to go back to your breath, they will dissolve again. Your body will relax. Pain will soften and disperse. Your mind can control your breath. Your breath can control your mind. Taking time to focus on your breathing is a two-way street: a bridge to a stronger, happier, fearless you.

The power of the breath has been so obvious to civilizations all over the world that techniques to develop it have always been taught. I've only practised a few: the Chinese qi gong – literally, energy work – which identifies and refines the use of energy in the breath; the yogi tradition which has multiple techniques from yoga nidra to hatha yoga for consciously using breath to develop energy and understanding, and the Hawaiian *ha* breath that I've described. These are my favourites, but as I explore the world further, I look forward to discovering more ways of working with the breath.

The early Christians knew all about the power of the breath to engender calm, stillness and consequent spiritual insight. Gregorian chant, a feature of monastic life from the 9th century onwards, uses the flow of the breath to draw out the prayer of the heart, the wish to spread and be part of the connecting web of energy that humans feel as divine love. By the time the Christian missionaries reached Hawaii in the 19th century, however, this tradition was no longer part of protestant Christian worship. The missionaries taught that their view of God was the only view of God. All other views were harmful. The Hawaiian shamans, whose role in their community was to heal and communicate with invisible forces, listened with curiosity. The stories of Jesus seemed to indicate that he did the same work as them. Would his priests also do this? But the Christian priests behaved very differently from spiritual leaders in the Hawaiian community. They spent more time talking about what Jesus had done 1800 years before than emulating it themselves. They didn't expect people to emulate Jesus. Although he was a human being, they were only interested in his understanding of the non-physical world. They did not believe that other human beings could emulate him. The Hawaiian shamans, on the other hand, did believe that. For them, a priest or spiritual leader earned his position by perfecting the physical and mental disciplines that allowed him or her to do what others could not do: walk on hot coals without burning their feet; heal wounds and cure the sick. The thing that astonished them most about the missionary priests was that they could not do this. They did not, apparently, know how to use their breath to procure visions and states of altered physical reality. The name they began to use for the priests, which soon became the common name for all Western outsiders to Hawaii, was 'haoli'. 'Ha' means breath, and 'oli' means without. 'Haoli' literally means, 'the breathless ones'.

Using the breath to travel into the perception of infinite love and compassion that includes the whole universe is as essential an element of Hawaiian tradition as it is of the yogi or Buddhist tradition. It is in this realm of a conceptual rather than a physical reality that 'miracles' happen. Here there is no fixed physical boundary, no inevitable result, only possibilities and choices. And those possibilities and choices have an effect on physical reality.

The word for this energy realm in Hawaiian is 'aloha'. Aloha means love, which includes romantic love, but is much more than that. It means the spirit that love engenders in us. Aloha is the choice to trust, to accept, to love, and to release. In your heart you are everything, see everything, everywhere. It may be only a momentary glimpse before you revert to the perceptions rooted in the senses that you normally use to operate in the physical world, but your ability to perceive your connection to invisible unformed energy has huge implications.

The essential nature of who you are has no boundaries. Having no boundaries, it is part of everything else. And having no boundaries, it is timeless. This means that you are both in time, having picked up impressions and reactions from experiences beyond your immediate physical existence, and outside it. The more you perceive of the impressions that have formed your current physical reality and choose to let them go, the more clearly you see the being you are. It is like lifting veils. Current difficulties are what prompt the enquiry in the first place. You ask yourself, "What is it in me that has created this situation or condition? Since all material realities are the product of cause and effect, I must be in some sense a cause of this reality that I'm perceiving now."

You may choose to accept this responsibility for your part in the situation you are in, or you may not. But acceptance, paradoxically, is the beginning, and the totality, of your power. It is the alpha and omega of love. When you accept responsibility, you begin to have the power to choose, to release and to change. Gradually, approaching through the lifted veils of your own past reactions, the clarity of the source of all our energy becomes more apparent to you, and something fresh emerges from within. The passage of the breath within you is a vehicle that carries you to this clarity.

Focusing on the river of your breath, your thoughts lose their tentacles. You see them, but they pass on by, allowing you to see beyond.

The best way to know more about how this works is to try it on yourself. Whatever the situation you find yourself in now, ask yourself this question, and see what comes up. Settle yourself alone in a place where you can be calm. Breathe steadily for a few minutes, observing the breath carefully to see its rhythm and make sure it is calm and even. Then picture in your mind the situation you are dealing with. Allow the feelings from the situation to be strong and present for you. Then ask yourself this question:

What is it in me that has created this situation that I perceive?

Stay calmly with the question and notice the reactions that come into your thoughts. When you perceive an answer, see if you can let go of the feeling that comes up. You can imagine yourself detaching that reaction from your heart like a physical object and allowing it to fall away into the earth.

There is a compelling example of how this works in practice in the work of a Hawaiian psychologist, Dr Ihaleakala Hew Len. Dr Len is committed to practising and teaching the Hawaiian practice of ho'oponopono, which means 'cleaning' or 'clearing'. Like the Buddhists or yogis, he says that our essential nature is obscured by the millions of pieces of data: reactions, emotions, assumptions, that we have accumulated. I have heard this likened to sand in a jar of water. When the jar is shaken the water is cloudy. When we allow the jar to settle, the sand falls to the bottom and the water becomes transparent, which is its true nature.

Dr Ihaleakala Len says the data plays like the hard drive of a computer in our subconscious and creates the reality we experience:

Perception is really the end product of data playing in the subconscious.[2]

For several years, Len was employed at the Hawaiian State Hospital to work on a ward for the criminally insane.

When I worked at Hawaii State Hospital, I worked with people who had killed, raped, and murdered people. I had to ask the question, "What is going on in me that I am experiencing this?" I'm experiencing a patient being violent. I'm experiencing staff going crazy, that sort of stuff, so having to take 100 percent responsibility for creating this experience. So I have to do this cleaning, and the cleaning, the ho'oponopono, is about going into the self, and specifically into the subconscious, where the data is and since everything is run by information, the information in my subconscious is dictating to me what I'm seeing, what I'm experiencing. So I just work on the data in me that I see as 'the other person'. So if I see you as crazy and goofy, if I erase that, you can't be that way. It's not possible. So that's what I mean by being 100 percent responsible.[2]

Dr Len would have been happy to work on the patients from home, with just their names and case histories, because he saw all the problems as himself. But confidentiality rules obliged him to go into the hospital. And gradually, just working in this way over four years, the violence stopped. Patients were no longer shut in exclusion rooms. They no longer had to be restrained. They were allowed to take part in team activities outside the hospital like jogging and tennis, and the average turnaround time from admission to release dropped from three or four years to three or four months.

The Hawaiian view is that the connections created between us and our surroundings by causes and effects create links as tangible as a network of ropes. These are the 'aka' or cords, that link us to people in our present lives and from the past. Sometimes these cords get knotted, creating tangles of causes and results that hold us in conflict with someone or many other people. You may have conflict within your own family that mirrors arguments going back generations that you know nothing about, and yet you are caught in repeating this pattern. You can free yourself by accepting these cords as literal, just as in the example of a tug of war. You can use the power of your imagination to cut them, to forgive and release others bound with them to you in the same thankless round of battles, being grateful to the current situation that has brought this to your attention. You can do this even before understanding the source and the cause. The understanding is likely to come later.

This simple process needs to be taken seriously to bring the powerful effects it can deliver. Treat it like a ritual. Offer a prayer to your surroundings with all their potent energy that enfolds you. Remind yourself that you are one among millions of human beings living on a continuous thread of consciousness through births and deaths that stretch back beyond your imagining and will continue long into the future. When you have settled and placed your energy in this way, picture the source of the conflict in the present before you. These words put you, your vulnerability and your love at the heart of the situation, and this energy from you dissolves conflict. Say them aloud to the person concerned:

Thank you for bringing this harm to my attention.
I'm sorry for what I have to make amends for.
Please forgive me.
I love you.[3]

Take note of the effect the words have on your body when you say them. The deeper you can focus your concentration on the subtle responses in your body, the more effectively you can free yourself of the conflict you've been bound by.

This isn't always easy to do, because we cling to who we think we are. In substance we are just different arrangements of minerals and molecules than all other material things, so we are linked to them by our physicality as they are linked to us. As we get closer to our animal form, the similarities grow, and yet our sense that we are separate and different intensifies. We are both animal and spiritual and we contain both.

As individuals, we are unique in our experience, or as Dr Len would put it, in the data we have accumulated. At the same time, we are part of everything else. Our greatest strength is in understanding this similarity and expressing it through our unique, individual selves. That's what a great artist like Shakespeare was able to do. In so doing, he speaks for all of us, for generation upon generation. Taking responsibility for our part changes things, miraculously. And you have that choice.

I think probably the most profound thing about the ho'oponopono, [is] that you can erase data. When the data is erased you are what Buddha called in the space of 'void' or what Shakespeare called in the space of blank and it is when you are in the space of emptiness, void and blank that the inspiration comes through. You are moved by perfect information as opposed to using dead information, but most of the time, we're dead. You don't have free will (at any moment 11 million bits of data are playing in you), but you have choice.2

Anyone who seeks spiritual understanding of life will agree on one thing: the human heart can be an engine of energetic transformation. Shamans, Hawaiian kahuna, sangoma, Catholic mystics, yogis, Sufis and Druids may have different languages and practices to bring this about, but the key to material transformation is the energetic transformation that love can engender.

There are documents, ancient treatises, schools of philosophy that explain why and how this might be so, and almost at once the human intellect is confused by them. The notion of escaping from our normal perception of separation between beings and between objects is profoundly challenging to our ordinary way of functioning in the world. We find it hard to perceive two realities at once, even though we can prove that both are true. A physicist can prove that a solid wooden table has spaces in the molecules that make up its structure. I know this is true and yet I cannot function if this is the reality that appears to me when I prepare to sit down and write. Even so, it helps me to be aware of that other reality. Sometimes I might need one reality to be true. Sometimes another. Allow your mind to be flexible and fluid. That is the nature of your being. When situations and experiences oppress you, you are not stuck. So long as you are breathing, you have solutions.

There is an ancient practice based on this perception of reality that comes from Tibetan Buddhism. You can find many teachers to teach it to you. However, I can explain it simply here. It is called *tonglen*. *Tong* means giving and *len* means taking in Tibetan, and this practice is simply taking pain and giving love. It has its origin in Indian Buddhism, and was written down in the 12th century as one of the Seven Points of Training the Mind by the Tibetan teacher, Langri Tangpa, and his student, Geshe Chekawa Yeshe Dorje.

In the 21st century the elements of *tonglen* might look slightly different but essentially this is the same practice. I like to begin by settling in a comfortable position with my back straight and composing myself by closing my eyes and thinking of something or someone that I love very much. This might be the sparkle of May sunshine on a new green leaf, or it might be the sweet touch of a loving child, or it might be the sight of my lover laughing, an animal that I care for tenderly.

Whatever it is, the thought should kindle in you the feeling of love, not with a sense of attachment or clinging, but the warm bright feeling of love in your heart. Then, bring to mind something that has oppressed you. This could be someone else's suffering, or the suffering of a whole population, or it could be your own suffering, your fear, your anger, your loneliness or your pain. Breathe this suffering in as though you were inhaling dark smoke. Let it enter your lungs and the region of your heart and see it transformed there by the bright light of love. Darkness is always dispersed by light. Allow the intensity of your remembered loving feeling to dispel the darkness and convert it into bright energy that you send back to the source of darkness as you breathe out. Again, breathe in the pain and the suffering. Let this penetrate your heart and see it transformed there by the loving energy that you generate. Send the loving energy back to the source of the darkness. Repeat.

This is all there is to the practice. You can find prayers to recite alongside the breathing practice, but I have found it very powerful just focusing on the transformation within me. When you are working on something in your own experience, you can perceive results quickly. You have no one but yourself to consult on how doing this changes what you feel. When you are working on the suffering of another individual, perhaps you will receive feedback in the form of contact from them or a spontaneous remark that will show you your work is having an effect. Of course, you will not go to them and say, "I have been doing this for you. How does it feel? Are you better now?" That would be like planting a tomato seed in the ground and then pulling up the seedling to see how it's growing! You must have faith and perseverance. That is the way things grow. Watch your own transformation and your own experience will grow the faith in yourself you need to persevere.

As your strength grows, you will want to use your energy for greater and greater pains: the pain of nations, of civilizations, of the earth itself. As the target of your loving energy expands, so will the time it takes for you to receive feedback of positive transformation. Do not attach yourself too much to results. The more you see of your own experience of pain, the better you understand its necessary role in helping you to grow. Our discoveries are always prompted by the experience of pain. In that way, pain is not bad, nor is it good. It is a necessary part of our evolution. So, as you tackle larger and larger areas of pain, do not allow the perception of that darkness to diminish the glow of bright love and joy within you. Do what you can and accept the evolution that will follow.

Your life and the experiences you gain each moment you are living are very precious. Your breath, and the effect it can have on you and your environment is very precious. It's a waste to allow ourselves to become so attached to a target we want to achieve that we forget to make the most of every day. In Odisha, in eastern India, I heard this story. A little while ago, when the state was still known as Orissa, a man travelled from his village to Kolkata on business. He did not often go to Kolkata, which was at least two days' journey away, and his wife had never been to the big city. When he got there, he found they were selling an unusual vegetable on one of the market stalls. It was a cabbage, but they didn't grow cabbages in his village. So he bought one for his wife. When he returned home, he gave it to her, and she promised she would cook it for their dinner the next day. The following day he came home in the evening. His wife had prepared dinner and set it on the table in front of him.

"Where is the cabbage I brought you from Kolkata?" he asked.

"Oh, it was no good," she answered. "I took the leaves off one by one, very carefully, but there was nothing inside, so I threw it away."

We misunderstand our lives often the way she misunderstood a cabbage. Breathe deep, accept pain and try to release it so it can gently change to joy.

Chapter 14

Beyond Soup

For now we see as through a glass darkly. Then we shall see face to face.

1 Corinthians 13:12

Many of us are familiar with those beautiful lines in the King James version of the Bible, published first in 1611. Paradoxically, while the culture of that age was fully able to accept mystery, meaning knowledge and power beyond human understanding, which many would call magic, this was also the age in which the scientific examination of natural phenomena really began in Europe.

Alchemy was accepted as a fact by no less a man than William Cecil, Elizabeth I's wily and influential Secretary of State. He sent a letter to Dr John Dee in Prague, who had boasted of his success with turning base metal into gold by means of alchemy, urging him to hurry home with the fruits of his experiments, "not to keep God's gift from your natural country."[1]

This was also the Renaissance, an era which began with a re-examination of those biblical texts that had underpinned the authority of the Christian Church for over one and a half millennia. New translations by Erasmus and Luther revealed new interpretations, and to many, the authority for understanding God no longer seemed to need to pass through anointed representatives, in the form of monks and priests, but to be available to each and every man and woman, speaking through their intuition, or, in another way of speaking, the energy of the throat chakra.

So far in this book we have predominantly explored energy that becomes tangible, in the form of food, sex, money, or relationships with other people. That energy is concentrated in the lower chakras, the densest energy in the human body. For most of us, this energy is the major part of the effort we put into our lives. We all need food, sleep, and a safe space to shelter, as a minimum. Most of us also need money, as well as love and relationships. This is not all we need by any means, but it's important to tackle the difficulties that can snarl up the abundant flow of these basic necessities as a preparation for expanding our horizons further. It can take time, but it can change the landscape of our lives dramatically.

The heart is the turning point because the heart chakra is chameleon like. Fuelling the physical by converting the invisible air into something tangible, it also motivates the physical to action. Hence its power. The more we concentrate on opening the heart and lungs, physically and metaphorically, the further we can travel, physically and metaphorically.

In this journey through the nature of our human energy, we have reached a point of balance in the heart, beyond which we must leave behind the tangible and launch ourselves into the unknown to go further. When we talk of the throat chakra we are talking of this realm, the creative heart of you, and, strangely enough, we need courage to trust its guidance and pursue its goals for this very reason.

At a subconscious level we are accustomed to 'knowing' things in different ways. Logical problems call for logical solutions, and we know we know that two plus two equals four. We may also know that we love our partner, but we may not understand why or even what 'loving' means to us or them. We are less inclined to trust those things that we know through feeling or intuition and more inclined to insist on the truth of those things that an 'authority' has stated to be true, even when those truths might contradict our experience. For example, that it is 'good for us' to eat three meals a day, or that we 'need' eight hours sleep. Yet our intuition, our imaginative experience, is a source of information about our environment that can lead us to dramatic breakthroughs in our personal life and in society's knowledge in general.

For hundreds of years of European history, the Church was the absolute authority over all knowledge. Its monks and prelates were the teachers, the creators of books, the doctors, the king-makers and the supreme political authority. 'Knowledge' needed to be approved by the Church authority or it could be dangerous to know it, as Galileo and Leonardo Da Vinci were too well aware. Approved knowledge was based on an Aristotelian understanding of nature: that God 'signed' everything in existence with its meaning or use for man. Out of this was born, for example, the doctrine of signatures, which classified the medicinal use of plants according to their appearance. More obvious examples of this are walnuts, which look like the brain and were considered to be good for brain function, as indeed they still are, but because of their silica content, not because of their appearance. Red plants, either red in flower or red rooted, were thought to be good for detoxifying the blood and for wound healing, as indeed many of them are.

The obvious problem with this simplifying approach to nature are the surprises and the many thousands of examples that do not conform to the doctrine. The suggestion that the key to knowledge was somehow 'holy' discouraged enquiry that would be regarded as 'heretical' or 'unholy'. What the monks in their ivory towers had never seen for themselves they made up. The book of natural history, that all young boys (girls learned from their mothers) would have been taught, was compiled by a 13th century monk named Bartholomew. This book was a product of the 'age of faith', if faith means 'the power to disregard facts of observation in obedience to statements of authority', as it has been defined by some philosophers. In that book, the moral attributes of creatures were mixed with their physical character, so that eagles are 'kingly', and the notion of a horse that roamed the forests with a long horn was described as fact, even though fishermen could have told them that the horns were found on the shores of northern seas and had once belonged, not to a horse, but to a whale, the narwhal.

The scholarly approach to nature in the 16th century was useless to anyone who relied on food and medicine from the natural environment. Farmers had a very different understanding but since they had neither money nor time for tutors and universities, two parallel strands of 'knowledge' existed side by side. There was the one that worked, that produced practical results in terms of a harvest or medicinal cures. And there was the 'educated' view, taught by tutors and universities throughout the Christian world.

The Renaissance was a long period of re-examination of the world and human experience which gradually undermined the medieval 'educated' view, by proving practical realities that were wonderful in their way, but which didn't conform to the Aristotelian theory. It's impossible to overstate how slow this change in perception of reality in Europe was. It could be said to have begun with a re-examination and retranslation of truths taught in the Christian scriptures in the early 16th century, which was accompanied by a re-examination of the phenomena of the natural world. Over a hundred years later, universities were still churning out the same Aristotelian theories of how the natural world worked, which led the English polymath and statesman Francis Bacon to quip:

*The students at our universities learn nothing but to believe. First to believe that they know that which they know not, then to believe that others know that which they know not.*2

Even the theory that blood circulates in the body by means of valves in veins and arteries, proposed in 1625 by Sir William Harvey after extensive dissections, was not accepted universally as truth for about 65 years.

We still deal with this dilemma every day. We tend to dismiss aspects of our experience which don't conform to our known reality because they make us feel vulnerable. Each of us makes unconscious decisions about what constitutes 'reality' and we incorporate this into what we do and the way we make plans. 'Truth', in the form of what we have been taught to see, is always something that we cling to. Other forms of knowledge we might experience are 'unbelievable' and potentially unsafe. The knowledge we have learned carries with it our self-esteem. It may be a doctorate or a profession. It may be our self-identity as a professional gardener or a good mother. Whatever it is, it is hard to accept a different viewpoint without sacrificing that part of our self-esteem tied up in our social position. Even if our way of seeing the world is hurting us, we tend to cling to it rather than trust our immediate experience in the moment.

Yet for the past one hundred years science has been showing us that the 'reality' we cling to is only a version of the physical world that our physical senses can cope with. Remember the reassurance of the *Times'* leader writer to his readers in 1919 that Einstein's theory would make "little difference to the practical world... We may measure our land and believe in our clocks as we did before Einstein."

We know now that he was wrong. Virtually every corner of human life has been affected by his discoveries, which have led us to technology from supercomputers to nuclear weapons. Above all, it is the connectivity between different parts of the planet, operating through satellite GPS systems and your mobile phone, that have had a dramatic effect on your life and measurably changed our practical world. Yet the *Times* writer was also partly right. Our physical senses are still attuned to the logic of gravity, the existence of parallel lines, the solidity of our environment and of our bodies themselves.

But in the throat chakra, the energy of our imagination and dreaming, we are living in the non-physical world. Looking back on the creations that have come out of this non-physical realm and are now part of our daily reality, we can see how this relationship goes: from the barely possible, to the persistent possibility, to the draft or experiment, to the thing that, in retrospect, seems ingenious, enlightened, practically perfect in every way.

Contemporary physical science measures things at the nano microscopic level and appears to be returning to a view of nature that is difficult to comprehend unless we allow ourselves to accept the paradox of two views of reality existing at once. Things are not as they seem to be when we get down to measuring them at this level. Physicists like Frank Wilczek, who is an American specialist in what is called Core Theory, at the cutting edge of experiments to investigate the nature of matter, have found they have to live with contradictory truths. His theory, arrived at through repeatable calculations, isn't something he would regard as random, like the visionary insight of mystics, which perhaps he would dismiss as unreliable. Frank Wilczek explains that we need to understand that the way we see things is not the way they are, but the way we choose to see them because it is the way we can manage, physically and intellectually. It is the vision of an external reality which is not the same as the essential reality. He arrives at this conclusion through creating a mathematical structure which allows contradictory particles to interrelate with each other and create mass or matter. He calls this structure the Grid.

A great lesson from the Core [the non-physical level that is beyond matter where these mathematical calculations make sense] is that the entity we perceive as empty space is, in reality, a dynamic medium full of structure and activity. The Grid, as we've called it, affects the properties of everything within it – that is, everything. We see things not as they are, but through a glass, darkly.[3]

This view of our world embraces a contradiction which is a step too far for everyday human senses, but familiar to mystics and healers of all generations. Firmly disassociating himself from anything that could be described as mystical, Frank Wilczek nevertheless reaches a central conclusion through the logic of mathematics that is so contradictory that only imagination can grasp it.

The deep structure of matter bears no relation at all to its surface structure.[3]

In the early years of the 20th century a brilliant young Bengali scientist called Jagadis Bose began to measure scientifically the invisible life of things presumed not to have consciousness: metals, rocks and plants. He was an unusual scientist for two reasons. The first was that he came from a poor family in Calcutta at a time when the British ruled his country, but nevertheless his brilliance was noticed, and he studied at Cambridge University in England where he was awarded a doctorate.

He was also unusual because, with the teaching of the Indian spiritual tradition behind him, he fully accepted the notion that God is in everything and therefore inanimate substances (the word 'inanimate' is from the Latin, meaning 'no soul, no life') have 'life'. This has always been evident on an emotional level to some. In the late 15th century Leonardo Da Vinci wrote in his notebooks, in the mirror writing that was intended to keep their contents from prying eyes, his view of the earth:

We can say that the earth has a vegetative spirit, and that its flesh is the soil, its bones are the arrangement and connection between stones which form mountains, its cartilage is the tufa rock, its blood the veins of water.

A similar understanding of the planet we live on has been

echoed by sensitives, poets, artists and people who live close to the earth ever since. In the last forty years it has been creditably presented as the scientific theory of 'Gaia' by the British scientist James Lovelock, who suggests that everything on our planet is part of a giant integrated self-regulating system, but this has often been dismissed as sentimentally zoomorphic by material scientists. Jagadis Bose was one of the earliest scientists who set out to prove that apparently inanimate materials respond to subtle energy from their environment.

Bose was inspired by his great friend and India's best-known spiritual teacher at the end of the 19th century, Swami Vivekenanda. Vivekenanda's outlook was different from that of a Western scientist of the day in that it was based on centuries of teaching inspired by the Vedas. Like Deepak Chopra, the Western-trained endocrinologist who has spent decades travelling back to the truths of his Indian heritage, he would have said:

Mind has remained a metaphysical riddle for centuries because it inhabits the physical world like a ghost. But that's a Western perspective based on our bias for solid, tangible things. We insist that the brain must be the source of mind because the brain is a visible object. The Vedic rishis adopted the opposite perspective, insisting that visible objects couldn't be the source of mind since the physical plane is the least conscious of worlds.[4]

Jagadis Bose experimented to demonstrate how these two views of consciousness fuse in our environment. He designed his own instruments to measure responses in plants, metal and rocks, setting them up in a long laboratory that is proudly preserved as a museum in his house near Kolkata university. His instruments fired signals from one end of the lab to the other to test how objects influence each other at a distance. Revered inventions, like his wonderfully named 'photosynthetic bubbler', are now displayed along the walls of this lab in Kolkata. They're considered so precious that I was forbidden to take photographs, whether from fear that I might try to copy the invention or some possibility that the photographs would degrade the instruments' spirit, I couldn't tell. But with these machines Jagadis Bose was able to show things that no one had thought possible until that time and even today many people do not imagine to be true.

He was able to show, with his *crescograph*, that plant growth is increased not only by light and temperature, but also by electric current. He showed how electrical pulses move all objects, not just mammalian tissue, so that there is always a correlation between movement and electrical energy. Jagadis Bose showed that rocks emit electrical energy and that metal responds to it, succumbing eventually to metal fatigue. All matter, he seemed to show, was a form of the invisible energy that we had only just begun to measure, as radio waves, as microwaves, infrared rays and now x-rays.

These observations and Bose's work have become part of the mainstream in our contemporary world. In this long laboratory Bose was able to generate the shortest electromagnetic waves then known at 5 mm and with these he succeeded in sending a signal received by a generator seventy-five feet away (35 metres). He was also able to improve on the work of the famous physicists Hertz and Tesla to create a workable x-ray. By extension of these principles, we began to be able to see inside a living human body. Gradually more and more of the physical mysteries the body enfolds are becoming known to us, and the intangible wonder of the possibilities open to us keeps expanding.

As physical theories about the nature of matter evolved through the course of the 20th century, there appeared to be a divergence between what could be shown to be true at the macrocosmic level and the movement of matter at the microcosmic level. Einstein's theory of relativity appeared to be incompatible with Niels Bohr's theory of quantum mechanics. The quantum physicist whose work made the greatest contribution to resolving the mathematical inconsistences between these two was David Bohm. The mathematics of quantum theory implied to him that there may be a process he described as 'enfoldment', through which any particular element in space has a field which 'unfolds into the whole and the whole enfolds into it.' His mathematics brought him to understand the universe in spiritual terms:

The essential quality of the universe is its subtlety, its intangibility. This quality is conveyed in the word spirit, whose root meaning is 'wind or breath'. That which is truly alive is the energy of spirit, and this is never born and never dies.[5]

Be realistic. Demand the Impossible!

I have been told that this was a slogan chanted by demonstrators in the wave of popular protests for change that swept Europe and America in the 1960s. To be honest, I am too young to have heard them myself, but this slogan has always enchanted me. When we emerge from our physical senses into the realm of our imagination this is the leap we are making. The impossible becomes possible and we have to learn to trust it over the voice of our rational selves to make progress.

The energy that our hearts give rise to is the energy of dreams, the energy of imagination and fantasy. We have the choice of whether to travel with our dreams or cling to the reality we know.

There is an Indian story about an old man who wandered from village to village begging food and shelter. He had no possessions at all except a blanket he wrapped around his shoulders to cover his nakedness and keep him warm at night.

One day, as he was crossing a river, he slipped off the bridge and fell into the water. There were crocodiles in the water, though it was not deep, and one clamped its teeth around his blanket as he struggled to escape. The villagers had seen him fall and gathered on the riverbank shouting instructions.

"Let go of the blanket!" they cried, as the crocodile's teeth came close and closer to his arms.

"But it's all I have!" the old man shouted back.

The story ends there. Did he let go of the blanket, or did he sacrifice the self he could be for the self he knew?

We do not like to let go of our story, however painful it might be. We have difficulty in embracing a new idea because we are stuck fast in one that has served us in the past. The innovative British economist, John Maynard Keynes put it this way:

The difficulty lies not in the new ideas, but in escaping from the old ones, which ramify, for those brought up as most of us have been, into every corner of our minds.[6]

A monkey can be trapped by a coconut shell filled with sweet rice. The hole in the coconut is big enough for him to reach his hand into to get the rice, but not big enough to remove his hand without letting go of the rice. Stuck fast to his hunting instinct, he falls prey to a human predator.

At the point of extreme pain or physical helplessness we may be forced to accept the unknown, despite ourselves. It is only when we do this that miracles happen. We call them miracles precisely because we do not understand and cannot explain how we can be experiencing something so different from what we know. The more we have learned, studied, and practised our knowledge, the harder it is to let go. This is the knowledge, after all, that has kept us safe and nourished us this far. Yet, hard as it is to trust it, this experience of discovering wonder occurs again and again to intelligent, well educated, perfectly 'normal' human beings. Many of us live to tell the story of our entry into the unknown.

In extreme survival situations, a voice that does not sound like it belongs to us takes over and directs us to follow. It happened to Steven Callahan on his boat, adrift in the Atlantic. Sometimes we die in these extreme situations and cannot communicate our knowledge in a way most humans understand. But those who go right to the edge, and live, bring back a tale of wonder that echoes in harmony with all the other tales we have heard. The neurosurgeon, Dr Eben Alexander, suffered brain death for a week after developing meningitis and when, to everyone's astonishment, he recovered his faculties and was able to reflect and ultimately tell his story, he told a tale that shattered everything he had previously thought 'possible' and yet was deeply connected to the emotional roots of his being.

Dr Alexander had experienced another reality while he was apparently 'dead'. He had been connected with a long-lost sibling who had, in fact, died many years before, and she had been a guide to the wondrous beauty of the physical world that he knew, in which he felt that everything about him was right, in love and in harmony with everything he could see and touch.

Dr Alexander was aware that his story seemed impossible. He deliberately avoided reading any other stories told by people who had been on the edge of life, in case his conscious mind influenced his memory of what he had seen and felt. Once the story was published, however, to the dismay of many fellow medics who assumed he must have got his facts wrong, he discovered the extraordinary unity in all the stories of near death experiences there are out there, and there are so many![7]

For each person this experience is deeply personal, engaging elements of their emotional memory that are unique to them and allowing them a direct communication with 'higher power'. Yet for each also there is wondrous love and beauty that enfolds their spirit, illuminating everything they perceive, and filling them with the conviction that they need to find a means to communicate to their fellow human beings that this is really 'who we are'.

When I was sick and dealing with a lot of dizziness, weakness and pain that I began to understand was emotional and physical pain intertwined, I discovered a beautiful recording of a guided meditation by the nada yoga musician Roop Verma. *Nada* is the Sanskrit for primordial vibration or sound, considered by Vedic masters to be one element of the essence of God. So *nada yoga* means 'union with sound', and Roop was a master practitioner of healing through the vibration of his beautiful playing of the sitar. His guided meditation, called *Experience Nada Yoga*, freed me in a way that reached out to me at the time. It was the kindness of his voice and his view of the universe that vibrated in my soul, encouraging me to release so many decades of fear and self-criticism that I had harboured to keep me safe.

"The universe is benevolent," he said. "Otherwise the human race would have died out long ago."[8]

You may believe this or not, weighted down as we are with continual pictures of human destruction of our planet and our fellow creatures. Yet, reflecting on my immediate environment, I was able to feel the benevolence of nature in abundance. I was able to drink in the comfort of my surroundings, the grass, the trees and the soft air, and gradually feel the bounty of what I had been given. There is so much in my life that is precious that I have not fought or struggled for, but stumbling along, have found in my possession. The relationships that blossom and give rise to new events and creations, the house that becomes a haven I never expected it to be, the ideas that gather weight and reality as I coax them along, even the tiny trees I have planted, I can now sit beneath and shelter in their shade. I am not responsible for any of this growth. I do not create it.

However, allowing myself to trust in the direction of growth and expansion which is the essential element of the universe we live in, teaching myself to accept the equally essential negative, which is death and destruction, urging myself to believe in the power of love, all this frees my energy to focus on creative future growth.

This energy of growth flows through our veins as naturally as the sap that rises through a plant. Children have it in abundance. It feels like endless possibility, unrestricted by known facts or physical laws. It feels like desire and trust, optimism and joy. It is not governed by the laws of logic, more by the laws of love and passion. It is the ability to pursue your dreams and a subtle guidance that will take you there. Adults tend to bury this energy under layers of guilt, recriminations, anger, reason, disappointment and regret. Nevertheless, this energy is available to you as long as you are living, and we do well to listen to the wisdom a child possesses.

My mother has always loved this creative energy in her as the best part of her being. As the months of her inability to operate independently have gone by, she is aware of her bodily strength leaving. Still she is optimistic that it might return.

Up until this point she has used her will to bring her dreams in to physical reality and launch herself into the unknown of her imagination. She has pushed her many fears out of the way, refusing to countenance darkness. When she has contemplated difficulty in the past, she has felt it might hold her fast. She prefers to experience life as a perpetual surprise. Childlike, when she encounters pain, she looks everywhere but at herself for strength.

She had come to me for a massage for several years because she was losing strength in her left leg and having difficulty walking. One of these times, I mentioned that I would be holding the first of my chakra workshops the next day: a new venture that I had been designing to give people the tools to help themselves.

"Can I come?" she asked.

"Well, yes, if you like. But you know, we will be working with the root chakra and this is all about your connection with the earth, and that is powerfully influenced by your relationship with your birth mother. It might be strange, you being there as my mother when I am teaching the class."

"Oh that's alright," she said. "I won't tell anybody that I'm your mother."

She left that day and I didn't expect to see her on the next. She had a habit of saying things 'for effect' that I had grown accustomed to. But just as the class was about to start, a small figure, twisted with age, tapped at the glass door. I swallowed my surprise, someone let her in, and we got on with the class.

Everything went well for most of the day as I explained how the immaterial energy of the root chakra makes itself felt in your physical experience and how to use the tool of change that is the human imagination. My mother participated in all the exercises and partner work, discovering in the process of pair work the powerful effect of her energy on other people. It is not something she had ever known, being accustomed to working by herself, but at the level of the throat chakra, this level of dreams, she seemed to sweep people effortlessly into another realm. Still she said very little during the day, and I managed to remember not to call her 'Mum', until right at the end of the day, when she asked a question.

"What *is* imagination?" she said, innocently.

I was completely floored. This, from my mother, who lived for her dreams and in her imagination every moment of her life she could manage. How could she not know what it is? Luckily, I did not have to answer. The participants in my workshop quickly came to my rescue with answers of their own. I still do not know whether her question was mischief or profundity. Did she want to know how it is possible for human beings to dream? Did she want an anatomical explanation of how the brain and nervous system work? Or did she simply not see something that was as natural to her as breathing? She never returned to the question in our conversations afterwards. She didn't want to analyse who or what she was. She feared this might destroy the magic of her life.

Now, at 95, growing weaker every day, she clings nevertheless to the possibility that she can regenerate her vigour by the effort of her will. She believes she will get better, that this pain is just a temporary interruption. In her dreams she stokes her joy of living and the power of human creativity.

"I think I need Vitamin C," she says. "If I could plant an orange tree, I could use the twigs to give me Vitamin C. You have one, don't you?"

"I have a lemon tree," I say.

How long do you think it will take you to harvest your Vitamin C?
I think it but I do not speak out loud.

She returns to the possibility of death which she feels the orange tree might defeat. I try and lay her mind at rest by speaking of it as an adventure that will free of her of the constant pain she has endured. In fact, on the rare occasions that I have inadvisedly yielded to her appeal for healing (healing someone in my family has never been a comfortable experience), this is exactly the picture I have seen for her. I have seen her flying out on a magic carpet woven from her heart, like Jasmine and Aladdin, thrilling to the joy of freedom and her bird's eye view of the beautiful world she loves. But she would like this to be a reality without the pain and fear of letting go of life.

Now, reluctantly, she seems to recognise that death is coming and responds in typical style.

"Let's have a party! I want all my friends to know!"

Exhausted, after five months of spinning plates to keep her happy and well cared for at home, we have succeeded beyond our expectations. She is loving the daily attention of so many people who love her and wants more! Like the party guest who turns up, ready to go, at 4am, my mother has worn us all out.

"We *are* having a party," I say. "It's been a continual party for five months now."

She laughs and goes contentedly back to her dreams.

Chapter 15

Creating the Future

What does it mean to have no data playing? That means you're free.
Dr Hew Len

As nature takes my mother to the end of her life, she is constantly asking me how she is going to die. She has grown accustomed to expecting me to produce solutions for all her medical, technical, financial and domestic problems. And I don't have the answer for this one. This disturbs me quite a lot until I realise she doesn't want the answer from me. She just wants company in this ultimate drama of her life. I am not providing answers. I am just keeping her company.

I am helping her in the bathroom one day when I feel I want to thank her for being my mother.

"I want to thank you for teaching me how to be selfish."

"Oh really? Did I? How did I do that?"

"By example."

She laughs, delighted.

She understands that this is not a term of abuse, although people focused on personal goals can be irritatingly inattentive to the needs of their loved ones. I am sure members of my family often wish I showed my love for them in a different way. But I am my mother's daughter. I drank, with my mother's milk, the wish to explore the life that has been given me as a personal journey. That means listening to my desires, encouraging myself to fulfil them, and allowing them to take me forward to discover more.

I am reminded of where I first heard the phrase, "Everyone needs a *little* bit of ego." It was from Roop Verma, the gentle and dedicated sitar player, who came from a family of scientists and doctors. His devotion to the inner spirit that his music expressed led him from his birth family in northern India, to Canada, to an ashram in New York State where he married and brought up an Indo-American family and managed to take his music to spread its wings all over Europe and the United States. In pursuit of this journey there were sacrifices, however. He was obliged to leave behind many people and places that he loved to the end of his life.

To make your dreams a reality you need to take a leap of faith. Once you settle old scores within yourself and let go of the drag of the past, you will find yourself increasingly free to be in this state. What might take conscious effort at first, becomes a way of living as your experience confirms the power of your choice.

Living at the level of the throat chakra feels like floating on a wave. It is as though the events you experience come before you as information in response to your thoughts and feelings like a kind of universal delivery service. You may be thinking intensely about something you want to do, and then a friend you haven't spoken to in a while gets in touch to ask a favour. In the course of conversation, you mention what you are thinking about and they put you in touch with a friend of theirs who would be interested. And so, by apparently random connections, your project moves closer to reality. This is the energy of the throat chakra. You examine incidents for their message and move forward on the path of least resistance. It is what the Hawaiians call 'living in the Flow'. It feels glorious: peaceful and exciting at the same time. But it can be hard to maintain!

Our dreams and desires are how we create our future. If we want our future to be different from our present, we have to examine the cause and effect that has led from the past to the present and let the past go.

Healing your life and your world is about allowing yourself to connect with the deeper energy that is your essential nature. In connecting with this energy, you can free yourself from the knots of thought and feeling that have kept you tied in an undesirable situation. The more we learn to free ourselves, the more connected we become, not just to our own deeper power, but to the essential power that is manifest in all the elements of the universe. It is a magnificent picture and a deeply fulfilling connection, which each one of us will explore in our own way.

Your open heart springs from an open mind, and an open heart delivers communication with the energetic realm of the intangible that becomes steadily clearer as you allow it to guide you. Once you learn not to judge in your habitual manner, in other words, possibilities appear before you, guided by the energy of your deep desires.

You are choosing now to invest in possibility, optimism, trust and acceptance, so that you can create a way forward rather than simply react to dangers. This is what Sri Yukteswar meant when he talked about the proper use of your intelligence:

Intelligence is rightly guided only after the mind has acknowledged the inescapability of spiritual love.

I used to believe that all spiritual traditions, particularly those from the East: Buddhism and Yoga, taught self-denial. My first encounter with Buddhism told me that the world I loved was an illusion, and that attachment to this world inevitably led to sorrow. The very word: 'samsara', used to describe our immersion in an illusion we call reality, had the sticky feel of the word 'sin' as it's used in Christianity, and I rejected it. It was as depressing as the concept of 'original sin', which is, I believe, the same idea.

Inevitably, humans are not perfect, and human desires cause many complications, but suggesting that just by being born human we are bound to do wrong, is an idea I found hard to accept. I turned my back on the teaching, not understanding what it was telling me. Years and years later, after experiencing the mixture of joy and pain that most of us recognise as characteristic of our lives, I began to unpick this teaching and explore it in depth. Much of what I have tried to explain in this book is guided by a deeper understanding of this ancient teaching than I had when I was younger, born through my own need for its wisdom.

It does not mean giving up our desires. Desire is the energy that shapes the future and arises continually in us like sap in a plant. To be sure that our desires are right for us we need to explore that deeper energy, the root of our being and what makes us happy on a physical level. Examining our desires takes time and self-reflection. It means understanding our motives, valuing ourselves and trusting our ability to learn. This is not often what we do. We tend to rush forward, adding our desires to our 'to do' list, and this has never been more true than now, when so many of us live in societies where material objects are easily come by. Alternatively, we reject our desire as too high, too far removed from the way we have seen ourselves in the past, and smother it.

Many possible desires arise simultaneously in our busy minds, and we have a tendency to aim, not for what makes us happy, but for success. Our natural sense of self-preservation prompts us towards safety, reinforced by the instincts of teachers, parents and others who do not know us as we know ourselves. For many of us, repeatedly taking the 'safe' route results in a feeling of frustration and disappointment in ourselves. We reach a point where we feel we are spending our precious life doing what we 'should' do, with no possibility of doing what we want to do. Yet, as we look around, the version of reality we live is quite unreal for some people. There is someone on the planet happily making a living from just about anything you can think of: tightrope walking, mud-wrestling, keeping pigs, growing salad, writing novels. The list is literally as long and as broad as our imaginations. Why should this person, who lives the way you would like to live, not be you?

Happiness that is genuinely satisfying is accompanied by the fullest exercise of our faculties, and the fullest realization of the world in which we live.[1]

So wrote the British philosopher, Bertrand Russell, when contemplating human happiness in 1930. Anyone who has worked hard to achieve respectability and success in their career that has left them feeling trapped and unsatisfied will understand what he means. I once had what I now describe as a 'proper job'. I was a BBC producer, and this opened doors for me in all sorts of places, accorded me a degree of respect I do not think I had earned, and was a stimulating and rewarding job. However, I became trapped precisely because it was a 'good job'. When the time came for me to explore new territories and develop other aspects of my being, there was simply no room for it in that environment, where things I perceive as reality now 'did not exist'. I felt I owed it to my family to stay, even though my instinct was telling me it was time to move on. I feared I would have trouble supporting them in an unknown world. In the end my body made the decision for me. I became so ill I could no longer function until I gradually learned to listen to the self my body was expressing. As it happens, I can support my family as well, if not better, than I could before, since I am happier and stronger than I was then.

We have so many dreams and desires that you would think we had perfected the art by now of making them happen. Or at least of being content with those dreams we have brought to fruition already. But that doesn't seem to be the way we are made. No sooner do we achieve one thing than we focus on the unexpected consequences or problems that it throws up in its wake. We look at the latest block that thwarts us and not at the chain of events that have brought us to this position or the part we have played in it. In spite of that, I believe that the universe we live in is disposed to enable us to make our dreams and desires manifest. It is a universe of continual change, where developments are prompted by energy, and we possess the faculty in our brains to focus our energy around imaginary reality until that imagination becomes something tangible. We owe it to ourselves to explore just how powerful that faculty is, once we release it from unnecessary restrictions.

It seems to me that nothing is so misunderstood as our dreams and desires. We praise and extravagantly honour people who make their dreams come true, and yet individually, so often, we tell ourselves we cannot have what we desire so there is no point in dreaming about it. Culturally, we school the dreams out of ourselves and consider that this is 'sensible' behaviour. I think it is insensible – a kind of somnolence or lack of feeling we impose on ourselves so that we will not cause ourselves too much pain by longing for something different from what we have made, like giving a chained dog a sleeping pill. It is not wrong to want to build something, to want to have something, to want to do something or express something, so long as we are prepared to accept that every thought and action has consequences, and that, while we can wish, we can only influence, we cannot control. Desire is simply who we are, and the universe is a manifestation of the characteristics of all the creatures within it.

As human beings we need to express the essence of what we are, just like a primrose needs to flower or an apple tree needs to fruit. Discovering how this essence can be expressed is part of the journey of our life. Yet we also need to accept that everything we create is independent of us once it has been created, and our creations, like us, weaken and die in time. Things we desire do not necessarily have the consequences we imagine, so we are creating not only what we wish for but the consequences for ourselves. This too is part of the journey of discovery we are living. We need to embrace two realities at once, as a physicist or a theoretical mathematician does.

I now understand this as the meaning of *samsara*: that all material things pass away. The permanence we like to cling to for the sense of safety it gives us is an illusion or *maya*, and the death of what we have clung to will bring us pain in proportion to the joy we have felt from loving it.

So how do we know which dreams we should pursue, and which will bring us happiness and which misery? Your own pleasure can come to your rescue. The healer I learned from, Martin Brofman, developed a kind of mantra that is useful to repeat to yourself as a guide to the path you're on. Try saying to yourself periodically:

I love where I am, I love who I'm with and I love what I'm doing.

Feel how this resonates with you when you repeat it aloud to yourself, concentrating fully on the meaning. We all find ourselves having to do some things we would prefer not to do some of the time, but if making this statement to yourself feels repeatedly impossible then you can reflect on what you would like to be different and better in your life.

If an idea returns constantly to your mind, you know it's not just a passing whim. If you have a recurring fantasy, which remains just that, then it is likely to be your own self that is blocking it from becoming the physical reality in which you live. So you can prepare the ground to bring it into being.

Much has been written about how to do this. Many people have made fortunes from putting forward the method they consider ultimately effective in turning what we dream of into a reality. There are countless perfect diets that promise a beautiful body and shining health. There is at least one empire built on persuading you to become the owner of a large house, fast cars and a successful business. On the more mystical level, 'The Secret' has promised you that you can get just about anything you want.

Once, when I was thumbing through an old book about yoga that belonged to my grandfather, I discovered some loose pages tucked into it that astonished me. My grandfather's experience in Bengal as a young man gave him a deep love of yoga, and in my childhood, I remember him more often upside down, standing on his head, than I remember him upright. So far as I knew, the physical postures taught in the yoga tradition were the only aspect of the philosophy that he embraced. In other respects, he appeared to be a perfectly conventional adherent of the Anglican traditions of his generation, whose passions were cricket, his pipe, Homer, ancient Greek poetry, his wife and his family, probably in that order.

The book I was now leafing through was one of the first to introduce yoga to the West, written by his contemporary while he was living in Bengal, Francis Yeats-Brown.[2] Its gentle encouragement to English-speaking readers to bend and move their hips would be scorned by the athletic Western practitioners of yoga asanas today, but the notes my grandfather had taken that now fell out of the book would, I think, surprise them. Given that the movements the book described were simple in comparison to the many complex *asanas* embraced by various schools of yoga we're familiar with, I was surprised to find on these pages a much deeper understanding of the philosophy that yoga enshrines.

Yoga means 'union'. That is to say that the disciplined movements of the body unify with the breath which leads to unity of mind, body and breath together. Unity of the breath and body stills the mind to the point where you perceive the unity of one with everything. The individual spirit is an aspect of the universal Divine so that union within, deep awareness of your personal microcosm, leads to understanding that you are not separate from your environment. The more you perceive the microcosm within, the more you see both your smallness and your vastness, in the continuous flow of energy between you as an individual and the play of energy beyond the individual self. You have power over the self and the macrocosm has power over you. This macrocosm we call God, and the teaching of yoga is designed to make you see and feel how you belong within it, as an emanation of primal light, sound and vibration.

The fact that every page of my grandfather's notes was headed 'MOST SECRET' piqued my curiosity. It was an irresistible invitation to read on. On these pages there were breathing exercises, which certainly would be familiar to most serious practitioners of yoga today. We know how powerful the way you use your breath is for the way your body and your mind function. Fifteen minutes daily of exercises like these and I suggest you would need little other help for anxiety, depression, insomnia, OCD, digestive, or blood pressure disorders. You'll find my grandfather's 'MOST SECRET' breathing exercises for you to put into practice at the end of this book. They're not quite the same as the ones I practise today, but they have the effect of activating all the deeper muscles of the trunk and abdomen which have a subtly energising effect on your whole being. This 'energy' that controlled breathing brings is universal or divine energy. It is something beyond oxygen which you convert to carbon dioxide in your muscles. 'Energy' or *'prana'* in the Vedic tradition, *'chi'* in the Chinese tradition, *'mana'* in the Hawaiian tradition, is the effect of the way this conversion takes place within you.

Yet this wasn't what surprised me most about my grandfather's 'secret' pages. What struck me was the uncompromising approach of his teachers to how to make the most of this elevated energy in your life. The 'MOST SECRET' pages urge you to focus attention on your mind like a laser beam, making no allowance for frailty. You are essentially Divine, the notes seem to say, and you must take care of the Divine energy your being expresses. His teachers divided the brain into 12 parts:

From the front to back they are concerned with these faculties:
- *Power of speech and writing*
- *Attention and application*
- *Intellect and knowledge*
- *Intuition and aspiration*
- *Emotions and feelings*
- *Spiritual inner understanding*
- *Personality, the small ego*
- *Individuality, the ego*
- *Aesthetics*
- *Art*
- *Love*
- *Power of creation.*

Concentrating on each of these aspects in turn, the yogis urge you to exercise your ability without limits in your imagination, so as to enhance the energy of each. This concentration of consciousness, in itself, increases each ability.

This list of functional areas in the brain corresponds roughly to areas of brain function identified by Western medicine, except that it incorporates experiences which are not generally given house room on a Western medical map. Medical scientists of the West have not identified an area for 'spiritual inner understanding'. Nor have they made a distinction between 'personality, the small ego', which you might take to be your style of behaviour and relating to others, and 'individuality, the ego', which you could interpret as your need for survival as an individual. Nevertheless, all these areas of experience are vital parts of our lives.

It has been accepted for a long time that certain areas of the brain naturally perform different functions, so that speech, language and concentration take place in the frontal lobe, for example, while memory, sensual and emotional experiences are processed in the limbic system, deep in the core of the brain. Even so, new research is showing our brains have large areas of apparently unused space, and a high degree of plasticity, so that it's possible for them to develop new neuron pathways to perform a function when the conventional area is damaged or missing.

Apparently indefinable human experience, such as 'spiritual inner understanding' or 'love', was precisely located on this yogi map. I assume this understanding was arrived at through intuition and meditative insight, and it will be interesting to see whether it is ever replicated using scientific methods of measurement. It may in time prove as effective and useful a map of the brain as the map of the chakras is of emotional energy in the body. But this was not the part of my grandfather's notes that surprised me most.

As I read on, I saw that making affirmations for oneself was a part of this yogic teaching. To say out loud what you wish for is a powerful thing. I always ask someone I am healing to do this before I begin. When you do this you are taking charge of the physical actions working at an unconscious level in your body. When the boss comes down to the factory floor and says emphatically and clearly what is wanted, everything can start to push in the same direction. You speak out loud because there is energy around us that we do not always see or feel. There are aspects of divine energy that do not take human form. It makes sense to ask for their help too.

It was this understanding, shining through the words, that impressed me so much in my grandfather's notes. I was familiar with affirmations, certainly. Experience has shown us that affirmations can have a measurable effect on performance, if we allow ourselves to believe wholeheartedly in what we say. But these affirmations were not limited by any mealy-mouthed rationalism. Why should they be? Experience is not rational. Most of it can't be measured, so when we make affirmations, why should we limit our desire to conditions we consider rational? My grandfather's Hindu teachers didn't. They recognised every being as a microcosm of the cosmic Divine energy ready to flow through us when we invite it in.

The 'MOST SECRET' pages suggest that every person should:

> ... *affirm these powers [of the human brain] and make a self-suggestion every day, so that they will grow in strength and ever remain in a healthy condition.*
>
> *Take any one of these powers out of the twelve, affirm it within yourself, and make a suggestion to the inner understanding – the sensory centre of the brain.*
>
> *One or two sentences of self-suggestion are sufficient to arouse the central faculty, which in turn quickens to life the power concerned.*

In other words, the verbal statements you make need your concentration and commitment at the deepest level. You need to feel the conviction of the statement in your body, and this in turn will wake up the faculty you desire. You should speak them only after you have stilled your mind with conscious breathing, either at the beginning or the end of the day, when your mind is not cluttered with other thoughts and responsibilities. But do not limit what you consider to be your abilities! 'MOST SECRET' gives sample affirmations that allow no compromise to the power you're capable of. Here's the affirmation for increasing your artistic ability, for example:

> *I am originality. The fountain of creative ability springs from within me, because I am one with Nature's artist. Nothing is beyond my powers. I can paint, draw, sing etc., exceedingly well.*

This is suggested for improving your mental attention and application:

I am all attention, and I will attend to the purpose of the evolution of my life and apply all the mental powers within me to anything I desire rightly; and I will not give up until I achieve my goal.

Be inspired by this example to align what you wish for with an open belief in your capabilities. Make a list of everything you desire in each one of the aspects of your life that are listed above, to the fullest of your imagination. Select one or two you especially want to focus on. Start to make these a part of your daily conversation with yourself. When you begin this practice, make a note which you will refer to again in months or years to come, and this will show you how you have changed things in your life.

You might think it's curious that philosophers who understand the visible world as an illusion created by the mind should have devoted so much attention to obtaining things, or situations, which would, by definition, be illusory. Yet it's precisely because of this philosophy that instructions for obtaining your desire have traction. If the perceived world is an illusion created by your mind, it has fluidity. You are offered a choice. By using your energy to focus and control your mind, you see what you have selected to see, and you have the option of changing the vision to something that you would prefer. Yet, whatever you choose, don't make the mistake of investing it with too much solid reality. You are keeping your balance between attraction and detachment.

It is as though you are the director of a film about your life. You can put anything you want into it, with enough attention and focus, and you can change the scene when you find it unsatisfactory. If you find that statement stretches your belief too far, then you again have choices. You can either disbelieve it and remain within your current vision of how things affect you in the world. Or you can experiment with some small achievable goals and see whether your experience changes your belief. That, after all, is what happened to me.

Twenty years ago, I would never have believed anything I have written in this book. My certainty is the result of experiment, leading to experience which has changed my belief about the nature of the world we inhabit. Good fortune, circumstances or intuition have led me to learn from widespread sources of human wisdom and discover the same essential teaching.

A Tibetan Buddhist monk and a Hawaiian kahuna easily recognise the resonance in their practices. They have a common understanding, not just of the physical laws of nature, but of the non-physical energies that resonate through the earth and the rest of our universe. The Dalai Lama visited a spot on the northernmost tip of the five Hawaiian islands, where the seemingly endless Pacific claws and tugs at the coast with all the power of an ocean that stretches to the nearest land mass five hours' flight away. When he was there, he is reported to have said:

"This is where spirits come into the world."

Later he went to the southernmost island of Hawaii, the so-called Big Island, shaped by two volcanoes. One rises so high above the clouds that all the international astronomy projects have their observatories there, to the discomfort of the god whose shrine at the summit they have overshadowed. The other is an active, destructive volcano, that recently wiped out many square miles of farmland and homesteads, leaving a black moonscape in her wake. On the southern tip of this island there is a place when the sea sucks wildly at the black cliffs. People go there to cast their lines into deep Pacific waters and catch inhabitants of the waters such as yellowfin tuna. It is a desolate spot somehow, even though it has not been turned to ash by mother Pele. It has a feel of the end of the world. When the Dalai

Lama came there, he said:

"This is where spirits come when they leave the world."

The earth-moving goddess Pele is not blamed or rebuked for explosions of anger that destroy homes and livelihoods. Her power is accepted, since, in the patient view of the Hawaiian people, she creates land of such fertility that they have traditionally been able to eat well and enjoy comfortable lives on her shores. The rumbling voice of the goddess reminds them constantly of their small power in mother Earth's hands, prompting them to be grateful for the bounty she showers on them, and never to take her power for granted.

This deep understanding of the natural voice in our environment is something that we have lost in countries where we are separated from nature by sophisticated commerce. In time we will pay a heavy price for our lack of understanding of the natural rhythm of our world. Commerce has been able to make use of natural bounty to shower humans with excess. When we don't need to fend for ourselves, we take everything we receive for granted and soon come to feel cheated if our demands are not met. But we can all take responsibility for harmonising ourselves with natural rhythms and reap the reward in hundreds of small ways that add up to our health and happiness.

The key points to bear in mind in preparing yourself to focus on obtaining a particular goal are these:

Examine your Motive

You must explore your motivation before you begin to pursue what you want. Your energy is powerful, and the energy of others equally so. If you use your energy to contradict another being then the energy is neutralised between you by the conflict. You need to see your individual desire as part of the expression of that macrocosmic pattern. So long as your desires do not harm another being, there will be no conflicting channel of energy from another whose needs have equal weight in the universe. The more you can align your desires with what benefits at least one other, the more energy you can share to propel your wishes forward. Your motive and the effect on others is a key part of achieving what you want.

Visualise

Tantra, once practised in India and still a part of Tibetan Buddhist practices, is walking on the line between apparent reality and potential reality. You focus your mind on imagined reality, on a great god or goddess with all their attributes. You do this in such detail that it absorbs all your attention. You must remember the god's clothes, appearance and furnishings. You must remember the hundreds of attendants, all their places and habitations. You must visualise their connections to each other and the thousands of connections beyond, stretching to the limit of your imagination. You must chant the god's name out loud and your appeal to the god for personal attention. The mental abstraction this produces is so intense that it overwhelms ordinary laws of physics. Preparing themselves in this way, people can walk across molten lava with their feet unscathed. This amounts to more than just turning off the pain gates, since the person who does it correctly can walk over hot coals with their feet unburned.

This may seem unattainable to you, but one thing is most important. You must *feel* the nature of the God: pure compassion, purest love, infinite creativity and healing. The essential attribute you desire will determine the deity you appeal to. As you immerse yourself in this practice, without reservation, you will unlock the power you desire.

Your mental and physical unity with the nature of the deity isn't intended to be with something 'out there'. The practice of imagining a deity that embodies the ultimate quality you desire to invoke brings a sense of union with the physical elements of which everything is composed. The elements of earth, water, fire and air make up your body, to which Eastern philosophies add the element of ether to describe the energy of the intangible. Different schools of practice put more or less emphasis on one area or another, but they all have in common the instruction to focus your attention on the elements you share with all the known world and allow yourself to explore their energy within you. Where you perceive blocks or limitations, do not turn away. Focus on releasing those blocks, calling on an elemental deity and all the assistant deities for help.

The nature of the energy that your goal embodies is more important than the shape of the goal itself. If, for example, you desire healing, you need the god who can bring the gift of life, the medicine buddha in many traditions, whose essence regenerates or replaces cells that have died in the body. If it is a loving relationship you desire, you must think about the essential components of that. This might be compassion, for yourself and the other person. It might be sex and sensuality. It might be procreation, the desire to have children. If you desire a fast car, you are looking for power, and you need to find that power in yourself, not from an external source. If you desire an abundance of money, you may be looking for protection and security. Whatever the essence of your desire, there will be a god or goddess, a mythical figure, who embodies it absolutely. This is the being whose essence you will draw into your imagination.

Let go of control

In calling on universal energy to achieve your desire you are reaching far beyond your individual ability. You are humbly searching to align your intention with greater energy. Another key teaching for obtaining what you wish for is to let go of the notion that you can control what happens. You can ask, but you must trust that the result will come in its own way at the right time. This detachment is an essential part of aligning yourself with the bounty of the universe we live in. You can accept and enjoy what is given. You can prefer some aspects of living to others and focus your energy accordingly. However, ultimately, there are bigger forces at work than you understand from the perspective of a single human life. As a very wise man said to me recently:

"Depression, darkness, death, these are also God."

Only with the understanding of our small power in the face of the great power which enables us to live, can we enjoy the best and use the worst of what life throws in our way to navigate further. When you look closely at even the darkest experiences of your life, you will find great teaching there. Growth begins in darkness. Persist in looking for the light.

Achieve your desire Hawaiian style

The Hawaiians teach a practice for achieving your desire which balances these essential points neatly and is refreshingly simple and practical. This is a characteristic of the Hawaiian style that makes their teaching so powerful.

Before you begin, settle yourself in a quiet place and sit comfortably. Bear in mind that your lower back and belly, the sacral area, is what the Hawaiians refer to as the Child. This is the area of your body that holds all your memories and corresponding emotions from the beginning of your existence to the present moment. The child is a powerful driver in your life and needs to be paid attention to. The child also needs to be loved, encouraged and taught, and will respond, like any child, with great love, energy and joy. Take your attention to this area and see how comfortable you can make it.

Then take your attention to the solar plexus, your upper belly and middle back. This is the area the Hawaiians call the Mother, the seat of your will, your self-identity, your rational thinking and responses. Just like any mother, she thinks she is running things in the body/home. She thinks she knows what to do and what the future will be. Yet taking all this responsibility on to herself, she often fails to see what other parts of the body/home are thinking and feeling, and her predictions for the future may be wrong. Her thinking can set up a destructive reaction to things that have not happened. Nevertheless, her will and vision set the course for the whole family. Take your attention to this area of the body and see how it is feeling. See if you can settle this area and focus on what you want to happen.

Now take your attention to the crown of the head and above it. Your crown, your physical brain and nervous system, have the capacity to reach beyond the limits of the known physical universe, into realms of imagination and fantasy, and beyond into a void which may be enlightening or terrifying depending on how you are prepared to perceive. This area, stretching from the crown above the head, is the area the Hawaiians call the Father. Take your attention to this area of your body and see how it feels.

Breathe out through the mouth as long as you can, making a *Haaaaa* sound, allowing the breath to come in through your nose and fill your body up from the base of the spine all the way to the crown of the head. Breathe out through the mouth again: *Haaaaa.* Do this three times, focusing on releasing any pressure or resistance you feel around your crown, forehead or scalp.

Focus your attention now on what you wish to have in your life. This is the Mother thinking. She is in charge of your conscious mind. Allow yourself to picture the deity who embodies the essence of what you want. Imagine the deity in all its attributes waiting there for your attention. Picture the goal you desire itself in as much detail as you can: what it will look like and how it will feel when you have it. Imagine that it is already in your life.

When you have a clear picture, take the image down to where the Child is. The Mother asks the Child how he or she feels about this image. She listens carefully to the response. You will find a very different perspective. This is where your fears and doubts live. This is where your joy, enthusiasm and contentment spring from. Whatever the Child comes up with, let the Mother respond. Let her see if she can comfort or convince the Child. Perhaps, on the other hand, the Child will convince her. If so, you may decide that's the end of the matter. But it's more likely that you will find a way to reassure the Child and get his or her blessing for what you wish to achieve. This is a negotiation to achieve a joint enterprise. To feel that you have the Child's agreement, you need to be able to imagine that the Mother and the Child can go forward towards this desire hand in hand. See them joining together, united behind this desire.

Now, imagine that they travel upwards through your body in a stream of blue light. They are going to present the Desire to the Father. Imagine this Desire emerging from your body like a blue flame at the third eye, the point between and just above the eyebrows. Imagine it travelling directly upwards from your body and being presented to the Father. Wait until you sense that the Desire has been received. Now take your attention back to just above the crown of your head and cut the stream of blue light. Let it go. Settle back into your body with trust that you have presented a clear wish to a greater power that has observed and will respond in your interests. Come back gently into your body and go about your life.

You may choose to repeat this exercise. If things don't progress in the way you hoped for, or an obstruction appears to come in your way, you can look again at the relationship between the 'mother' and the 'child', between your will and your unconscious, and see whether there is something lurking in your unconscious that you hadn't noticed before. But don't repeat it too often. Your desire is planted by this process like the seed of a tree. You have used your imagination to choose the seed and prepare the ground around its root. You have 'announced' to the universe your desire to see this tree blossom and fruit, and this clear intention has an energetic echo with circumstances that enable its ripening. When you doubt that is happening you begin to close down the channels that allow this energy to flourish.

It's your doubt itself that needs attention. Your thinking is a creative arm of your being. It can open up possibilities and it can close them down. When we assume that something is possible and it comes to pass, generally we pay it no more attention. I assume that if I need to run to catch a bus, I can do it with no problem. But if I have had an injury or a weakness in my legs that I have been working hard to recover from, then catching this bus at a run may be something I have dreamed of, a scenario I have pictured in my mind many times. Catching this bus will be something of a miracle then, and once I am sitting safely in it, I can reflect on the combination of mental preparation and physical application that has brought this 'miracle' about. My body's recovery has been directed by my mind, guided by my desire.

When the goal you have in mind involves the energy of other people you may feel you have less control and doubts creep in. Perhaps your goal is to write a best-selling book, and then you must come to the attention of all those people who will buy your book and please them. Do you want that attention? Perhaps your goal is to have a lasting loving relationship in your life, and yet this means accommodating someone else's wishes and desires. Are you ready for that?

The energy of other people is the great unknown until you know your own self deeply and thoroughly. Examining your mental habits and desires, using the exercises in this book, will allow you to clarify what has helped and hindered in your relationships with other people. You will discover how understanding your own energy gives you the tools you need to make effective changes in your life. This shows you the power that lies in your hands to create change. It will also allow you to see what helps and hinders those around you. As the clarity shines brighter on your life, by some subtle miracle, doubt, scepticism and self-consciousness give way to trust, integration and creativity. You are no less intelligent that you were when you were full of doubt and scepticism. You are just choosing to use your intelligence in a different way.

You are beginning to align yourself with the great energy of space, that is within you and beyond you, of which your structure is created, just like the structure of everything else. In knowing yourself, your feelings, your body and the influence of your mind, you are exploring an infinitesimally small part of the great universe, discovering subtlety and fluidity in your own complex being. You begin to pay attention to the voice within, a voice distinct from the conventional mutterings of your day to day mind which prefers to concern itself with those things that are recognisable and defined.

The voice that you hear within you is like a deep echo of a distant drum beat that translates itself into a random thought on waking, a gut reaction, a persistent idea that irrationally draws your attention, a spontaneous decision that leads you to a particular place or person. Listen to this voice. It is your truest guide.

Your intuition speaks like a breeze. It is subtle, like a persistent tide, but its voice is not loud. As you explore your own energy more deeply, you discover its power, but you also begin to recognise the flow of energy in the people, animals, animate and inanimate elements of the environment you walk through. You notice how each moment of your day is a moment that can never be reclaimed. Your time is precious. Perhaps you begin to use it better. You begin to take time to examine what you are doing and why you are doing it. You may slow down, but you will be no less effective for that. You will notice, and other people will pay attention too. This is what it means, I believe, to honour the self. Your life and circumstances are a uniquely precious possession that you have been entrusted with to steer harmoniously through the universe for the purpose of discovering its pattern.

My grandfather's list of affirmations recognises the essential truth that is at the heart of being human as expressed in the philosophy of yoga. The life within us is the absolute purity of creative divinity expressed through matter that is already the creation of the past. Absolute energy is temporarily expressed in the architecture of cells, nerves and muscles that constitute our physical being. The more we acknowledge the complexity of our being, the more we can cultivate its potential. The process of cultivation, whether it is challenging ourselves intellectually or physically, is a process that hones our ability and makes it shine, in the way that only careful polishing and cutting can turn a diamond from a colourless rock to a brilliant object. The practices of yoga are all designed to lead us further along this path of polishing, not for our own satisfaction, although the practices do bring health and happiness, but as a form of respect for the total creation we are part of. That part of it which is in our care: our bodies; our lives, we make the most of, so that the pattern of the whole sparkles.

These notes on cultivating different areas of the brain and human abilities by feeding them with the power of positive thought seemed to me an important aspect of the practice of yoga that many modern interpretations in the west have overlooked. I was puzzled as to why my grandfather's notes should be headed 'MOST SECRET'. If this instruction is something that would help any human being to make the most of a precious life, shouldn't it be offered as widely as possible? Or would the yogis who taught this practice have followed the habit of so many religious teachers from all mystic schools in the past of guarding their knowledge carefully? That way they could ensure it wouldn't fall into disrespectful hands and maintain their power and authority at the same time. It was my mother who cleared up this mystery for me as I wondered aloud about it one day.

"But you know he worked at Bletchley during the war."

Bletchley Park was the intellectual hub of the British war effort during World War II. It was the home of the famous codebreaking operation led by Sir Alan Turing that enabled the Allies to anticipate German strategy. My grandfather had little to do with the codebreaking team. His job at Bletchley was to prepare soldiers going into battle for potential capture and teach them how they might escape. He had been a prisoner of war in World War I and sent to a camp called Holzminden which became famous for a dramatic mass escape. My grandfather chronicled the escape plan in a book he published in 1920.[3] He wasn't one of the escapees, but he was regarded as complicit and transferred to a high security prison on Stralsund. High security or not, he managed to escape from Stralsund in a typically downbeat fashion. He forged a passport, assembled a set of clothes that allowed him to pass for a workman, and walked out of the gates. Speaking very little German, he managed, even so, to get all the way back to England, something few escapees achieved. So, in World War II, he was recruited to teach young soldiers.

Perhaps, as the war went on, there were fewer and fewer recruits needing his instruction, or perhaps circumstances had changed so much between the First World War and the Second that his advice was no longer useful. Whatever the reason, he clearly found time to think about yoga and perhaps practise it in his office at Bletchley. This was the reason for the heading that had puzzled and enticed me. In Bletchley Park, information was carefully guarded. Every piece of paper came ready stamped with the words: 'MOST SECRET'.

Chapter 16

Mission Fulfilled

All creation, streaming out of the self, is just the self.
Song of Ashtavakra[1]

My mother's agony now is living a reality that confuses her. All her adult life she has felt she can make choices about how to live her life and she has indulged them to the full. Now, even her choices about her own body seem to be out of her hands. I have bags full of medicines which she has been given to counter the side effects of the drug that is keeping her heart pumping. The doctors know this drug is actually also killing her, fatally damaging her kidneys, but we are on a journey where the parallel lines will meet at infinity. Death will outrun the effects of the drug, but we don't know how or when that will be. My mother says she would like to just stop taking the pills that are keeping her going, but the medical professionals seem to think they can't allow that. Disgusted by the suggestion, a nurse in the team that is now visiting to care for her exclaims:

"This is not Switzerland!"

A young GP in the team has gladdened our hearts by openly saying that we are helping our mother to have 'a good death'. None of us actually know what that looks like, although we feel we know what it means. Peace. Love. Letting go. The nurse bends her head over the GP's notes and clucks with disapproval.

"He's got a lot to learn."

My mother is dismayed by the sensation of losing control, tormented by alternating acceptance and fear she can no longer avoid. Her torment manifests in a litany of symptoms that do not allow her, or anyone else, to sleep. Ultimately nature is in charge, and, much as she loves nature, her courage fails her at this overwhelming aspect of it. The continuum of energy which has given life to her body is leading her down to the point of no return, to the darkness, the void devoid of every familiar sense. Naturally, she is scared.

She would like to know where she is going so that she could have the illusion of control, but the picture that appears before her is black. She does not know. A part of her still takes refuge in every aspect of her body she can command.

"Look how strong my legs are!" she says intensely when she has been levered off the bed so she can wobble on to the commode. These remnants of her physical strength interest her far more at this point than the philosophy of Buddhism she has immersed herself in for decades. And then, one night, everything changes.

"I suppose what I feel is fear," she says, while she rubs the knuckles of my hand, as though she were trying to make them shine.

I've never heard her name her fear before. She has always been too busy fighting it. At the time I merely think, *Of course!*, while I urge her to look into that darkness to go forward, the way I remember I used to do as a child, when I was sure there was a monster hiding under my bed. I would leap on to the bed from a safe distance, until eventually I taught myself to look directly into that black hole under it. When I looked for my fear, I would find it was gone. I encourage my mother to do the same now. Later, I realise that this is what she was already doing.

That night, the restless agitation which has made her want to escape on limbs no longer strong enough to hold her is gone. The nursing team, tired of being summoned to inject her with the tranquillising drug that is the only thing that can defeat this restlessness for a few hours, decide to link her to a machine that drip-feeds the drug into her body. Her breathing softens and settles. She sleeps on her side like a baby. Only a tiny pressure from the hand I know so well shows me that she is conscious and can still hear me. Peace. Love. Letting go. In less than 48 hours she is gone.

After death, the character of a person shines out from the place they occupied in life, like the powerful scent of a flower. For some reason, I could look at my mother's work after she died: the paintings, etchings and printed books she made with such care and passion, and see her spirit burst from the pages in front of me. I could not do this when she was alive. I'm not proud of that. It was just the way it was. She would show me what she had been working on and I would look at it critically, wondering if other people would see something in it that I didn't. They did, but I wasn't sure what they were seeing. I would mutter some faint praise or encouragement that she scarcely heard. She always rejected criticism, on the surface at least. She preferred to trust her instinct and she was her own champion.

When she died, it fell to me to trawl through all the things she had owned or created in her life and find a new home for them. Looking at the etchings I had grown up with that blazed with so much vibrant energy, I began to understand why I had been so mealy-mouthed in my appreciation of her efforts. This powerful personality threatened to extinguish me. I was rooting, as we nearly all do, to find the point and purpose of *me*. My mother's passionate character and her demands on me got in the way. I could only find myself in separation from her, and the more she kept drawing me back to her, the more I longed to be apart. As I grew older and stronger, it became a two-way barrier, each of us wary of the other's power.

I remember the tulip. A tulip that grows from the parent's seed, instead of its own roots, will have streaks and variations of colour that were hugely valued by wealthy 17th century gardeners for their exotic fragility. But, as those who invested fortunes in these valuable 'varieties' soon discovered, to their cost, those exotic streaks were in fact a sign of disease. A healthy flower comes from a bulb that has taken the time to develop roots and make its own connection with the earth.

Some people are clear from an early age what the point of their lives is and where they want to position themselves in relation to society. Our current Prime Minister, Boris Johnson, is apparently one of those people. According to his sister, when he was asked as a child what he wanted to be when he grew up, he answered, "World King." Being Prime Minister of the United Kingdom is a long way from that, but the tortuous journey that has carried him to his current position could only have been predicted in the inner territory of his self-belief and desire. My mother was an artist from childhood, using her eye to arrange people and places in a way she found aesthetically pleasing. When she was sixteen, she persuaded her younger sister and friend to drape themselves naked around trees, and sprawl on beds with apples in their hands while she photographed their beautiful bodies. She entered the photographs in a national newspaper competition which published them and awarded her first prize. Naturally, she was delighted. No one asked the fourteen-year-old models how they felt.

It's much easier for most of us to see the point of other people we know or read about than ourselves. We lead busy lives, envisaging one goal after another and working hard to reach it and maintain what we have created. Yet we are dogged by a nagging dissatisfaction and a sense that there is more to discover about who we are. We may come to feel discovering the 'point' of us is a mission we can't postpone any longer. We look restlessly for teaching and guidance elsewhere. If we are lucky, we find someone or something that acts as a guide to the treasure we hold in ourselves.

My luck was to discover that my own body is a powerful guide, in tune with parts of myself I had been too busy to pay attention to for years. When my brain tumour was discovered, it was found to be sitting on my pituitary gland. The pituitary gland lies directly underneath the hypothalamus, which in turn is most closely connected to the limbic system of the brain, where memories, emotions and reactions to pain and pleasure are recorded. These parts of your nervous system distribute the hormones that balance water and heat in your body. Together they help control your heart rate and, in women, distribute oxytocin, the hormone responsible for lactation and maternal bonding. The pituitary controls skin pigmentation, the release of hormones that control growth, regulate energy, stimulate the adrenal glands on the kidney to produce adrenalin, and sex. With all these vital functions for human life it's not surprising that the pituitary is often called the 'conductor of the orchestra'.

When I was challenged by a life-threatening condition, my initial instinct made it clear to me with its powerful voice what I wanted to do with my life. I wanted to write, and I wanted to work with people to help them out of pain.

The series of fortuitous connections that led me forward on this path look, in retrospect, like the 'Flow' I have been talking about, but I had so many fears and reservations at the time this is not how it felt. My father's other daughter, my half-sister, led me to a healer, Martin Brofman, who not only provided a map to help me understand my body and its messages, but also led me to discover my capacity to heal. According to Martin's map, the tumour itself, which affected my whole nervous system, had its roots in my relationship with my father, but its position on the pituitary suggested tension in me about my mission or purpose. My inner emotions, as yet still ignored by me, nevertheless coordinated perfectly with my physical symptoms as described by his map.

The initial physical problem had been double vision. There was a dissonance between the way I functioned for work and the way I wanted to express myself. The tumour that caused this problem, because of where it was, spoke of feeling disconnected and unrecognised by 'authority', in the shape of my father, or bosses or teachers, but also of a frustrating lack of direction. Like many people, I looked for an authority outside myself that I could trust as a guide. In my illness and the deep introspective pause that my body forced upon me, I found a voice that led me to the guide within, the internal voice I have talked about.

Martin used to liken the area of the pituitary, the brow chakra, or third eye, to a firefighter, positioned high up with an overview of the forest below.

"Whenever there is a forest fire," he used to say, "and the firefighters are down on the ground trying to put it out, they need someone who has an overview to tell them where to go. There will be this one firefighter high up on a tower who will be able to see where the fire is spreading, feel the direction of the wind and so on. He will communicate with the people on the ground and tell them what they need to do. Your brow chakra is like that, the part of you with an overview, directing the mission."

When people talk of a higher power, often referred to as something you communicate with through the third eye, it's easy to feel as though this something is quite disconnected from the life you lead. Yet the part of you that has access to a wider view and comprehensive energy is still part of you, just like your stomach or your little toe are essential parts of what you are. If you are to sense your unity with and between all things, this extends to the minutest part of your physical functioning. People sometimes look upon such a sensation of union as an escape from the humdrum physical self, which it can be from the point of view that you become unaware at that moment of your body. But you cannot disregard parts of your body, your life or of your society because they do not function well. They too are an expression of the divine. Your interaction with them will lead you deeper along the road of discovery so that you can bring your own life to fruition.

If you look for guidance to fulfil an unsatisfied sense of

purpose in your life, you need to look within yourself first. You will be guided by feelings within your own body, and by emotional reactions that stretch back to the moment you were born. I am reminded of a conversation I had with a fisherman in Hawaii one day. We were standing in the ancient holy site of Pu'uhonua, where the Hawaiian ancestors and their traditions have been honoured for centuries. As we looked out at the endless ocean he said:

"We didn't look at the sea to know when it was time to go fishing. We looked up into the hills." And he gestured behind him.

Before the white missionaries and subsequent landowners came to Hawaii, the islands were occupied by extended families. Each family or tribe occupied a stretch of land that went all the way from the volcanic peaks of the interior to the black rocks of the shore, a distance that stretched over tens of miles. Although some members of the extended family were settled by the sea and specialised in fishing, they were in contact with other members of the family who were farmers in the hills. When the crops in the hills were setting seed, they knew that the fish in the sea were spawning, and that soon there would be fish in abundance they could harvest without depleting the catch.

"So we would watch how the plants in the hills were responding to the cycles of the moon," he said. "Then we would know what was happening beneath the waves."

When you feel dissatisfied with your life and cast about for the 'point of you', it's much easier to see what other people achieve than yourself. You look at their successes, of course. You do not see their doubts. But we all have a purpose. We all contribute to the movement of humanity and the evolution of the planet. Your achievement may have been biological, creating or nurturing a younger person. How beautiful is that! Or it may be the expression of a personal perspective, in music, speech, writing or painting that creates a harmony through which other people can see their world reflected. Or it may be another form of service, looking after the wounded, protecting the vulnerable, catering to people's needs to provide food, shelter, or comfort. It may be discovery, adventure, information, that you bring back to humanity for the benefit of your species and the planet.

Whatever it is, you can be sure that what you are 'meant' to do will be what gives or has given you the most pleasure and satisfaction. It may also have given you the most agony, pain, and fear, but that should not stop you from doing it. When you are facing a difficult situation, or a pause in your life, not knowing where or how to go forward, you can use the life you have lived so far to evaluate your course and direction.

Look at the things you have done in your life. List what you feel have been significant choices or actions and put alongside them the answer to these questions:

"What prompted me to do that?"

"What did I hope to achieve?"

"What satisfaction or pleasure did it give me?"

"Do I feel the same way now?"

It is much easier to determine these things in retrospect than while you are doing them. It is sometimes better to look backward to find the way forward. This leads to another interesting way you can glean important lessons about the tools you have at your disposal going forward.

You are partly your mother and partly your father, although you are unique. You are not like any siblings you have who may have experienced the same parenting as you. In spite of your differences from your siblings, your mother and father are vital to your being. If you accept that you made a choice, at some pre-conscious level, to be born to these parents, why did you choose this particular recipe and how have you been able to use the ingredients in your life so far? Is there an ingredient or a combination of them that still needs to be expressed?

When you begin to think like this and peer into the origins

of your being, you begin to see more and more clearly how the threads that come from your parents' ancestors and your parents' reactions to those threads are expressed in you. If you start by considering the character and qualities of each parent, in so far as you know them, you will reveal a pattern in your own life that expresses a major theme about who you are and you can decide how you want to respond to it. Do you want to take that forward or is there a quality that you need to find a balance for?

I've talked a lot about the paradoxes of existence that fascinate me. Over and over, as I was discovering things about myself and my life that I had been blind to for decades, I was finding that what felt like the truth was the space between two opposites. The way forward, the path of greater discovery, consists in accepting and embracing those opposites and in so doing, understanding your place in the whole. My physical ailments neatly expressed my inner feelings of discontent, as I've said, from the initial symptom of double vision, to the sense of disconnection from the 'authority' or divine, expressed by the father, that burst open in me after he died. This doesn't mean that everyone who experiences this separation would have similar symptoms. It just means that those aspects of experience were important to me, forming signs on the journey of life through which I am learning to express the Divine.

When I look at the characters of my mother and father, the differences between them are startling. Almost every characteristic that occurs to me to describe each one is expressed by its opposite in the other. My father was loyal and dutiful. My mother was a rebel. My father was musical. My mother couldn't hold a tune. My father was secretive and tactful. My mother was passionate and outspoken. My father was a gameplayer. My mother hated games of any kind. They did have things in common. They were both children of mothers who had grown up without their fathers, carried about from place to place by *their* mothers, clinging to the fringes of friends and family in a more or less desperate bid to find security and support. Both my mother and father were good looking and charming, knew how to make themselves agreeable, and haunted by the fear of poverty, as their mothers had been.

The characters of my mother and father and the differences between them have been significant for the choices that I have made in my life. I am married to a man who is in many ways my opposite, and I have found value in that, teaching myself to embrace the difference and express myself as I wish to in spite of it. My mother and father, on the other hand, found it impossible to live together and separated when I was a baby. Peering into the lives of my parents, I can see how consistently I have chosen to find unity in opposites, in a practical sense as well as a physical one, and I am grateful for the richness that has delivered me.

After my mother died, as I trawled through the hundreds of sketchbooks and notes of her artistic work she had carefully stored, the consistency of her creative drive shone out at me. Her style changed considerably over the years, from the precise early watercolours and detailed sketches, to the careful technical work of etching and printing and, later, the free poetic drama of her paintings. More striking than the changes of style was her apparently fluid process of reinvention and discovery. When she encountered an obstacle, she diverted her creative drive along another channel. When the printing press became too heavy for her to handle, she turned to wood engravings and monoprints. When her studio burned down, destroying plates and equipment, she turned to painting. She drew and printed her next book on a computer, teaching herself Photoshop and ingeniously combining it with watercolours, though she was already in her eighties. After she died, and I began turning out cupboard after cupboard, this stream of expressive beauty lay all around me.

I wanted to honour that continuous creative lifetime somehow before it was dispersed, so I decided to put it all together: the sketches, doodles, and unsold work, and mount an exhibition in her studio. I felt that I wanted to show the branches and flowers of this expressive stream in the environment that she had considered the best place on earth. It was hard work, mounting the display and promoting the event, but on the days of the exhibition, the sun glowed and the 'best place on earth' showed off its glory. Friends and family helped me, but even so it was a scramble to manage people arriving, inspecting and selecting paintings and prints to take away with them. Suddenly, in amongst hundreds of pages of rough prints that I hoped to find a home for, I spotted a scrappy piece of paper that grabbed my attention. Swiftly I drew it aside, with the sense I had found something precious.

That piece of paper hangs beside me now as I write, mounted in a frame. It's a shabby piece of cartridge paper, with a stain on it. It has a hastily drawn sketch of some plant that looks like verbena but could equally well be cow parsley or carrot. Beside that, in her not very legible handwriting, my mother has written words that tell me she too perceived the power of paradox:

World is water
Air is light
After day there comes the night
Look into the space between
To find the things you have not seen.

When you dig deep and do what your intuition prompts you to despite all the obstacles, you are likely to encounter a sign at some point that indicates you are on the right path. That 'sign' might be meaningless to anyone but you, but you will recognise it with a resonance that you can feel in your body like the vibration of a hammer on a gong.

I had been searching for guidance outside myself that would take me deeper into knowledge of the divine within myself. I wasn't sure where to go. I had found Martin's teaching and gone deeply into healing. I felt in tune with the messages the physical body could whisper to me and yet I wanted to plant the seedling of my spiritual understanding in deeper soil. I cast about for a structure to twine myself around and continue growing, but none seemed to be what I was looking for.

As you know, eventually I set off for India, landing in Kolkata and heading down to the ashram that was founded by a pupil of Sri Yukteswar less famous than Paramahansa Yogananda. The ashram just outside Puri in Odisha is home of a branch of Kriya Yoga, founded by Paramahamsa Hariharananda and headed since his death by his pupil, Paramahamsa Prajnanananda. The ashram teaches a form of meditation which you need to make a commitment to study. It's not like picking up a book which you can discard when you've digested the contents. You make a commitment to practise before you really know what you'll be doing. This happens at an initiation ceremony. No initiation, no knowledge.

I've been suspicious of this kind of thing most of my life. I have liked to explore, try things out and see where they take me. I could, of course, promise to practise and then break my promise, but that is also foreign to my nature. Yet I had followed my nose and found myself in the ashram which had kindly agreed to mount a special private initiation ceremony for me. The person who would perform the ceremony would arrive soon, I was told. For a few days after I arrived there was no more information, so I enquired again.

"Don't worry," they said. "The brother is aware that you are here and he will come. Just be ready. Someone will call you."

I spent the rest of the day in a fever of doubt and dispute with myself. I walked up and down the paths dotted with steles informing me that almost everyone needs a guru, and a guru is a friend who is a guide to yourself. I longed to walk out of the ashram, over the dunes to the sea. I chafed at the regularity and smooth discipline of the place and skipped the evening meal. The next morning, I was woken by a knock at the dormitory door.

"We are ready for you. Come to the door of the small hut by the lake at 6am. You need to bring five flowers and a small amount of money as a token for the donation. We will bring five fruits from the kitchen."

I lay back on the pillow and thought, *So this is it. You're really going to do this. Quick. what's the date?*

It seemed important. It was the 19th November. As soon as I realised the date, I remembered something else. 19th November was Martin Brofman's birthday. The idea of a 'guru' and commitment to something he didn't already know was foreign to Martin's nature too. He had a tendency to explore and try things out before adopting them with any kind of loyalty. This inbuilt scepticism is probably what made him such a good teacher for me. He never asked for any commitment. He was certain about what he was teaching but he never wanted people to take things on trust. He never wanted to be treated like a guru.

Martin was gone now. He had died two years before. But in the darkness of the dorm room that morning I felt his presence. *"It's my birthday. Come celebrate with me. Here's my present to you."* The hammer hit the gong.

The cabin by the lake was a very special place. A single-storied mud-walled terracotta building with a thatched roof, I realised gradually, by the wooden sandals at the door and small mementos all around, that it had been Hariharananda's home in the ashram he created. It was the place where he slept and meditated, looking out over the beautiful lake where water lilies bloomed. I was honoured to be given initiation within its walls.

Under the porch at the entrance there was a statue of

Ganesh. Ganesh is the elephant-headed god whose special gift is to cut through obstacles and reveal the illusory nature of the 'reality' we perceive. One version of his story says he was such a good-looking god that he was carried away by vanity over his appearance. Shiva, the source of creation, told him his appearance was an illusion and from that moment he would assume the head of the first animal to emerge from the jungle. That animal was an elephant. I have always loved elephants.

Waiting by the door to enter, I watched an old monk anoint Ganesh with sandalwood paste and place a garland of flowers around his neck, performing his prayer in front of the statue as he did every morning and evening. I was reminded of the ceremony of Kali I had witnessed in the Kalighat in Kolkata, its noisy formality so very different from this monk's quiet devotion. The monk, I felt, was honouring the truth that the world beyond the physical one we know is part of the world within. Accordingly, he would be ready, when his time came, to slip fearlessly through non-being into another way of being.

Chapter 17

Acceptance

What is the purpose of life? You say God, but when you study the scriptures that doesn't make any sense. You need to attain a state of peace, happiness and bliss, and if you have attained peace, happiness and bliss, then that is called God. If you have not, then you are worshipping, adoring and believing in God who is not God.[1]

As I write this, we are counting the dead, worldwide. For the first time in our experience, war is everywhere: war against a thing that is a speck of the size of the breadth of one of the hairs on your head. If that hair were a foot wide, our enemy would be the size of a poppy seed. This virus is an enemy we know very little about, except that it has spread from the animal kingdom to humans who have no defence against it. The hunted are revenged on the hunter. The virus has achieved something we could not even have imagined six months ago: it has suspended 95% of international flights; turned oil sucked from the earth into a worthless commodity; made poorly-paid cleaners into heroes and the richest executives useless. It has cleaned our planet's skies and waters, forced us all to treasure the earth and the food we can coax from it, and to make the most of what we have in our present life.

We have suspended commerce and are weighing up all our normal activities because, in nearly every country in the world, we are trying not to die faster than our medical services can cope with. The doctors themselves are powerless against this virus if we have the misfortune for it to enter our lungs. Our bodies fight it and in so doing our lungs become so choked with mucus that we cannot breathe. It is not the first battle of this kind humanity has faced, but in our interconnected, ingenious, fast-moving, technical world it is shocking to find ourselves powerless against this tiny enemy. An experienced doctor in New York keeps a journal of what he is going through in the emergency room and posts it on Facebook, drawing us into a glimpse of each other's reality:

It is a hard thing to tell a healthy and functional person who felt fine and well six days ago they may be dead in a day or two and humbly ask how aggressive they want us to be. A chance to live comes with the risk of dependence on life support and pain. The alternative is the guarantee of an imminent but peaceful death.[2]

For those who are not on the front line of the battle, under social distancing rules, when only 'essential' tasks permit us to leave our homes, time opens up like a flower in bloom. It has that quality of freshness and depth. We are forced to look to our roots, to our need for the security of shelter and food. We are forced to share these things with our loved ones, so that shelter, food, and love become again all we need to think about. The rest is noise. Whatever you have in your life that is beautiful shines more brightly. You have time also to confront the shadows in your life and defeat them. This is healing. We can look to ourselves to solve the problems we face. This experience serves to show us how precious our time is. And how far from that way of living we have travelled.

We find ourselves isolated in a world more interconnected than ever before. Our responsibility to ourselves is to find peace and happiness within, and to offer the love and strength that peace brings to each other. Once, nearly three decades ago, I travelled by plane, train and bus to Ladakh, in the folds of the Himalayas, to meet the Dalai Lama in person. I learned a lot from that meeting, but I am happy to say that today the 84-year-old Dalai Lama shares his wisdom on Facebook.

The outbreak of this virus has shown us that what happens to one person can soon affect every other being. But it also reminds us that a compassionate or constructive act, whether working in hospitals or just observing social distancing, has the potential to help many... Photographs of our world from space clearly show there are no real boundaries on our blue planet. Therefore all of us must take care of it and work to prevent climate change and other destructive forces. This pandemic serves as a warning and only by coming together with a co-ordinated global response will we meet the unprecedented magnitude of the challenges we face. Sometimes some friends ask me to help with some problem in the world using some 'magical powers'. I always tell them the Dalai Lama has no 'magical powers'. If I did, I would not feel pain in my legs or a sore throat.[3]

There is no magic that can resist the forces of the universe. We live from them and within them, but also we *are* them. We reflect those forces, just like the moon mirrors the light of the sun. We can, if we choose, interact with them. Astrologers point to the conjunction of the energy of the planets Pluto and Saturn that occurred in January 2020, to explain how familiar life came to a juddering halt worldwide in this year. Saturn is the planet associated with power and restriction, and Pluto is the planet of death and rebirth. A conjunction between those planets has not occurred since 1982. At that time, I was living in a poor, underdeveloped country named the People's Republic of China. Many Chinese people were starving, suffering from the effects of the government inspired Cultural Revolution. Revolutions of another kind were under way worldwide, however, which have transformed the whole human world, including China, in ways we could not imagine then. 1983 was the year the first mobile phone was sold, the year that the Internet officially launched, and the year that Microsoft introduced the first version of Word.

Change is happening all the time, though normally we travel too fast to notice it. We create problems, overcome them, and change our world. We are a force on a planet that yet has its own way, where life will continue with or without us. For our own sakes, we need to focus our love and energy on all the life our planet supports. We heal the wounds we perceive so we can enjoy the comfort of our home, this earth. We cannot heal all wounds at once, but we need to start somewhere. We can start by giving ourselves time to heal our own.

When I am trying to explain how I think healing works to people, I sometimes use the metaphor of a three-layered cake. The bottom layer of the cake, which we can call the chocolate layer, is our physical body, and this is affected by physical things. Pharmaceutical drugs, viruses, bacteria, herbs, food, water, exercise, massage, our physical environment, all have an effect to a greater or lesser extent on this layer. The effect is different for each one of us because we have another layer, which we can call the vanilla layer. This is the layer of our thoughts and feelings, memories, desires and fears. I describe it as 'above' the layer below because it is more powerful. What is within us affects the reactions of the physical. We have enormous power to understand and interact with the energy of this layer and, in so doing, influence the physical. As a healer, this is the layer I work with.

There is another layer which I'll call the icing on the cake. This is a layer beyond human understanding. It determines the circumstances of our life, when and where we're born, who we're born to, whether we grow up in a refugee camp or a loving middle-class home. Some people consider these circumstances random, and so refute the existence of this layer of our being or choose to ignore it. Yet the more you explore yourself in detail, from how physical parts of your body link to emotional aspects of you, to memories and imagination that relate to the history of your parents and the place and time you were born, the more you begin to perceive there is a pattern in everything. The pattern of existence may be beyond human understanding, but we are gifted with the ability to be conscious of the little things. Awareness of what we do and how we are yields glimpses of the power we are part of and the role we play in it. As above, so below. We may not understand the totality of the spiritual layer of our being and it is one we do not control, but this does not mean we are disconnected from it. We can communicate with it and gradually learn to understand its voice.

The sensitive point of communication with this energy in our physical body is the crown chakra, though understanding comes via the interpretation of the 'third eye'. Physically, the crown chakra describes your brain and your nervous system. Energetically, it controls the pituitary, the 'conductor of the orchestra', which once went so haywire for me. It is influenced by your relationship with your father, just as the root chakra is influenced by your experience with your mother. By extension, the energy of your crown chakra influences your relationship with authority in your life, whether that is with teachers at school, bosses at work or police and, sometimes, doctors. The crown chakra contains the energy of the Divine in formless purity.

In the chakra 'map' the crown chakra is at the top of the line, just as it is in the body. The map follows the energetic polarity of the spine. The word for spine in Sanskrit is *Merudanda*. *Meru* means the poles, as in the north and south pole of the earth. *Danda* means a staff or vertical axis. As Paramahamsa Prajnanananda has pointed out in his book about the union of physical with non-physical energy:

This is an illustration of the polarity in life being the root cause of boundless flowing energy.[4]

The crown represents the masculine, while the root is feminine, in the Hawaiian teaching, the Christian and the Hindu. The earth is the divine feminine: the yin or darkness of created matter.

The heavens are the uncreated source of all, the absolute, the yang force. They are inseparable, magnetically interconnected in all forms.

Describing something as physical which is not physical, we tend to fall back on the certainties of our external senses: up, down, back, front, and so on. But the 'map' of the chakras denotes a sphere, a bubble of existence that we experience physically as a line or separation. The energy of the crown is essentially at the core of us, not a layer on the top. It is another paradox we need to adjust to, and see in two ways at the same time, just as, in my cake analogy, we all understand that the powerful middle layer is inside, invisible, not sitting on top of the physical. As we dig deep, working from the external layer of our interaction with our environment and our circumstances, we gradually begin to perceive the core.

After my mother died, I found little notes scribbled in a diary. It was not a formal diary: just one with dates and appointments that was small and light enough for her to carry around as she trotted into her ninth decade. She had been taking notes from her teacher, Lama Chime Rinpoche, who was himself about to enter his eighth decade. As he grew older, more exhausted with students presenting the same problems over and over again, Chime's teaching grew simpler, more direct. Or perhaps that was the effect of my mother's scribbled notes. But this one stood out. It is the essence of the teaching of the Tibetan Dzogchen tradition.

"One Taste," she wrote.

That is to say, the perception that ice and water are the same thing, in different conditions. In this understanding, there is no 'good' and 'bad', no 'life' and 'death', no 'physical' and 'immaterial'. They are all different conditions of the same experience.

Mystics, who see our consciousness as part of the divine energy that is the source behind all physical forms, teach that this element in us never disappears, but merely takes on different forms when it ceases to be a part of who we think we are. This is the observable pattern of nature, as water converts to steam, bones to humus, and coal to gas and ash with the addition of heat that converts them. Christianity and Islam teach that one lifetime is enough for humans to be united with the supreme non-physical energy that is the creative source. The yogis and the Buddhists teach that each lifetime is a lesson that can take us closer to the bliss of this absolute state, and each human birth is an opportunity, a privilege that offers learning, like the chance of going to school.

I've had my own lessons to learn about the crown chakra. If you do not have a close relationship with your father, for one reason or another, you are likely to experience this disconnection as feeling unrecognised or unappreciated by bosses and teachers. You are likely to be resistant to authority. What's more, since you are so resistant to authority, you're likely to be the last person to recognise it!

For several years I helped Martin Brofman to organise the healing seminars he came to teach in the UK. I enjoyed helping him. The seminars were always insightful. I gained a lot from being at so many of them and developed my skills as a healer. But they were intense and exhausting to organise. For the participants they were four days of an immersive experience that allowed them to cast off many of the habitual limitations of the way of being that had brought them to seek healing. For the organiser this meant advertising, inviting, fetching, carrying, hosting, partying sometimes late into the night, ensuring all were well fed and sheltered, while also healing and being healed over four intensive days. Martin was exacting in his standards and always looked for everything to be the best it could be, which usually meant better than it was. This aspect of his character allowed him to develop a radical and effective method of teaching the gift of healing, but it could make him demanding when it came to the more mundane aspects of life.

Generally, we worked well together, but this harmony broke down dramatically at the end of one four-day seminar in Brighton. It had been particularly intense for me from the point of view of what I still needed to heal in the crown chakra aspect of my energy. I had decided before the seminar to have another MRI scan to make sure that the tumour I believed to be gone had in fact disappeared. The scan was booked, due to take place a couple of weeks later, but I didn't know at that point what the results would be. In the course of the weekend I had hardly slept. I had felt overwhelmed by compassion for my father, not the man I remembered, but the young man he was before I was born. I'd been up early in the morning, standing on the cliffs with the sea air blowing in my face, buffeted by waves of understanding and sympathy with him I'd never felt before. Giddy with the effect of this, or perhaps from exhaustion, I made some remark to Martin in front of the class as I sat down in my place at the start of the final session. I can't remember what I said. It was a light-hearted remark and I thought no more about it.

The afternoon wore on, and I became aware that something was wrong. Martin was in a spectacularly bad mood. As the participants were leaving, he asked me if I would drive him to London on my way back to Kent, roughly a 120-mile round trip, saying he didn't feel like taking the train. Reluctantly, I agreed, rapidly packing up the seminar paraphernalia, while the necklace I was wearing, with stones the colours of the chakras, burst into a hundred pieces on the floor.

When we got in the car, the thundercloud of Martin's fury burst over me.

"You disrespected me in front of the class! You have no respect for authority! While we are working together, I am the authority and you need to remember that!"

Mentally I resisted the onslaught. *He's behaving like a diva!* I said to myself. I focused my attention on finding the right road in the dark and driving rain while he continued to rail at me.

"If you were in the Marines, you'd never get away with speaking to your superior like that! They would crush you!"

Out of the corner of my eye I saw him smash a fist into the palm of his other hand. I stifled the urge to state the obvious and say that we were not in the Marines. I simply said, through gritted teeth:

"No authority I have ever worked for has spoken to me in the way you are speaking to me now."

As I said it, the words had an unexpected effect on me. I was still angry and felt he was being grossly unfair. I had worked my socks off to make the seminar go well and it had been a spectacularly powerful and successful weekend. At the same time, I realised the reason that no authority had ever spoken to me in this way before. Because I didn't like authority. I had specifically chosen authorities that did not express themselves in this way. If BBC bosses or my Cambridge University tutors had been displeased with me, they generally just turned away and looked for what they wanted in another place. It was polite, indirect and non-confrontational. Just like my relationship with my father in fact. My father only shouted at me once, as I remember, when I accidentally trod on his golf ball that had been neatly positioned on a tuft of grass.

After dropping Martin close enough to his hotel for him to get a taxi, I drove home amid a turbulent mix of emotions. A succession of realisations exploded on me. I remembered rebelling against my mother as a four-year-old child, when she reproved me for being rude to her. I told her I couldn't be rude to her because she was my mother and I was going to leave home. Then I ran up the stairs while she chased me with a hairbrush, knowing I could outrun her. I was the rebel daughter of a mother who was herself a rebel. She had disastrous relationships with teachers during her brief school career, accidentally burning down one school and being expelled from another for throwing a pudding basin at her teacher. I had had a much more conventional relationship with teachers and bosses, but I could see now that there had been no confrontation because I simply hid who I was.

When I told my family what had happened with Martin, they too roundly judged that he had behaved like a diva, but the next morning I was surprised to find myself thinking of *The Taming of the Shrew*. Still harbouring more than a little self-righteous indignation, I felt a fragile glimmer of humility. This is what happens to Katherina in Shakespeare's play, I thought. She finds herself ready to concede, to accept what she does not know or understand. The moon is the sun and the sun is the moon, if the authority wills it so.

Acceptance paves the way for understanding, which paves the way for love. Submission, acceptance, devotion. These are extremes of the yin force that has the most intense magnetic attraction for the purest yang: unformed creative energy. It has taken me many years to learn that.

By the time I spoke to Martin later that morning I found I was able to apologise to him for behaving thoughtlessly. He was in no doubt that he was dealing with resistance in my crown chakra. I chose to let that resistance go, regardless of my previous habits of thought in similar circumstances. I gave up the need to judge that I was 'right'. Over the next few days and weeks, I felt folded in waves of love and support. Martin was part of this wave, encouraging me with minute attention throughout the process of the MRI, until the ultimate inspection of the images with my consultant proved that the brain tumour had gone. It was an important lesson, possibly the most important lesson I learned from Martin, because it broke through the comfortable restrictions of my ego. As it turned out, it was the last time Martin and I worked together.

I don't teach a workshop on the crown chakra, because I

believe that each person will find their connection to the Divine in their own way. As you strip away the layers of resistance in all the other chakras, you become more and more open to loving the power of the universe that holds you. Its guidance becomes more readily part of your daily life. But there is an interesting exercise Martin taught me which you can use to explore the character of your reactions and habitual style of thinking.

The distinction between the information delivered by your external senses and your internal ones is mirrored in the two sides of the brain. The notion that mental activities are entirely localized has been discredited by the work of many doctors and scientists who have been demonstrating the adaptability and the plasticity of the brain, but nevertheless there is a tendency for different areas of the brain to take charge of different tasks you encounter. So it has been said for a long time that organs on the right side of your body are controlled by the left side of the brain which tends to operate better at tasks of organisation, logic, deduction. Conversely the organs on the left side of the body are controlled by the right side of the brain which tends to handle spatial sensations, impressions of colour, dreams and imagination.

This may be already something you experience in your life if you are left-handed and notice a distinction between your way of approaching a problem and that of someone you know well who is right-handed. Yet undoubtedly you use both these faculties every day of your life and there is likely to be more that your brain can offer you if you explore.

To do this, close your eyes and settle your body in a way you know well. After a few long steady breaths, imagine walking into the chamber of the left-hand side of your brain. What do you see? Do you see colours, monochrome, furnishings or perhaps numbers? Do you just sense an atmosphere? Let yourself linger and feel what this chamber is like.

Then go and visit the right side of the brain. Does it look

different? Is it easier to get into or harder? Lighter or darker? Sense the ambiance of this side and see whether it feels different from the left.

After a while, imagine that you invite the right side of your brain to visit the left. When this right side enters as a guest into the left side, does it see things differently, want to rearrange the furniture, or let in more light? How would it be if the right side of your brain lived there in cooperation with the left side?

When you have done this, take some time to invite the left side of your brain to visit the right. What does the left see there? Can the left side see form and meaning in the information that is presenting itself in the right side of your brain? Are there treasures to uncover, dark and secret spaces?

Imagine you could make a bridge between the two sides, an open door where each was free to visit the other at any time. If you repeat this experience you will find that the picture within gradually becomes clearer. Things on the left side of the brain may become more colourful and softer, more fluid. Things on the right side may become lighter and brighter, more distinct and recognisable.

When you have digested some of the things your brain can yield to your imagination when you go exploring in this way, then you can try to apply these insights to something in your own life. Consider a problem you are facing or something you would like to achieve. Present it to the left side of your brain. What do you see? Then present it to the right side. How does the mind react? If the reaction is different, see if you can imagine each side of your brain tackling the problem in its own way. Then imagine them tackling the issue together. Remember the information they tell you.

As soon as you can after this exercise write the information somewhere you will see it every day. Try to remind yourself to apply it to the way you want to go forward. Stick to this approach when there are difficulties. Often the best advice we can get is our own advice that we've forgotten! From time to time repeat the exercise and see if the inner landscape has changed.

These days when I meditate it feels as if I am turning on a tap. I use the practice to clear my mind, to strip away the data I have accumulated. I see the information go and it leaves its mark on my understanding, but without it I begin to feel the clear air of freedom. Into this vacuum comes the bright energy of my environment which flows into me as I flow with it. It teaches me to switch from time to time from my external visual sense to my internal visual sense, where I allow myself to look at something without seeing lines and perceive instead the energy that flows from it. Sometimes I may switch from my external auditory sense to my inner auditory sense and hear the voices of the dead, the vibration of the earth or the testimony of trees. Everything around me becomes my teacher and so my friend. I have lost my resistance and fear of the word 'guru' because I see that there is a teacher in everything I encounter.

There is a story in one of the old Vedic scriptures, about a sage who was asked to name his guru. He answered there had been twenty-four. Intrigued, his listeners asked him to name them.

I have taken shelter of twenty-four gurus, who are the following: the earth, air, sky, water, fire, moon, sun, pigeon and python; the sea, moth, honeybee, elephant and honey thief; the deer, the fish, the dancing girl Pingala, the kurari bird and the child; the young girl, arrow maker, serpent, spider and wasp.[5]

Plenty of energy has been devoted to determining what he learned from each guru, but the essence of this story is that everything is imbued with the same essential divinity, expressing it in different forms.

I am still counting my gurus and evaluating their lessons. Martin Brofman never wanted to be a guru, as resistant to authority as I was myself. But he taught me the unlooked-for discoveries that come from sacrificing your ego to authority. He taught me that a teacher doesn't have to be perfect to have something perfect to teach you. He was a friend and guide through the thickets of unrecognised aspects of myself. My dog was one of my gurus. He taught me how devotion works, that devotion comes before the reward, not the other way around. Because of his love and devotion to me, I was ready to do everything I could for him. He also taught me the nobility of acceptance. I pray I can die as swiftly as he did when my body tells me it is time to let go.

Sometimes it takes me years to understand the lessons I am learning. Sometimes they come to me instantly. I looked up one day at the trunk of an oak tree, bursting powerfully into leaf above me. *That*, I thought, *is how we are, like leaves on a tree.*

There are billions of leaves on this tree and each leaf cannot see the shape of the tree for all the others in the way. It has no idea how big the tree is or where its roots are. All the leaf knows is that its job is to gather as much light as it can, transform it into energy and feed it back into the tree. In exchange the tree gives it life and makes it grow, storing the energy from the leaf and sending it down to unseen roots. One day the leaf will have served its purpose. The cells will begin to close at the top of its stem, it will fall to the earth and feed the tree in another way as it decays. But while the leaf lives, it is connected to the great tree. It has its own stem through which it sends energy and receives growth and form. A leaf may only partly understand its role, but it can always feel the power of the tree within.

Chapter 18

Most Secret – *Breathe*

There is an Indian proverb or axiom that says that everyone is a house with four rooms, a physical, a mental, an emotional and a spiritual. Most of us tend to live in one room most of the time but, unless we go into every room every day, even if only to keep it aired, we are not a complete person.
Rumer Godden, *A House with Four Rooms*

If you would like to 'air every room' to explore the practices referred to in this book, you can hardly do better than incorporate a daily habit of conscious breathing into your life. If you do this regularly, even for ten minutes a day, you will begin to notice changes in your health and strength. You will also give yourself a powerful perspective on things that trouble you in your life on a daily basis. You can render yourself completely 'safe' in the breath, able to surmount emotional ups and downs and contemplate fears and anxieties with a cool eye, determined to cut through them.

Cultivating the breath is an essential part of health and a counteraction to many modern diseases, from high blood pressure to anxiety. It is important to do all the breathing as slowly and steadily as possible, never forcing yourself or straining, but working within your limits and gradually extending them. These are the exercises my grandfather mentioned and I like to think of him practising them in his office at Bletchley Park, gazing out of the window at the movements of men and women in uniform as they hurried from hut to hut outside. I give you the exercises here, just as he wrote them down.

From 3-30 minutes:

Stand erect with your hands at your sides, and draw in air by contracting the walls of the stomach; then slowly let the air out, but keep the stomach contracted. Distend the walls of the stomach as far as possible and slowly draw in air. Repeat.

From 5-15 minutes:

Lie on the floor and raise the right leg up, keeping the knee stiff, at right angles to the body. Lower the right leg and when the heel rests on the ground, raise the left leg. After doing this several times, raise both legs together.

Increase gradually from seconds to minutes.

Stand erect. Fix attention on the air that is going out: 'expiration', and slowly breathe out until the lungs are empty. Pause, counting slowly. Fix the attention on the air that enters the system: 'inspiration', and breathe in, counting as above.

Note: Don't on any account strain. Let the increase in suspension, either way, come gradually, as it surely will.

Rhythmic breathing

The rate of the pulse is the rate of the heartbeat. Determine this rate from the pulse by placing your third and fourth finger lightly on the midpoint of the underside of the wrist. Count the beats of blood pumping under the fingertips. Then draw in a full breath for a period of 6, 8, 10, 12, 14 or so heart beats. Retain the breath for a period of half the selected number of heart beats. Exhale in the same manner.

During this exercise, which can be carried through lying down, the mind should be fixed on a point between the eyebrows and a mental picture made of the numbers as they are counted.

All these exercises can be done at any time during the day, but first thing in the morning when the mind is at its calmest is preferable, even if this means rising half an hour earlier than usual.

Anatomy Of The Non-Physical In The Physical Body

Each part of your physical body corresponds to one or other of the elements, as shown in this chart:

ELEMENT	BODY PARTS associated	EMOTION associated
Earth	Root: skeleton; bones; spine (in general). Nose; teeth; legs; feet; hips; elimination: lymph; kidneys (see also solar plexus); testicles; vulva	Relationship to Mother/Earth Insecurity Fear; Mistrust, or converse: Trust Instability Will (action) Physical safety
Water	Sacral: womb. Vagina; penis; ovaries; prostate; lower back	Store of emotions; Memory; Appetite/ desire for food and sex; Instinct Unconscious Dreams Joy, Pleasure
Fire	Solar Plexus: upper abdominal organs, liver, pancreas, gall bladder, kidneys (see also root), skin; muscles; eyes and eyesight; jaw; face	Individuality Intellect Self-confidence Anger Power; Freedom Will (thought)
Air	Heart: lungs; breathing; immune system; breasts; thymus	Love Relationships Connection Inner communication Balance

Ether	Throat: arms; hands; fingers; thyroid; shoulders; ears and hearing; voice; speech; singing	Intuition, inspiration Desire (wishes) Communication (outward expression in speech/music/art etc.) Fantasy; Daydreams
Mental Body	Brow: Behind centre of eyebrows. Hormonal balance. Vision (thought); the way you see	Centre of individual consciousness Seat of cosmic intelligence Eternal knowledge of self and the Universe
Causal Body	Crown: Top of the head. Brain; Hypothalamus and Pituitary Nervous system	Relationship to Father/Authority Seat of Cosmic Consciousness Isolation; sense of being misunderstood or unseen. When energy rises through the spinal canal to this chakra individual consciousness merges with cosmic consciousness.

Notes

Chapter 4: The Quest

1. *"Before printing, Old Wives Tales were ingeniose: and since printing came in fashion, til a little before the Civil Warres, the ordinary sort of people were not taught to reade; nowadays, Bookes are common and most of the poore people understand letters, and the many good Bookes and variety of Turns of Affaires have put all the ould Fables out of doors: and the divine art of Printing and Gunpowder [a reference to the traumatic English civil war] have frightened away Robin-Goodfellow and the Fayries."* Aubrey's Brief Lives, 1881, 67-8.

2. *Times of London.* 28/11/1919, Anon Leader. Einstein noted that the paper was pleased to describe him as a "Swiss Jew", whereas in Germany he was described as a "German man of science". He quipped that should his star fade, and his theory be disproved or disapproved of by the scientific establishment, then no doubt the epithets would reverse, and in England he would be described as a "German man of science", in Germany as a "Swiss Jew"!

3. *"Approximately fifty years after BH Kim, the presence of the PVS inside the blood and lymphatic vessels, cerebrospinal fluids of the central nervous system, and on the surface of the various internal organs was indeed confirmed by various techniques developed by the SNU team. The most significant unconfirmed part is ironically the PVS in skin, which is supposed to be the acupoint. BH Kim claimed that the acupuncture meridians extended into the PVS inside the mammalian body, which still needs to be verified because the techniques used for the PVS inside the body do not appear to work for the PVS in the skin. ...*

   We strongly believe that the thousand-year-old acupuncture therapy and traditional eastern medicine will become in a true sense a scientific medicine when the entire network of PVS and its roles in mammalian body are fully uncovered. This will then shift the level of oriental medicine from traditional wisdom and art with a long history to the biomedical sciences in a true sense. Furthermore, it will also bring a paradigm change in regenerative medicine: cancer, immune deficiency or hyperactivity, pain control, stem cell therapy, and other important issues in human health care in general."

"50 Years of Bong-han Theory and 10 years of the Primo Vascular System," by Soh, Kang, Ryu. *Evidence-Based Complementary and Alternative Medicine*, Volume 2013, Article ID 587827.

4. *Change Your Mind, Heal Your Body*, Anna Parkinson. London: Watkins, 2014.

Chapter 5: Interlude

1. *Ayurveda and Life Impressions Bodywork*, Donald VanHowten. Twin Lakes, WI: Lotus Press, p. 49. With grateful thanks for his permission to quote this.

Chapter 6: Rooting For Mother

1. *For Those About To Change*, Alfonso Vonscheidt. Hampstead House.
2. *Be Here Now*, by Ram Dass (Richard Alpert). Crown Publications.

Chapter 7: Hunting Treasure In the Dark

1. You can find a recorded version of this meditation and others referred to in this text on my website: www.annaparkinson.com.

Chapter 8: Rediscovering Innocence

1. Research by Michael Merzenich, referenced in *The Brain that Changes Itself*, Norman Doidge. London: Penguin, 2007, p. 80.

Chapter 9: Sex and Spirit

1. *Memories, Dreams, Reflections*, CG Jung. Fontana Press, 1971, p. 19.
2. *Jnana Sankalini Tantra*, Paramahamsa Prajnanananda. Motilal Banarsidass Ltd., 2006, p. 19.
3. This area is reputed to be the first place where Buddhism took root. King Ashok considered himself a follower of the Buddha's teachings 350 years before, although he was said to have murdered his brothers and killed or tortured thousands in battle. In 262 BCE he took over the ancient kingdom of Orissa. Eight years later he changed his name to *Devanampiya Piyadasi*, meaning 'he who looks on with compassion, beloved of the gods'. He decided to make his land a model of compassion and respect for life, arranging for stones and pillars engraved with messages to be placed beside key roads of his realms in India, Nepal, Afghanistan and Pakistan. One, deciphered in C19th, read:

   "Everywhere has Beloved of the Gods, King Piyadasi, made provision for two types of medical treatment: medical treatment for humans and medical treatment for animals. Wherever medical herbs suitable for animals and humans are not available, I have had them imported and grown. Wherever medical roots or fruits are not available, I have had them imported and grown. Along roads I have had wells dug and trees planted for the benefit of humans and animals."
4. *Adrift: Seventy-six days lost at sea*, Steven Callahan. Bantam Press, 1986, pp. 175-8.

Chapter 11: Finding Intelligent Life

1. See *The Brain that Changes Itself*, Norman Doidge, London: Penguin, 2007, for a series of fascinating experiments.
2. See *Mind Over Medicine*, Lissa Rankin. Hay House, 2013.
3. *The Autobiography of a Yogi*, Paramahansa Yogananda. Self-Realization Fellowship, 2004, p. 146.

4. Albert Einstein, from *Einstein on Cosmic Religion and Other Opinions and Aphorisms*, Dover Publications, 1931.

Chapter 12: The Heart of the Matter

1. See *Love and Survival*, Dean Ornish, MD, Harper Collins, 1998, for many controlled experiments into the powerful effect of love and relationships on heart health.
2. A hydrogen atom is 99.999% empty space. If an atom were the size of a melon, the nucleus would still be invisible. Around it electrons are constantly moving, absorbing and giving off energy. This beautiful description of the way electrons move is by physicist Roger Barlow in theconversation.com: *"electrons dance – there is no better word for it. But it's not random dancing – it's more like ballroom dancing, where they move in set patterns, following steps laid down by a mathematical equation named after Erwin Schrödinger. These patterns can vary – some are slow and gentle, like a waltz whereas some are fast and energetic, like a Charleston. Each electron keeps to the same pattern, but once in a while it may change to another, as long as no other electron is doing that pattern already. – If you touch [a] table, then the electrons from atoms in your fingers become close to the electrons in the table's atoms. As the electrons in one atom get close enough to the nucleus of the other, the patterns of their dances change. This is because an electron in a low energy level around one nucleus can't do the same around the other – that slot's already taken by one of its own electrons. The newcomer must step into an unoccupied, more energetic role. That energy has to be supplied – by the force from your probing finger. So pushing just two atoms close to each other takes energy, as all their electrons need to go into unoccupied high-energy states. Trying to push all the table-atoms and finger-atoms together demands an awful lot of energy – more than your muscles can supply. You feel that, as resistance to your finger, which is why and how the table feels solid to your touch."*

3. *Chogyam Trungpa: His Life and Vision*, by Fabrice Midal. Shambhala Publications, 2004. Pema Chodron quoted p. 161.
4. Mr Crisp Live, *The Wit and Wisdom of Quentin Crisp*. USA: Alyson Books, 1998, p. 154.
5. *Aion: Researches into the Phenomenology of the Self*, CG Jung in *Collected Works Vol. 9.*

Chapter 13: Heart Medicine

1. *Svetashvatara Upanishad 1.15.* A poetic metaphysical text, composed around 5th century BCE, whose name means 'carried beyond on a white horse'. The text explains the Divine Soul is in everything and accessed by each individual through self-knowledge and self-discipline.
2. Dr Ihaleakala Hew Len interview in 2001 with Carla Galstaun, YouTube video. See also June 11, 2014 by zerolag. biz.
3. The full ho'oponopono prayer, as taught by Dr Ihaleakala Len's teacher Dr Morrnah Simeona, is as follows:

   "Father, Mother, Child as one.

   If I, my family, relatives and ancestors have offended you, your family, relatives and ancestors, in thoughts, words, deeds and actions, from the beginning of creation to the present, we humbly, humbly ask your forgiveness. Let this cleanse, purify, release, cut all the negative memories, blocks, energies and vibrations and transmute these unwanted energies into pure light. As it is said, it is done, and set free."

   There are some good short courses to learn the full implications of this powerful prayer in the Netherlands and USA. See www.aloha-o-ka-i.org.

Chapter 14: Beyond Soup

1. Letter, William Cecil to John Dee, quoted by Edith Sitwell in *The Queens and the Hive*, Macmillan, 1962, Appendix A.

2. "The Advancement of Learning" Essay by Francis Bacon, 1605.
3. *The Lightness of Being*, Frank Wilczek. NY: Basic Books, 2010, p. 179.
4. *Life After Death*, Deepak Chopra. Random House, 2008, p. 218.
5. Dr David Bohm, interview with David Suzuki for *The Nature of Things*, CBC Radio, 26 May 1979.
6. *The General Theory of Employment, Interest and Money*, JM Keynes. December 1935, intro., p. vii.
7. *Proof of Heaven*, Dr Eben Alexander. NY: Simon and Schuster, 2012.
8. *Experience Nada Yoga* guided meditation by Roop Verma: www.roopverma.com.

Chapter 15: Creating the Future
1. *The Conquest of Happiness*, Bertrand Russell. Published 1930.
2. *Yoga Explained*, F. Yeats-Brown. Victor Gollancz Ltd., 1937.
3. *The Tunnellers of Holzminden*, by Hugh Durnford. Penguin, 1920.

Chapter 16: Mission Fulfilled
1. *Song of Ashtavakra 2:4*. The Ashtavakra Gita is a dialogue between the sage, Ashtavakra, and Janaka, a king in what is now the Indian region of Bihar. Dates vary from 400 BCE to 1300 CE. It is a discussion about the nature of the soul and reality and denies the existence of any external or objective reality. In a conversation between Janaka and Ashtavakra, pertaining to the deformity of his crooked body, Ashtavakra explains that the size of a Temple is not affected by how it is shaped, and the shape of his own body does not affect himself (or Atman/soul).

Chapter 17: Acceptance

1. From a lecture by Swami Rama on a famous Tantric text called the *Saundarya Lahari* or *The Waves of Beauty* which praises the feminine aspect of creation or Mother Earth, the Goddess Sri. *Sri Vidya* (learning the goddess) (2/41) Swami Rama YouTube 6/08/08.
2. Jason Hill, New York Presbyterian Hospital, April 16th 2020 Facebook feed.
3. Dalai Lama Facebook page, April 2020.
4. Paramahamsa Prajnanananda, *Jnana Sankalini Tantra*, p. 108.
5. Lord Dattratreya, one aspect of supreme creator Vishnu, *Srimad Bhagavatam*, Canto 11, Chapter 7, 33-35.

Author Biography

Anna Parkinson is a former news and current affairs producer with the BBC. In 2002 she was diagnosed with a brain tumour and her quest to find a cure led her to discover healing. Her journey to health brought a profound change in her outlook, and for the past sixteen years she has been a practising healer. She continues to write and teach lively workshops she has devised to convey self-healing 'tools', both internationally and at the College of Psychic Studies in London. She is also invited to give talks on healing and the traditional uses of plants based on her book about the work of her 17th century herbalist ancestor, John Parkinson. Anna lives in Kent in southern England with her family. For events, blogs and more publications see Anna's website at http://www.annaparkinson.com.

Previous Titles

If you enjoyed this book, you might enjoy Anna Parkinson's earlier books:

Change Your Mind, Heal Your Body
London: Watkins Publishing, 2014
"When modern medicine has no cure, the answer lies within."
This was the author's accidental discovery when she was diagnosed with an inoperable brain tumour. She tells how she found a healer who showed her not only a way to successfully heal the tumour but another way of seeing the world. This book is a profound yet accessible story of healing the mind and body. Part memoir, part practical guide, it gradually draws the reader from a world of fact and logic into a world in which genuine healing is both possible and realistic.

Nature's Alchemist: John Parkinson, Herbalist to Charles I
London: Frances Lincoln Ltd., 2007
John Parkinson's most beautiful book of plants, *Paradisi in Sole, Paradisus Terrestris*, first published in 1629, dedicated to Queen Henrietta Maria, has been treasured by generations of gardeners ever since. Anna Parkinson was so fascinated by this book, handed down through her family, that she set out to uncover the life of the man behind it. The fruit of original research, this lively biography tells the story for the first time of how an outstanding gardener used his beloved plants to help him survive one of the most turbulent periods of British history. *Nature's Alchemist* was voted one of the best 10 books of 2007.

Note To Reader

Thank you for purchasing *Beyond Sex and Soup – Living a Spiritual Adventure*. My sincere hope is that you will find this book relevant to your own life, and that you experience the benefits of putting the methods described into practice. Any benefit to you justifies all the creative effort I have put into synthesising what I have learned. If you have a few moments, please do add your review of the book to your favourite online site(s). This feedback helps me and other potential readers too. Please visit my website for further resources, recent blog posts and news of events coming up. You can also sign up here for my newsletter: http://www.annaparkinson.com.

Sincerely, Anna Parkinson

Your Simple Path
Find Happiness in every step
Ian Tucker
A guide to helping us reconnect with what is really important in our lives.
Paperback: 978-1-78279-349-6 ebook: 978-1-78279-348-9

365 Days of Wisdom
Daily Messages To Inspire You Through The Year
Dadi Janki
Daily messages which cool the mind, warm the heart and guide you along your journey.
Paperback: 978-1-84694-863-3 ebook: 978-1-84694 864-0

Body of Wisdom
Women's Spiritual Power and How it Serves
Hilary Hart
Bringing together the dreams and experiences of women across the world with today's most visionary spiritual teachers.
Paperback: 978-1-78099-696-7 ebook: 978-1-78099-695-0

Dying to Be Free
From Enforced Secrecy to Near Death to True Transformation
Hannah Robinson
After an unexpected accident and near-death experience, Hannah Robinson found herself radically transforming her life, while a remarkable new insight altered her relationship with her father, a practising Catholic priest.
Paperback: 978-1-78535-254-6 ebook: 978-1-78535-255-3

The Ecology of the Soul
A Manual of Peace, Power and Personal Growth for Real People
in the Real World
Aidan Walker
Balance your own inner Ecology of the Soul to regain your
natural state of peace, power and wellbeing.
Paperback: 978-1-78279-850-7 ebook: 978-1-78279-849-1

Not I, Not other than I
The Life and Teachings of Russel Williams
Steve Taylor, Russel Williams
The miraculous life and inspiring teachings of one of the World's
greatest living Sages.
Paperback: 978-1-78279-729-6 ebook: 978-1-78279-728-9

On the Other Side of Love
A woman's unconventional journey towards wisdom
Muriel Maufroy
When life has lost all meaning, what do you do?
Paperback: 978-1-78535-281-2 ebook: 978-1-78535-282-9

Practicing A Course In Miracles
A translation of the Workbook in plain language, with
mentor's notes
Elizabeth A. Cronkhite
The practical second and third volumes of The Plain-Language
A Course In Miracles.
Paperback: 978-1-84694-403-1 ebook: 978-1-78099-072-9

Quantum Bliss
The Quantum Mechanics of Happiness, Abundance, and Health
George S. Mentz
Quantum Bliss is the breakthrough summary of success and
spirituality secrets that customers have been waiting for.
Paperback: 978-1-78535-203-4 ebook: 978-1-78535-204-1

The Upside Down Mountain
Mags MacKean
A must-read for anyone weary of chasing success and happiness
– one woman's inspirational journey swapping the uphill slog for
the downhill slope.
Paperback: 978-1-78535-171-6 ebook: 978-1-78535-172-3

Your Personal Tuning Fork
The Endocrine System
Deborah Bates
Discover your body's health secret, the endocrine system, and
'twang' your way to sustainable health!
Paperback: 978-1-84694-503-8 ebook: 978-1-78099-697-4

Readers of ebooks can buy or view any of these bestsellers by
clicking on the live link in the title. Most titles are published
in paperback and as an ebook. Paperbacks are available in
traditional bookshops. Both print and ebook formats are
available online.
Find more titles and sign up to our readers' newsletter at
http://www.johnhuntpublishing.com/mind-body-spirit
Follow us on Facebook at https://www.facebook.com/OBooks/
and Twitter at https://twitter.com/obooks